THE BEST
SPIRITUAL
WRITING
2000

THE BEST
SPIRITUAL
WRITING
2000

EDITED BY
PHILIP ZALESKI

INTRODUCTION BY
THOMAS MOORE

HarperSanFrancisco
A Division of HarperCollinsPublishers

HarperCollins books may be purchased for educational, business, or sales
promotional use. For information please write: Special Markets Department,
HarperCollins Publishers, Inc., 10 East 53rd Street, New York, NY 10022.

HarperCollins Web site: http://www.harpercollins.com

HarperCollins®, 📖®, and HarperSanFrancisco™ are trademarks
of HarperCollins Publishers Inc.

FIRST EDITION

Library of Congress Cataloging Card Number 98–12368
ISSN: 1525–5980

ISBN 0–06–251670–1

00 01 02 03 04 ❖RRD(H) 10 9 8 7 6 5 4 3 2 1

Contents

PHILIP ZALESKI

Preface

This has been the year of lists: the ten best wines, the fifty worst films, the one hundred greatest people of the year, decade, century, millennium. Our passion for enumeration may grow ludicrous at times—can a list of the hundred best lists be far around the corner?—but the impulse seems wholly admirable, a desire (one could even call it a religious longing) to praise the highest and damn the lowest, to mark the transcendental extremes within which we carry out our mundane lives.

In keeping with this fin-de-millennium tradition, I spent the last months of the old century compiling, with the help of a panel of distinguished writers and thinkers, a catalog of the one hundred best spiritual books of the century. Such a project, we believed, had considerable merit. It would honor the great spiritual writers of the last one hundred years, it would provide a reliable guide for those searching out the modern classics in the field, and it might shed some light on the nature of spiritual writing and thus on the book that you hold in your hands and its confreres in The Best Spiritual Writing series.

Participants in our panel included Joseph Bruchac, Frederic Brussant, Lawrence Cunningham, Natalie Goldberg, Ron Hansen, Kabir Helminski, Rodger Kamenetz, Harold Kushner, Lawrence Kushner, Thomas Moore, Huston Smith, Helen Tworkov, Christopher de Vinck, John Wilson, and David Yount. Each panelist nominated as many books as he or she thought appropriate.

The only criterion was that the book must have been published for the first time during or after 1900; our aim was to take the spiritual pulse of this century, not of earlier ones. New translations of old works were thus ineligible, ensuring that the roster would consist of something more than one hundred ancient scriptures in modern dress.

Over two hundred books were nominated. It fell to me to make the final selection, adding the few key works that had been overlooked by panelists (invariably books from the first decades of the century, half-buried by the silt of time), and winnowing the heap down to one hundred winners. It wasn't easy. Almost every nominated book deserved to make the final cut. Moreover, I wanted to prepare a list that, without any sacrifice in quality, would reflect the full spectrum of world religions, at least insofar as that spectrum has shone through English-language translations. As a help for readers short on time or patience, I also drew up a list of the *creme de la creme,* the ten best spiritual books of the past one hundred years.

Here, then, are the hundred best spiritual books of the century, arranged alphabetically by author. The top ten are in boldface:

Adams, Henry, *Mont-Saint-Michel and Chartres*

Agnon, S. Y., *In the Heart of the Seas*

Anonymous, *Alcoholics Anonymous*

Anonymous, *The Gospel of Thomas*

Balthasar, Hans Urs von, *The Glory of the Lord*

Barfield, Owen, *Saving the Appearances*

Barth, Karl, *The Epistle to the Romans*

Bernanos, Georges, *Diary of a Country Priest*

Black Elk, *Black Elk Speaks*

Bonhoeffer, Dietrich, *Cost of Discipleship*

Letters and Papers from Prison

Buber, Martin, *I and Thou*

Tales of the Hasidim

Camus, Albert, *The Plague*

Chapman, John, *Spiritual Letters*

Chesterton, Gilbert Keith, *Orthodoxy*

Daumal, Rene, *Mount Analogue*

Day, Dorothy, *The Long Loneliness*

Dillard, Annie, *Pilgrim at Tinker Creek*

Dunne, John, *The Way of All the Earth*

Eisely, Loren, *The Immense Journey*

Eliade, Mircea, *The Myth of the Eternal Return*

Eliot, T. S., *Christianity and Culture*

The Four Quartets

Endo, Shusako, *Silence*

Florensky, Pavel, *The Pillar and the Ground of the Truth*

Foster, Richard, *A Celebration of Discipline*

Frankl, Victor, *Man's Search for Meaning*

Gandhi, Mohandas, *Autobiography: The Story of My Experiments with Truth*

Greene, Graham, *The Power and the Glory*

Griffiths, Bede, *The Golden String*

Guardini, Romano, *The Lord*

Guenon, Rene, *The Reign of Quantity and the Signs of the Times*

Malcolm X, *The Autobiography of Malcolm X*

Maritain, Raissa, *Journals*

Maugham, W. Somerset, *The Razor's Edge*

Merton, Thomas, *New Seeds of Contemplation*
  The Seven Storey Mountain

Muggeridge, Malcolm, *Something Beautiful for God*

Newman, John Henry, *Meditations and Devotions*

Niebuhr, H. Richard, *Christ and Culture*

Niebuhr, Reinhold, *The Nature and Destiny of Man*

O'Connor, Flannery, *Wise Blood*

Otto, Rudolf, *The Idea of the Holy*

Ouspensky, P. D., *In Search of the Miraculous*

Peck, M. Scott, *The Road Less Traveled*

Percy, Walker, *Lost in the Cosmos*

Pirsig, Robert, *Zen and the Art of Motorcycle Maintenance*

Ramakrishna, *The Gospel of Ramakrishna*

Reps, Paul, *Zen Flesh, Zen Bones*

Rilke, Rainer Maria, *Duino Elegies*

Rosenzweig, Franz, *The Star of Redemption*

Russell, George William (AE), *The Candle of Vision*

Schimmel, Anne-Marie, *Mystical Dimensions of Islam*

Scholem, Gershom, *Major Trends in Jewish Mysticism*

Schumacher, E. F., *A Guide for the Perplexed*

Schuon, Fritjof, *The Transcendent Unity of Religions*

Singer, Isaac Bashevis, *Collected Stories*

Smith, Huston, *The World's Religions*

Steinsaltz, Adin, *The Thirteen Petalled Rose*

Suzuki, D. T., *Essays in Zen Buddhism*

Suzuki, Shunryu, *Zen Mind, Beginner's Mind*

Tagore, Rabindranath, *Gitanjali*

Teilhard de Chardin, *The Phenomenon of Man*

Teresa, Mother, *A Simple Path*

Therese of Liseux, St., *The Story of a Soul*

Tillich, Paul, *The Courage to Be*

Tolkien, J. R. R., *Lord of the Rings*

Tomberg, Valentin, *Meditations on the Tarot*

Traherne, Thomas, *Centuries*

Trungpa, Chogyam, *Cutting Through Spiritual Materialism*

Underhill, Evelyn, *Mysticism*

Weil, Simone, *Waiting for God*

Wiesel, Elie, *Night*

Yeats, William Butler, *Collected Poems*

Yogananda, Paramahansa, *Autobiography of a Yogi*

It is impossible, I believe, to survey this list without a surge of hope. The assembled titles argue that, in the midst of the most violent century in history, marred by world wars, genocide, nuclear attack, and the rise of communism and fascism, we have enjoyed a remarkable efflorescence of spiritual writing. It tells us that just as great saints arise in times of persecution and turbulence, so too do great spiritual writers. "Adversity introduces a man to himself," as the folk saying goes; and meeting oneself is an essential step on the path to wisdom.

The list suggests, too, that professional qualifications have little to do with being a good spiritual writer. Popes, priests, rabbis, monks, and nuns pepper the list, but so do scientists, poets, economists, and statesmen. The authors on the list represent not only a wild diversity of vocations, but a wild diversity of faiths, including, but not limited to, Buddhism, Christianity, Hinduism, Islam, Judaism, and the primordial traditions. What almost all have in common is literary excellence. Here the great poets—Eliot, Hopkins, Rilke, Yeats—lead the way. The novel also makes an important, if underdeveloped, contribution. Fiction grapples always with a handicap in its dealings with spirituality, the inevitable tendency toward didacticism, sentimentality, or pastiche. It may be that children's literature—above all, C. S. Lewis's *The Chronicles of Narnia*—represents, in its lightness of heart and purity of intention, the apex of narrative spiritual writing in this century.

There are some curiosities on the list. A few of the books—*The Gospel of Thomas,* Gerard Manley Hopkins's *Poems,* John Henry Newman's *Meditations and Devotions,* St. Therese of Lisieux's *The Story of a Soul,* Thomas Traherne's *Centuries*—were composed before the twentieth century, but remained unpublished until modern times. Two volumes—*The Gospel of Thomas* and *Alcoholics Anonymous*—are anonymous, while a third, *Meditations on the Tarot,* was published anonymously, although its author has been revealed since as the Catholic esotericist, Valentin Tomberg. Several books—Hans Urs von Balthasar's *The Glory of the Lord,* Lewis's *Narnia* septets, J. R. R. Tolkien's *Lord of the Rings*—are multi-volume works; we fudged a bit here so that they could take their rightful place on the list. A number of the selections, including Hopkins's *Poems,* Ramakrishna's *The Gospel of Ramakrishna,* and Ramana Maharshi's *The Spiritual Teachings of Ramana Maharshi,* are compilations assembled after the authors' deaths. But the strangest fact, to my mind, is the brevity of the works on the top ten list. Most are under two hundred pages. Great truths do not require great length.

The best of the century tells us something about The Best Spiritual Writing series. We see that certain themes remain constant, as if hard-wired into the soul: the struggle with evil; the quest for God; nature as theophany; the sense that we inhabit two worlds, one divine, the other human—all too human. We see, too, that the writings in the annual collections don't burst out of the blue, like Athena from the head of Zeus; they evolve from a rich tradition of religious reflection that dates to the beginning of this century and, in truth, to the beginning of civilization. Truly, there were giants on the earth in those days. Each essay or poem in this year's compilation, however humble or ephemeral, contributes to—and thus changes—this colossal tradition; each plants a seed for next century's list of the best spiritual books.

As always, submissions are encouraged for subsequent volumes of *The Best Spiritual Writing*. Please send writings to Philip Zaleski, 138 Elm Street, Smith College, Northampton, MA 01063. The best way for a periodical to submit material is to add The Best Spiritual Writing series, at the above address, to its complimentary subscription list.

Many people helped in the production of this volume. My thanks to John Loudon, Gideon Weil, Meg Lenihan, Liza Hetherington, and the entire crew at Harper San Francisco; to Kim Witherspoon and David Forrer of Witherspoon Associates; to Thomas Moore; to all others who contributed in ways large and small, and, as always, to my beloved Carol, John, and Andy.

Introduction

During the first three decades of my life I was green and easy and thought I knew what was what. When I was nineteen I spent a full year as a novice in a Catholic monastery where spiritual reading was the order of the day. I was forbidden to read newspapers and magazines or even books on philosophy and history. The focus was on the spiritual life, and so I read biographies of saints and books on meditation and prayer, and I remember dipping into the gray area where psychology and spirituality intersected. I was quite sure what the spiritual life was all about and where I was headed with it.

The spirituality that issued from this protected life and selective reading had an Icarian quality—I kept flying closer to the sun and my questions to the spiritual director gradually turned more and more rarefied and idealistic. The monastery grounds were like a launching pad for UFOs. I looked skyward and felt an increasing distance from "the world."

Years later the inevitable fall took place, first with leaving the community and discovering that the vow of poverty was quite different from the condition of poverty. I learned that love, romance, and sex only looked like bliss from a distance but were actually invitations into the thick and thorny foliage of a life lived without the artificial protections of monastic walls. But my real splashdown took place during the many years I practiced psychotherapy. For me this work was an initiation into the underworld of human experience that I had only read about in a distant way in the dense quiet of monastery gardens. Step by step, day by day, crisis after crisis I entered the lower half of life that I had been spared until my thirties, and I felt a change come over me as my ideals darkened and my sense of possibility transformed into a sense of the workable. I felt overshadowed for the first time in my life. My lower body stirred to life. Painfully and reluctantly, like the Virgin pulling away from the angel in Botticelli's *Annunciation,* I learned to live in the presence of earthier passions.

In doing therapy I had the sense that the work was not entirely on a dream or two and didn't try to analyze them as much as let them overshadow us and reveal the slightest hint about the mystery taking place in life. This required an attitude that was new to me, a kind of receptiveness I had never had before and didn't know was possible. It demanded not only intense mental awareness but even more a physical opening and an emotional rawness. My own complexes and neuroses were as much involved as those of the people looking to me for guidance. I had to face my own density and failure in order to see the dramas unfolding in the person with me and in the space between us. It was not at all a matter of applying textbook learning and drawing on safe ideas and being clever with practiced techniques.

I now consider those twenty years of daily entering the dreams of people, far more complex than they would ever appear on the surface, as the second stage in my initiation into a spiritual life. And yet the literature suggests that part two of my process was psychological and part one spiritual. As I experienced them they were both spiritual and both psychological, and I don't have any means of separating these two dimensions even for therapeutic or theoretical purposes. Therefore, and I guess this is the point in starting this way to introduce a book of spiritual writing, I don't know how to define it. The spiritual seems to me to be entirely and intimately woven into the rest of experience so that any genre of writing could be spiritual if the serious spiritual concerns come to the fore.

Of course it's easy to spot the spiritual in essays on meditation or appearances of angels or quests for explicit religious meaning. Clearly there is a spiritual literature concerned with experiences that have little to do with the paltry conditions of an ordinary life lived on an ordinary plane and overshadowed by complexity. But it's also clear that some kind of spirituality arrives only after profound struggle and emotional entanglements, that perhaps rises like a clear sky after a dark and stormy rain. Rilke says that God has to be mined from the earth as we stoop over in the underground shaft of our personal strivings and difficulties. Alchemists described the process as hefting a pickax and very slowly digging for the spirit in the lowlands of mountains and at the edge of flowing waters.

So maybe it's the case that spiritual writing is like Dante's *Divine Comedy*, beginning in a clouded fall into and below the plane of living, up through a variety of sufferings and torments, and issuing in choirs of angels and the display of an unfolding rose. But I also sense that Beckett and Pinter and Anne Sexton are spiritual writers because they look so closely and honestly at the absence of obvious meaning in the human condition and yet at the same time demonstrate their love of humanity through their enjoyment of the humor inherent in the human condition. Their characters don't come up into any paradiso but they show that something transcendent shines through in the honest attempt to deal with a life.

The spiritual also shows itself when you feel turned inside out, like Marsyas of old, who for not recognizing a divine influence in music had his skin torn away like an animal hunted down and snared, an image perhaps for what happens when real art gets hold of you. We used to call the spiritual dimension the interior life, but I don't think that referred to a life shut off from external concerns as much as the life of the soul that stood in some contrast to the life captured merely by the senses.

The struggle to love and be loved, to make a living and provide for your family, and to keep sufficient sanity to get along in the world is a path toward spirit as sure as a retreat from life in some hothouse of spirituality where the way seems direct and transparent. For myself I trust the path through the daily muck much more than the route that goes around it or above it or passes through it like an angel gliding transparently through a solid door. The spirituality that issues from engagement has blood in it and is grounded. It has come from somewhere and we have dragged our soul along as we have endured the passage and therefore emerge as a person of character as well as spirit. Herakleitos is famous for saying that daimon is character, which I might read as an appeal to let all spiritual effort release the inchoate soul and create a personality of considerable substance.

Maybe then the problem of identifying the spiritual is simply a subtle one requiring a sharp eye and a talent for reading the resonance of events. To perceive the spiritual in a slice of life or a piece of art we may have to make a good story of it, because a story has the uncanny ability to raise the spirit out of the flesh like bread rising yeasty in a warm place. You will notice, I think, how many of the selections here come in the form of narrative, which guarantees that the spiritual will not be sliced away from the soul.

I do think that Philip Zaleski is a perceptive man who knows the value of contextualized spirituality and is not seduced by the obvious, which would be too weak because of its excessive simplicity. He also recognizes that good language is a kind of body that keeps the spiritual humane, connected to the life we all lead rather than serving as an escape from that very life, a tendency that sits like a trap in all forms of the spiritual. For that reason I feel a special honor and opportunity in writing these words preparing you, the reader, for an exercise that in my monastery days we called spiritual reading—a different kind of reading where there was no intention of being informed but only inspired. By inspired I mean breathed into, not motivated toward action.

The old theologians said that the task of spirit is to feed the soul and to keep it seeded and alive. Spiritual reading does this by lulling us into reverie and by enticing us to live momentarily at least in a multidimensional world of nuance and resonance. These words have a celibate kind of sexuality about them, like the message of the angel who informed Mary that at that very moment she was conceiving something wonderful even though she wasn't acquainted with sex. They make the soul swell and for a brief time take valuable ascendancy over literal and practical life.

Dante prays to God as Apollo, "Enter into my chest and inspire me, as when you tore from Marsyas the sheath of his members." When the torments of ordinary living tear us inside out we are ready to be filled with the spirit, and this book shows us in so many ways how life organizes itself for that very purpose, so that even though the struggle may seem entirely secular, its effect is to make us ready to recognize and receive the spiritual.

Therefore in doing spiritual reading one has to make special effort to read past the literal depictions in the words and grasp the more subtle resonance on which the spirit is conveyed. Only at this level of refinement do we have access to the spirit as it enters the soul and gives new life to the body. We may need an education in spiritual reading so as not to make the common and basic mistake of focusing on the literal rather than on the implied, on the loudest notes rather than on their overtones.

I feel so strongly about the value of finding spirit under the skin of ordinary ordeals that I am suspicious of spiritual writing that goes too plainly and directly for the higher atmospheres. It can be done, of course, but in my view is rarely successful or effective. That's why I enjoy the Zen parable, the Sufi tale, the mystic's poem, the African recital, the Biblical story, and the personal narrative. Spirituality has special forms that are powerful—the psalm, the prayer, the meditation—but they might best prepare us to read the denser and less direct story in which the incarnated spirit shows itself only to the perceptive eye. In some spiritual traditions only a sharp teacher can yank the spiritual motif out of the seemingly naive tale.

The art historian Edgar Wind says of the tale of Marsyas, "the flaying was itself a Dionysian rite, a tragic ordeal of purification by which the ugliness of the outward man was thrown off and the beauty of the inward self revealed." Ordeals of purification represent one theme among many in which we can spot the spiritual in the apparent secular context. Incidentally, there is a wealth of spiritual insight to be found in the art history of a writer like Wind— yet another complexification of the very idea of spiritual writing.

I have been called a spiritual writer and yet I never think of myself as such a thing. Could this unselfconsciousness be a prerequisite? Is it helpful not to go about spiritual writing directly? Or is it a misnomer in my case? I write about the deep soul, which is intimately connected to the spirit but is not identical with it. My hope is to get the soul that enlivens ordinary days and gives meaning to ordinary ordeals linked more closely to the spirit to keep spirituality honest and safely grounded in the common humanity rooted in our weaknesses. The spirit inspires, but it is the deep soul that keeps us connected, empathic, and compassionate. These might be good signs to look for in spiritual writing. Without the soul, spirituality can be dangerous to your health and to the common good.

Once I was standing at the back of a lecture hall when I overheard two people talking about the spiritual speakers they had heard in person. About me one of them said, "Oh, he's not as inspiring as the others." I took the comment as a compliment. In my view, spiritual writing need not always inspire and thrill. Its first task is to give our ordinary ordeals deep context and tools of transcendence. It should help us get through life rather than above or around it. It should turn us inside out, peeling back our skin of literalism, and remind us to hear the divine and angelic music that sounds through in any good piece of writing of any genre that has been inspired by a muse and directed toward the slightest transcendence of our ordinary days.

CHRISTOPHER BAMFORD

In the Presence of Death

from *Lapis*

For Tadea Dufault Bamford (1947–1996)

*Rose, o pure contradiction, to be no one's sleep
under so many lids.*

Rainer Maria Rilke

Two years ago, I was granted the gift of accompanying my wife Tadea over the threshold. It was not the first death at which I was present, but it was the first that I attended with the fullness of my being. It was an experience I shall never regret, a grace for which I am grateful. Psychologically, physically even, the personal loss, the pain, the grief, the disorientation remain—to be lived through, transformed, never to be forgotten. Not to be gotten over, certainly, but to be understood, illuminated, and gathered up in the greater light of the gift that came with them. The gift and the disorientation came together. It is not possible for me to imagine them apart. Both remain. I cannot say I have brought them together, but I have come to understand that life is praise and lamentation, and that these two are very close, perhaps one—and that they are transformative. Despite the almost constant sadness, confusion, setbacks, self-pity, and other burdens of ordinary egotism, I feel the wound, the opening, and sometimes the joy, the certainty of knowing that meaning exists, even if I am not yet able to cognize it fully.

Sergius Bulgakov, the Russian Orthodox priest and sophiologist, tells of a near-death experience in which he beheld two figures of light and recognized that they accompany each one of us through life. On one side, the Crucified One; on the other, radiant, serene, golden with light, the Risen One. These two figures frame the reimagination of death I am trying to live.

But it is with the gift that I wish to begin.

Tadea died very quickly—about six months from diagnosis to passing, about a month from when medicine gave up to when she died.

During that last month, I was with her about twenty-three hours out of every twenty-four. Tadea, or perhaps I should say death, "Brother Death" as St. Francis calls it, was my teacher. She sat very quietly, very consciously, with a certain peace and patience. She resisted nothing. The day consisted mostly in attending to the details of her care. Mostly she couldn't eat, but she was always willing to try, knowing that was important to us. She had to be moved fairly regularly, an enormous bank of fifteen or so pillows constantly rearranged so that her posture and seat were slightly different. There were periodic bouts of vomiting, mostly bile, and some indescribably clear fluid. People visited and the ones who stayed mostly sat with her in silence. While she could, she knitted, and read a little. But soon that made very little sense, so she just sat, communing with whomever was with her, reassuring us in some way that all would be well. In the beginning she had been afraid of dying, while at the same time strangely realizing that it was something she could do. But everyone around her thought only of healing and life. There was really no one she could talk to about dying. All of us with her would hear nothing of it: we wanted only positive thinking. So she went on that inner journey by herself. And, by this time, she knew she was dying, while the rest of us still prayed for healing. So she just sat quietly, waiting for us to understand that all was as it should be.

Looking back, what seems most significant is the transformation that occurred in the experience of time. Everything slowed down, expanded, became qualitative, rather than quantitative. Those weeks seem like an eternity, which I still inhabit. Each day stretched out until it became like a whole life; and within that life the full presence of every moment was itself like a day—a summer day with its flora and fauna, night stars and day stars, its sunrise and early morning, mid-morning and noontime, its long afternoons, evenings, and nights.

In a word, with its routines and rituals, its different kinds of silences, the time surrounding her passing became rhythm. Not in any mechanical way, but in the most alive way imaginable. Time became a set of Chinese boxes, in which each moment, each movement, contained others within others, like a fugue within a fugue, so that I thought if I could but unpack one it would contain all.

To some extent, too, life took on the atmosphere of a dream or a memory. Daily reality ceased to be linear and became more like a field within which relations, connections, emerged and disappeared, often several simultaneously. In that sense, time became space-like. Or rather, the experiences of time and space became so closely united that one could not separate them. Time became spatial, extended, volumetric, dense, while space, that is, the sickroom and the phenomena within it (the icons and flowers, the minerals and crystals, the vomit pail and the piles of papers and books and medicines, as well as the ever-changing light and air, the sounds and symphonic silences, filled with insects, breezes, and scents) became temporal, a rhythmic dance.

As in a dream, a great deal was happening continuously but instantaneously—as it were in the twinkling of an eye—within a context of changelessness. Huge meanings were palpable, but not graspable by the conscious mind. And as in a dream, I acted without reflection, without questioning. I found myself "living without a why"—repeating the same small tasks and gestures that a bedridden patient requires, always the same, always different. It was a life without discursive thought. As in a dream, too, it was difficult to concentrate, to focus in the usual way. And yet I found I gave my whole being, not just a part, to whatever activity was at hand.

To use another metaphor, time, each moment, became a gift, a grace. It was as if all rested in God's hands. Everything was given over and became gift. I no longer experienced the movement of time, the current of life, as horizontal—as having a before and after, a past and a future, the one in some sense behind, pushing, and the other ahead, approaching—but as vertical. Each moment came as a miraculous opportunity. A gift that was realized, received, in the giving back. Because of this, the room was filled with a sense of sacrifice and also with gratitude and wonder: gratitude for every perception, every moment; wonder at the enormity of life, its perpetual abundance, and at death's being a part of it.

Probably sensing this, Tadea would not tolerate any negative feelings in the room. Nor any overly discursive or philosophical conversation. No sermons, please, she said. No sad faces. No resistance. No pretense, no disguise. It seemed she wanted only the truth that we are, the reality of the moment. Around her, only praise or affirmation seemed appropriate.

Indeed, permeating everything and implicit everywhere was an atmosphere of devotion and prayer, praise and service. Every day unfolded almost as a liturgy. So time also became liturgical, the enactment of a divine service in which not just I and the others around me but the whole universe participated, with enormous love and reverence. None of this was heavy. It was nothing formal or organized. It was magically light, as if somewhere musicians with an extraordinary touch were playing through the world and us and thereby raising the hard materiality of the world into a song of praise. Holy! Holy! Holy!

When life is lived in the continuous presence of death, which is the presence of God, it is as if every moment becomes an offering, a communication, received from and given to the spiritual world—by which I mean the greater life of heaven whose entrance, though everywhere, is most obvious in death, which raises the life that is death into the reality of higher life.

Three days before it came, we knew.

The day before we knew had been extraordinary. Previously, Tadea had been vomiting for hours—pitch black bile-like tar. That morning she woke up bright and cheerful. We had been attending the little Catholic Church at the bottom of the hill—the Eucharist especially had meant a great deal to her. But recently she realized that she had never been baptized. She thought it time to take the step. So, this last morning before we knew, the priest came and baptized and confirmed her in Christ. Friends and family stood around the bed. Tadea sat straight up, wide-awake, smiling, even winking when appropriate.

Next day, I stopped the little rituals that had to do with physical healing. Otherwise, outwardly all continued as before. Though her body was ravaged and wasted—she weighed less than eighty pounds—she sat there patient and awake. And yet already everything was different. There was an awesome and still beauty about everything. Her physical body was there, now weakened almost to the extinction of life. It was about to return to nature, bearing the marks of suffering, to carry into the earth the inscription of so much experience, of so many trials, mistakes, joys, disappointments, of moments of crystal clear consciousness as well as so much lived beneath the surface in the dark valleys of a soul's journey. But though she still sat with the tablet of her body, her presence now filled the room. Or rather, presence filled the room. Presences. The room became quieter, the silences more intense and filled with reality. There was a heightened sense of being, an exceptional clarity of perception, an interiority to space and silence I had not suspected before.

Looking back, I would say that I felt for the first time the perspective of heaven. And this changed the meaning of everything. Prayers, for instance, became much less personal. As I said the Lord's Prayer, holding Tadea's hand, I could feel that I was not saying it for myself, by myself, or for us alone, but that a vast chorus of beings, stretching to infinity and back again, was joining with us in a much greater cause than whatever personal desire I might subjectively have. It was now clear that the healing visualization we had been doing—imagining the golden stream of the spirit showering down and washing away all impurity—had to do with purification in a much larger sense than physical healing. One could feel beings gather.

Tadea died at 11 A.M. on a Sunday morning, surrounded by her brother, her three daughters, and myself. That morning, we washed her face with Kiehl's lotion and freshened her cheeks with rose water. We brushed her teeth. She rinsed her mouth out herself, holding the glass in both hands. We combed her hair. The sun flooded in through the windows, rich and golden like wine.

She sat up very serene and straight. Her eyes were closed, and a smile played on her lips. For three days, she had been unable to lie down for fear of vomiting. She was uncomfortable, mostly from lying in bed for a month, and she was physically weak from lack of food and because she was already leaving her body, but she was in no pain and was taking no medication, except for a blood thinner.

At about 9:30, she suddenly raised her voice, as if to someone leaving the room, and said, almost sang, "'Bye!" "Who's leaving?" I asked. "I mean a generic good-bye," she said.

We sat around her on the bed. "I could guzzle the ocean," she said, enjoying the thought. Again, she seemed to smile. Then she said, "It's too bright, I can't see." Thinking that she was referring to the morning sun pouring through the windows, we pinned blankets over the windows, slowing the liquid golden flow to a trickle. "It's not cooperating . . . ," she muttered. Soon, it must have been: she smiled again.

Just before eleven, she asked to be put on the commode. She felt herself leaving. I lifted her onto it. Her face was very pale, bloodless, like marble. She could no longer hold up her head. I supported her as she did her business and then clumsily lifted her back onto the bed. She tottered slightly, then steadied herself, smiling, perhaps at us, but it seemed more likely at some inner experience of her own. Finally, she opened her eyes unnaturally wide and leaned forward ever so slightly as if entering into whatever it was that she was seeing. Then she was gone: no longer a sensible being in the sensible world. Her breath continued for a few moments. Then ceased. Time, which had been slowing down all through the last weeks, stopped. I thought of St. Therese realizing there was no time in heaven. The heavens opened and time ceased. Tadea's journey in an earthly body was over. Physically, she was gone. Grief became the rupture between heaven and earth.

But the liturgy continued, life continued, on both planes. Her body, though it was only her body, had served nobly in the service of her life and was a sacred, numinous thing, to be handled and regarded with awe and reverence. The children bathed, oiled, and washed her with tenderness and love. The house was filled with people. There was an enormous sense of stasis, of in-betweenness, liminality. It was as if, like her, the space we occupied lay between worlds, not yet there, no longer completely here. Unaccustomed to the concrete reality of the spirit, of the living experience of what had before been just the philosophical problem of two worlds, we moved around in an air of trance.

Time was thick with memory—memories bursting with life that poured endlessly from the abyss of loss each person felt. Everyone was moving around absorbed in individual thoughts of her, all of these forming a dense knot that as it were recapitulated her life. Tadea's presence was extraordinarily strong. She seemed gone, but not away. For the moment, lost from this world, but safe in another. What was the way back? How to join the two worlds?

The undertaker came and took her away to pump out the fluids. Forty minutes later, she was back. We dressed her, carried her downstairs, and laid her in a plain pine box in the living room. For three nights, she lay there, someone always with her. The fourth, she lay in the ground.

The experience of her death intensified. The gift—or, I should say, the giving, for it was an ongoing process, always changing, always transforming—never stopped. It was a continuous initiation, one not yet over. I understand now that it is the initiation of life itself. It is as if only death reveals the meaning of life. As if in death the whole of life—its task, its meaning, its fruit, above all, its mystery—is laid bare. But that is to run ahead of myself. Whatever little understanding I may have has come slowly, accompanied by inner tumult and confusion, tears, pain, and much foolishness. I am still in the midst of it all.

Right at the beginning, within days of her passing, I was given some little talismanic gifts, which I think helped me immeasurably to engage the process of what was to come. First—and this is so obvious, but it came with a startling newness—I realized that her life, that each person's life, is a spiritual journey. I do not know whether it was she or death who taught me, but the lesson I learned was that life was not about getting or doing, but about creating virtues in one's soul. I understood, seeing her life unfold before me, as it must have unfolded before her, that what she had sought all her life—through all the messiness, confusion, and struggle of a human life—were certain spiritual aptitudes or faculties. In her case, freedom, trust, spontaneity, the courage to lead from the heart, openness to the joyful intimacy of the present moment—and, above all, perhaps, the virtue of "peace." And that, in a sense, dying was a step on that path, a momentous step perhaps, but the right step for her, at that moment the ripe fruit of her life. Realizing this, I suddenly felt enormous gratitude for having been permitted to be part of her journey. This gratitude filled me entirely. I felt enormous gratefulness for having known her and having been part of her life. And this feeling, opening me right up, spread to everything. Love of God and all God's creation. I encountered every soul, every being, every living thing with the mantra "What do you seek in me? What can I give you?" And I realized how close gratitude is to praise, to sheer affirmation, as a fundamental gesture. And how close praise is to love, for, as the Troubadours knew, through praise the lover lays down self and becomes one with the beloved.

At the same time, I was also confronted with the abyss of all my shortcomings in our life together, all the ways great and small in which I had let Tadea down. I knew that to dwell on these would have been catastrophic. But I was given the gift of recognizing that the way across the abyss of guilt lay in reconciliation or confession and forgiveness. For days, then, I moved through the house, reliving her life and our life together, as she must have been doing where she was. Filled with gratitude, I distilled all that I had learned from her into lessons that I would now take into my life. At the same time, I was overwhelmed with compunction at my weaknesses, falls, and blindnesses. And I realized, painfully, that there was nothing to be done but to seek forgiveness, to forgive and, through the process of forgiveness, find forgiveness. And forgiveness was granted, coming over me slowly over many weeks like a fine rain. Finally, release came, and a new task, when I stood at her grave, and heard her say, clearly, "Now, make a new life." Easier said than done.

Looking back—and perhaps this is true of all initiations—I found myself plunged in the midst of paradoxes. It was as if death itself, and the fact of death, anyone's death, one's own certainly, and especially the death of a loved one, illuminated the fundamental paradox of life. Immediately, on first encounter, this paradox took three basic forms: three related but separate struggles I had to pass through.

First, Tadea was away, but she was not gone. Nor was her journey finished. It continued, wherever she was. That made "wherever she was" a human place, as human as earth, for I knew that she had not left herself behind when she left, but had taken all that she was with her, that she was not one whit less who she was where she was now than she had been when among us. Indeed, I suspected she was more herself, truer to herself, there. All this meant that not only was heaven a human place but that life, her story, was endless; that all our stories are endless. And that to understand the meaning of an endless story—mine, hers or yours—would require a new way of being in the world. And a new way of listening, an endless listening. For we are not used to stories that have no end. We know neither how to live them nor how to tell them nor how to listen to them.

Her presence was so powerful that I could not believe that she was gone. She was here, but not here. She was dead, but she was alive, she was living. That both were true, I knew with absolute certainty. I opened every closet, I ferreted through drawers, I wandered from room to room looking for her. I expected her to appear at every moment. I couldn't believe she would not come back. That I wouldn't find her standing where she ought to be standing, doing what she ought to be doing. On the other hand, I talked to her constantly, knowing that she was where she was, not here, and that she would not return to visibility, to the sense world. And I knew that she heard what I was saying and thinking and feeling, for sometimes she would respond in clear and distinct ways. I also understood that my relationship to her was changing, becoming different from what I had experienced while she was on earth. So many people mourned her passing, and each one had his or her own experiences. I recognized then that the dead belong to everyone—that they have a relationship to all the living and that they are "big" enough where they are so that each of these relationships could be unique and intimate. At other times, too, I understood how the dead participate in our lives, in the life of earth, that they never leave the earth, as it were, or lose their love for it, as Christ likewise is with us to the end of time.

The more I lived, then, with this paradox of "gone but not away," the more it began to resolve itself for me into another that I called, felt, thought of, and lived, as the paradox of heaven and earth. I also thought of it as the Great Life and the lesser life. Joa Bolendas, the Swiss mystic and visionary, had relayed a message to me from Tadea. Joa had received it from her dead brother, Wilhelm. He had seen Tadea and heard her saying as she looked toward the earth, "Love me, and live with me in the great life." But what was the relationship between life on earth and the Great Life? Was the Great Life present on earth, if only we could live in it? Or was it present always? Death opened this paradox for me, and the more I lived with death, with the reality of death as a part of life, as present in life at every moment, as its depth, the more the question for me became one of heaven and earth, invisible and visible, and how to integrate, or even unite, these. I realized that if I were to shut death out of life, pushing it into a realm of impossibility, then I would allow death as the absolute limit and negation of life to define life, and so sever heaven and Tadea forever from earth and me.

Both heaven and earth were now powerful realities for me. I had been given a visualization, which as I practiced and adapted it, brought me as it were imaginally into heaven. In this imagination, Tadea and I are floating down a river of liquid light. I am floating headfirst, face down. She turns me over to face the blue sky. She turns me round, so I float feet first. But I am in a numbed, comatose state. She wakes me up. I awake as if emerging from a dark tunnel. I see where I am. We float into a quiet pool, play for a while in the water, and then clamber out, and walk through a light-filled desert-like landscape, where we meet Mary and Jesus, and kneel before them in prayer. As I say, this brought me imaginally into heaven, and united me with beings present there, but at the same time it strangely kept heaven and earth apart, as separate realities.

This disjuncture, the rupture—which I came to understand was the teaching of grief—focussed with exceptional clarity and penetration the third form of the existential paradox Tadea's death posed for me. This was the paradox of old life/new life. Certainly, it was the hardest thing to realize that Tadea was never coming back. But did that mean that, if I wanted to remain close to her, I had to be where she was? And if it did, how could I be there and here? For certainly I had to be here: here was where my new life would be made, would come. I had to continue to grow and change. I was unwilling to accept that I had to make a choice: there or here. Live here, forget there; live there, forget here. I refused to choose. There had to be a third way, a middle way—a paradoxical place where one could be a being of light and an embodied, passionate, volatile, struggling earthy human with a life to live in the human world of earth in the twilight of the twentieth century.

Thus the journey continued, both the same and different. Many of the experiences that I had come to know during Tadea's dying remained and even intensified. But at the same time I felt myself split into three: as if my journey took place in three worlds, and it was my task somehow to make them one. There was the world of what I called Heaven, or the Great Life, with which I sought to stay in constant contact—through prayer and loving thoughts, and through the awareness that heaven surrounds us at all times and may speak to us in many different, subtle ways. Internally, I experienced intimations that thoughts and feelings and impulses of will were prompted and sometimes finished not by me, but from somewhere else. And externally, in nature and in situations as humdrum as driving, I recognized signs that I was thought of. There was almost a kind of reciprocity in this—as if my awareness of heaven was simultaneously heaven's awareness of me. Very few of these intimations, however, were overt or startling, and when these came they came so quickly that mostly I was left with just the startle, the content gone, as when one awakens from a dream one knows occurred but cannot remember. Mostly, it was just a feeling, a sense of presence, a conviction, even, of heaven's hiddenness within our world. I knew it was there, even if it did not reveal itself. It was as if death had revealed the hiddenness of life and was at the same time itself that hiddenness. So, while living with heaven's presence, I also lived with its hiddenness.

And, all the while, constantly, overwhelming all my efforts to make sense of all this, waves of loss came hard and heavy. Loss, too, became a world, a journey. At first, Tadea's absence was hallucinatorily strong. There was a feeling of dismemberment. Of an abyss. My conscious mind kept repeating, "I can't believe it. It's impossible." I had suffered loss before—in childhood and in divorce. But this was different. It forbade any illusions and would not allow itself to be rationalized. It simply was and is—a great truth. And yet, gradually, what felt for months both like an amputation that had severed an organ of my being and like an oppressive, amorphous, tangled, congested cloak of darkness and unknowing, clarified. The part that was made up of my own anger, my sense of betrayal and abandonment, my survivor's guilt, and my fear of the unknown, slowly dropped away. The wound, the gap, the abyss remained. I still had no sense of where to go, what to do, and why. "Living without a why" no longer worked. And yet, around the edges, I began to recognize that this feeling of loss and disorientation—that death itself, for the living—could also be a threshold, a bridge to new experience. Indeed, I came to think that death is "threshold" itself, and that, insofar as I am able to not separate it from life, life itself becomes the threshold it seeks to be, forever and abundantly opening into newness.

And at the same time, like the stranger at one's table, the third paradox came home to roost. There was my actual new world, my new life. That I would have to make, but how? I felt like a newborn child. Nothing from my old life worked anymore. The habits, the routines, all my old ways seemed dead, like a dead man's clothes. I did not want to wear a dead man's clothes. And besides, they no longer fit. I wondered desperately how you make a world. I kept trying, inventing transitional objects as an infant does when making its world. Useless, of course, both the trying and the desperation. I realized that I could not make a new life with my thick head. That I would have to learn a new kind of patience and openness. I am still trying.

And so I began to live in what I learned to call "the middle voice." This is a grammatical category in ancient Indo-European languages used to denote the action of verbs that are neither active nor passive, but, as it were, both at the same time—as, for instance, when what is received is what is given: the gift as both what we give and what we receive. In ancient times, this grammatical voice was used to express, in ritual and liturgy, the mediation of the divine in human action. But as I lived into the experience of death and tried to hold death and life, heaven and earth, together in a single gesture, it came to have a more universal application. For I came to understand that the dead, and so the whole invisible world, are always with us, seeking to participate in all we do and all that is done on earth and that all our actions ask to be mediated, shared, by them.

I came to realize, too, the deeper meaning of what Rudolf Steiner meant when he said that humanity is the "religion" of the gods (as the "gods" are the source of our religion). He meant that the earth herself as we experience it with all our senses, faculties, feelings and so on, is the religion of the gods. I understood then that the beings of heaven, including the dead, look to our experience to allow them to participate in heaven in their "religion of the earth" and that thereby everything that takes place on earth takes place in heaven as well. So we are all called to be priests offering the liturgy of our experience to the spiritual world, thereby allowing it to participate, on its side, in its liturgy of service to the same evolution of the cosmos and the divine.

In other words, seeking to be true to the unity of life and death, heaven and earth, seeking an integrated duality, a cooperating polarity, gave life a sacramental quality. And I realized, too, that from the point of view of heaven only selfless experiences (actions, feelings, thoughts), or experiences offered up, even ever so slightly, so that they are somehow not for oneself alone but for the world, have value—that to the angels and the dead, experiences that are really only self-feeling, wholly closed in on themselves, are infinitely saddening, because they exclude heaven.

None of this, of course, came all at once; nor easily; nor was nearly as heavy as it sounds.

It was a sort of alchemical journey—separating the fixed from the volatile, the spirit from the body, and then reuniting them. In the first weeks, I lived, in a sense, more in heaven than on earth. It was as if I had actually passed over the threshold. My earthly part had to struggle to keep up. Things were certainly happening around me, destiny continued to mold and call me—after all, I lived my life on earth—but events on earth took a considerable time to filter through, or rather I did not realize what was going on, what new sequences of events were precipitating, until I came back over the threshold—crashed, as it were, and the world fell apart.

During those weeks before the crash, as if in a dream, the supersensible reality of the deathbed vigil continued—the changed sense of time, the sense of the world as liturgy, the feeling of gratitude and gift in every moment. Insights, too, kept coming, who knows from where, to help me perhaps, disconnected, but part of a whole. The first was the realization, focussed by death, that all of creation participates in every moment. At church one Sunday, celebrating the Eucharist, I recognized that just as all humanity (and thereby also the earth herself) was present and invoked and united in the sacrificial breaking of the bread, so too all the dead (and all the angels and spirits) were also present—that in some sense all humanity, whether embodied in heaven or on earth, is united, a single being. The sense of interconnection, of kinship, of solidarity, was overwhelming. I had a real sense that all are members of one body, speakers in a single conversation, and I understood that while living with death as the end of life has perhaps helped us evolve our individuality, it has also set us one against the other and promulgated the Darwinian world of each against all. It now seemed the reality was quite different. Life was without end. Therefore, every human being was connected to and responsible for every other. There was nothing of which I knew of which I could say: "That's not my responsibility."

At the simplest and the deepest level, this came down to the love of God and the love of every individual soul I met. I vowed to serve God and to serve every soul. To carry these in my heart and to rejoice in them for their own sake. I understood, too, the subtlety and gentleness this requires.

In fact, it seemed everything now taught and demanded subtlety and gentleness—a kind of delicate, watchful patience and the ability to wait, without expectation, but with open heart and mind. Strangely, I experienced this above all in nature. It was as if all my senses came alive in a new way. I had never experienced the rhythms, the colors, the diversity, and the infinite richness of life so powerfully. I became aware of a vast current of life pulsing fecund and abundant through the world. Birds particularly took on a heraldic role. I had never noticed so many or, perceptually, entered into so intimate a relationship with them. They seemed the very embodiment of life between and uniting worlds. I could not speak the language of the birds, but I could understand why angels are always depicted with wings. And somehow this current of life was related to the transformed sense of time, where time became space, and unfolded not in lines, but in intricate, interwoven rhythms. Standing transfixed before nature— before a tree or a rock, or watching a bird, or the proliferation of weeds and herbs in an overgrown, unheeded corner—I had a profound sense of movement in place, of this current of life or time as a vortex opening vertically, uniting all worlds. And at each point, at each rhythmic vortex, I could sense the participation of heaven in earth. Perhaps it was my imagination that the early morning fog, coiling and trailing over the landscape, dense and white, was somehow fructifying the vegetation in ways undreamed of by botanists. Perhaps it was my imagination, too, that the dead likewise care for and love the earth as if it were their garden and rejoice in and in some strange way share in my perceptions.

Nor was this sense of the rhythmic vortex of time, in which all heaven sought to participate, limited to single perceptions of individual things. It also contained them all. So that the seasons, too, and the great round of the year, came alive for me in a new way and became a palpable, living whole, participated in by the gift of death.

On my side, no matter how great my disorientation, pain, and confusion, I was and remain filled with gratitude and, what is so close to it, praise. In heaven, says Elizabeth of the Trinity, each soul is a praise of glory. Each soul there, praising, lives no longer its own life, but lives in love, and knows as it is known.

I made a vow to receive all that came to me as a gift and, in the middle voice, transform it, make it human, and offer it up as gift of praise to the beauty, the truth, and the goodness of existence.

Thereby, I found myself loving the world more than I ever had.

I understood then that life itself, each moment as it becomes experience, perception, feeling, cognition, is such a gift—given in the receiving, received in the giving. I knew too that this giving and receiving demands absolute trust and confidence, nothing held back, no protection, no barriers, radical openness and receptivity.

I struggled with the problem that the concept of the Great Life was of no use if it did not give meaning to this life—the life of the soul and human heart, with all its brokenness, confusion, and pain. But then I realized that just as the Risen Christ is the Crucified Christ, nothing of our experience is lost or worthless in the eyes of life. That, indeed, as Julian of Norwich affirmed, "in heaven our sins will be not shame but glory to us."

Thus my life continues, a stammering liturgy, forever seeking to bring earth into heaven, heaven into earth, and forever falling back and down into the various abysses that hold the worlds apart. Sometimes there is conversation, sometimes there is holy silence, often there is a dark pit, close to depression, sleepless nights and pointless days. Rarely, but with a sweet promise, there is song. I think of the lines of the poet Hoelderlin in "Celebration of Peace:"

Much have we learned, from morning on,
Since we have been a conversation and listen to each other,
—but soon we shall be song.

LIONEL BASNEY

Immanuel's Ground

from *The American Scholar*

When I was a boy, there was a camp meeting in my town. Since then it has become a Summer Family Conference and convenes in the facilities of the local college. But in those days it was a genuine holiness meeting, such as used to be common in American country places. The parents of those who came to the conference lived, then, in screened cottages and dormitories on the elm-roofed camp-ground, where their parents had lived in tents with plank or straw floors, and used washstands beneath the trees. It was the middle generation I knew. They were a new population, in town every third week of July; the plates on their large secondhand cars read Ohio and Indiana and Florida. They held three services a day in the tabernacle, preaching and singing and praying. After supper, fanning themselves in the hot westering sun, they listened to missionaries describe the work in Africa, while the supper dishes clinked and someone whistled in the camp kitchen across the gravel drive.

I am writing of events forty years ago, in rural New York State, but these events represented something far older, as old almost as the national frontier once it had crossed the Appalachians. Camp meeting grew out of revivals flaring along southern rivers in 1799 and 1800, among people who, cheated on land and without a cultural fabric, made up a new culture on the spot. Two generations later, great vacation camp meetings, such as those at Ocean Grove and on Martha's Vineyard, were built by a Protestant hegemony setting out to reframe American life. Two generations after that, after war, boom, and the Scopes trial, the hegemony had withered to an embattled minority trying to keep itself alive in the minds of its children. Ours was a small, obscure camp meeting. Few came, compared with the crowds on Martha's Vineyard, though our tabernacle was often full on Sunday nights. No one would come to argue with us, at least; no one bothered the cars in the stony parking lot, under the streetlight in its haze of insects.

The cottages on Martha's Vineyard, with their frilled eaves, have gone into American architectural history. Our tabernacle was just a roof of unplaned lumber above a concrete floor—closer, therefore, to its origins, the barn and the preaching-shed. I would distract myself from the sermon by tracking with my eyes the intricate raftering, the swing beams and purlins, the braces around the posts that held the roof up. Or tied it down. The design worked in the Gothic way, converting mass to suspension. The more wood that had gone into it, the lighter it had become. On stuffy evenings the ushers would slide the hangar doors open on both sides, leaving the roof seemingly without walls, floating on the uncertain air like a linen of rough pine. "I tell you. . . !" the preacher would shout, and above his voice, and above our singing, the tabernacle seemed to brood, impassively, with shadows under its wings.

The surrounding towns called ours "the holy city." It was officially dry, no hotel or bowling alley, its life dominated by the alliance of the college and the one big collegiate church. The town stood on plateaus let into the west wall of the river valley like balconies—one for the school, another above it for the campground, smaller ones, like lofts, for houses. To reach the campground, you wound up from balcony to balcony and finally bent a steep hairpin curve into the trees. The camp meeting hill was a kind of promontory over the long opening of the river, above the cornfields. Thrust out like a pulpit or castle keep, it was the first thing you saw of the town as you came from the north. You couldn't see the buildings, only the scrubby slope and the high battlement of trees. From among the trees, you couldn't see the valley.

Nor could you see the town, the college, or the lofts of houses. The campground was closed in. Eleven months of the year it was all but deserted. In summer, before and after the meeting, it was all but wild. Birds filled the trees and flung themselves through the air in front of you. Squirrels scrabbled tail up and tail down on the huge trunks and yelped back at the jays and crows, and at you, the intruder.

On the side of the tabernacle away from the road, weeds grew calf high right up to the cement sill. The grass was gray with dust that the rain huffed up from the clotted ground. Snakes lived there, sidling off as you walked out into the gravelly worn space, vaguely a drive, that curled around the tabernacle and separated it from cottages, dormitories, and kitchen. Even in front, the ground was raw and stony, the grass unmown. There were no monuments in the town square of this little temporary settlement. Its monument was itself—that it was just this, just here, that these were the circumstances of the repeated moment when people turned to face the reality they knew could not be negotiated.

When we think about religion, this is what we are looking for—the cultural traces, the formalities, of that encounter, so that by recording and understanding them we might come to understand the encounter itself. It had, for the plain people, the shape, the sounds, the smell of that grove and its wooden shed. You carried the meeting away with you when it was done, in memories of nights that were like the scars of home or of breaking away from home. Corners of the campground, or of the tabernacle itself, would go away in minds to the ends of the earth.

We walk up to the tabernacle in the hot late afternoon, after supper. The July sun has dulled the trees. The college lawns rust in the weeks of heat. Now the white light going orange lies like an abrasion on the tabernacle's matte-white walls. People are arriving from all directions. Their motion, the heated cars pulling up, the exhaust in the ballooning dust are not motion at all, but a property of the frozen heat and light. We live close enough to walk, across the scalded plain of the campus, onto a path as steep and narrow as an escalator trailing up the hill. None of this seems like motion either. Nothing seems to move. Everything is happening in the same moment. In the expectation of God.

The college falls away beneath us as we climb. The path peters out into a rutted, sandy patch of weeds and empties us into the grove. The grass, ropy as kelp, is rank with beaded, unripe ragweed and hoary dandelions. From the cottages and parking lot people assemble, the women with faces lowered into blossoms of shared gossip, the men carrying their jackets over their forearms. Children run and screech among the elms. There is a gush of organ music from the tabernacle. We walk deliberately toward it. I feel caught on a hook, my breath coming fast already.

Now the sun angles in from the deep west, and the white walls shine with light as sharp and flat as acid. Inside the tabernacle it is darker, stuffy. The wide doors are slid back on both sides, the air comes in, the tabernacle roof is airborne above us. The crowd stands with a grumble of chairs and feet; the organ punches the last phrase of a song everyone knows, in the quavery Hammond blat that is like batting in the ears; and we sing.

Around its edges the crowd is still frayed and gathering, people hurrying to places, the ushers walking quickly back up the aisles and signaling to each other to bring people down to empty seats in front. We sit down, the lath folding chairs crackling, and are welcomed. The presiding minister's smile seems to me rank pretense; but perhaps he is not afraid. I watch the line of ministers on the platform. They sing without songbooks, leaning over to speak with one another, nod and smile among themselves; their faces scan the crowd like searchlights. They join the song or leave it for a phrase, beating time on their knees with their Bibles.

They sit in a slight shadow. In the early evening the platform seems dim. All around us the tabernacle is ringed with windows and open doors. As the service begins, it is dark inside and the windows are full of daylight. As evening comes on, the windows grow clear, as if they were display cases in a museum of the real world: you can look out (in) on summer foliage, western New York, 1955. Then the lights are switched on and the room is ringed with darkness. The tabernacle gathers light into itself, holds it, until it is a ship blazing in the dark, the only survivor of the light. Late in the sermon the doors are still open, and the night outside is intense.

There is my family, sitting on folding chairs on the extreme western edge of the crowd, by a door. There I am, I can see myself; I seem composed, grave, but I can feel the terror behind the gravity in the child's round face. He is afraid of the approaching sermon and of what may come next, the call of God, the encounter.

With half his mind, however, he is listening to the crickets outside. He is holding to the world out there, making it real. Sometimes there is a sudden rise in the wind, whipping up dust and blowing through the wide doorway. The wind ruffles sheet music on the piano—the pianist grabs at the pages, smooths them back, rearranges her books—and in a hymnal lying open on an empty chair the pages flap and settle. No one but the boy seems to notice.

Sometimes there is rain. The air suddenly rouses and freshens, turns its cool lining outward, with the clamminess of the storm in its folds. There is a rush of wind, like the swell of an excited crowd, and the trees out of sight above the roof edge hiss and shush. Raindrops wash across the threshold like a scatter of grain and then begin to hammer steadily on the concrete. The roof bellows. In the myth time I am inhabiting, it seems inexplicable that the rain goes on regardless of the sermon. There is a voice in the storm. Which voice should I be listening to? There are two worlds, and I am sitting in both.

But the two worlds are most distinct and intense on perfectly still evenings, when the tabernacle is warmly yellow and the night seems to draw close to hear the preacher shout. The oldest sound outside, a sound so native to that northeastern summer as to be its natural form of silence, is the pulse of crickets. The preaching is an active sound, the crickets' sound contemplative. The preacher drives us toward decision, doing something, standing up, going forward. The sound outside leads you back to the summer evening— isolating, quieting, interiorizing, the song of a world that wants nothing, in which I could want nothing. At the moment, tormented by the preaching, I want that outside world with a desperate pathos. Even the passing of an occasional breeze raising its shallow applause among the trees does not disturb the stillness beyond the light.

Nothing moves. I sit in two worlds. This is myth time: summer, religion. The small enclosed grove, on the hill, is divided between light and dark. The portly women fan themselves, absorbed in the sermon. The evangelist wipes his neck. I can see myself, there, the grave dark face containing its terror and curiosity. The preacher is still calling to me; the evening is still at the door.

We leave the tabernacle and outside it is dark. "It was so dark," my mother writes me of the campgrounds of her childhood. "There were the little lights on tents here and there among the trees—but it was so dark." In the countryside, the city grid fifty miles away, we are in something like the actual darkness of the planet with the sun out of sight. Camp meeting stranded you in the night and gave you a little light to make it tolerable. It was like being stranded in time and having no more to go on than our small clearings of language. Camp meeting was in a clearing, too, the columnar trees stirring in their invisible tops. I doubt a plane would even have noticed us below—a few porch lights, the one streetlight in its steam of bugs.

The preaching, of course, appealed to brilliantly explosive light, fire falling from heaven (as it was said literally to have done during the Welsh revivals of 1905) and the light on the Damascus road. Our songs were wiser. "Let the lower lights be burning, / Send the news across the waves." Something about a hymn sung in our shopworn voices injected modesty into the project. "God has given me a lifeboat," D. L. Moody liked to say, "and told me, 'Moody, save all you can.'" The *Titanic* of Western culture was, after all, going down. It is a complex image, spiky. There is the triumphalism of watching what Hardy called "this vaingloriousness" disappear; there is also the tragic modesty of being able to do only a little. And the lifeboat lantern is hard to see past. It is so dark.

I have tried, but I can't recall the tabernacle lights being switched on. It must have happened. We felt the fall of dark. The light seemed not to vanish but to come inside, shrinking and brightening. Things narrowed and focused as the service went on, first to the pulpit, then to the altar rail, the point of energy and desire where people, kneeling, disappeared behind the people who were standing, and then in a minute voices would rise above the singing—"Glory! Hallelujah!" The dark outside served the purpose of the meeting; or, actually, the service had accommodated the gigantic event, the arrival of night, adapting itself in a triumph of cultural invention no less significant for being unconscious, simply accommodating the unavoidable: camp meeting was an outdoors phenomenon.

Culture is invented when circumstances are welded together with the widest intuition of their meanings. Religion can be had anywhere, any day, for a set fee, but faith is time- and place-specific. This is why the Bible says, *Now is the hour of salvation. . . . Now, if you will hearken. . . .* But there is also the observation, *You do not know the day or the hour. . . .* This makes the specificity of faith urgent. We must be, we were, endlessly accountable for what we did in a particular meeting on a particular night. *Be watchful, therefore.* Back we go to circumstances: the call is to presence and attention. The world is about to change around you.

At Cane Run, Kentucky, the Jerusalem of the camp meeting pentecost, you can enter the cramped log church that was standing on the ridge in August 1801, when the enormous "union meeting" began. The church is clean, restored, and quiet; its keepers have encased it in a stone basilica to keep the weather away. The revival itself, by contrast, was loud, out-of-doors, seismic, unpredictable. We can only guess how many people came, but they overwhelmed the preparations; the meeting expanded like a storm, or many overlapping tornadoes, and people a mile off could hear its heavy, abiding murmur, like the sound of a battle. While the meeting lasted, the rules of normal culture vanished. The little church has a slave balcony, but outside, slaves and masters marched side by side and women and children preached. From then on for a century, the signs of the American pentecost would be night and fire, forest and cleared place, marching, fainting, falling, and crying out, the midnight parade under flaring pine knots, the sacramental meal in a grove by a river.

Of course when the torches guttered and stank in the damp mosquito-thick dawn, things went back to normal. But what does it mean for things to be normal? More changed at Cane Run than styles of worship. Camp meetings were one source of abolitionist politics and so involved the causes of civil war. They involved its causes in a looser way: they were part of war's imaginative economy. Crossing over Jordan into campground, tenting there, the "hundred circling camps" with their altars and their "righteous sentence" read out in torch light: such images are not chosen or designed—rather, exuded, almost, from intense experience—but they made war plausible and therefore possible.

A new iconography is a new history: a set of conditions in which unprecedented things can be deliberately done. Any intensely religious event is an intensely worldly event. It remakes the world itself by affecting the meanings of the most comprehensive, least avoidable conditions. A religious event that does not change the meaning of light and dark, fire and water, food and drink, field and city, war and peace, birth and death, slavery and freedom has too superficial a connection with us. One that does can create culture.

Not a new mind, but a new world. Conversion changes the actual; things look and sound different. Different conduct, naturally, is required; people change their hopes and common practices. Cranmer's Third Collect for Evening Prayer—"Lighten our darkness we beseech thee"—does not say whether it is physical or spiritual darkness that is to be illumined. This is the prayer's great accuracy: what seems to be praying is the human condition, physical and imaginative at once. Cranmer's writing has the power of Shakespeare's. "The dark and vicious place where he thee got / Cost him his eyes," Edgar says of his father—not that Gloucester's punishment is proportionate, but that, having put himself in the line of darkness, he couldn't calculate or restrain the terrible darkness that might come. If Macbeth murders sleep, he will not sleep. Skeptics who mocked the camp-meeting exhorters for their ecstatic behavior were said to have been struck blind, suddenly groping and stumbling where they had been jumping and howling a moment before.

A circuit rider named Johnson is picking his way through the malarial Indiana woods at night. It is perhaps 1815. He and his horse blunder off the invisible track, slide twice into a ravine, and scramble out. He loses the horse altogether and stumbles on, falling into a river, and then, having recovered his mount, sits drenched and wretched in the utter lostness of the wilderness. The horse is half-asleep; it shifts and stamps. Johnson asks himself where he is. Immediately the answer comes, a hymn line—"We are marching through Immanuel's ground"—and he kicks the horse forward onto Immanuel's ground and is located, a few minutes later, by someone hearing him sing as he rides.

Indiana into Immanuel's ground: the conundrum lies in how it occurs. But then what do we know about religion? We have hardly advanced beyond William James: "If you ask *how* religion thus falls on the thorns and faces death, and in the very act annuls annihilation, I cannot explain the matter, for it is religion's secret, and to understand it, you must yourself have been a religious man of the extremer sort." Setting the condescension aside, James has two important things right: it is the "extremer" case—the genuine believer—who provides the crucial data; and the religious do understand.

But that will not be enough to say, and the condescension cannot be set aside. There are two languages here, two resources of explanation, and James will accept only one of them, that of science. The religious understand, but not in a language James can hear. The gap is as wide as the coming of secular culture, as sharp as the mind-body problem; it is the abyss Kierkegaard insisted on to renew the urgency of faith. Religion can be had anywhere, for a set fee, but it does not correspond to, it only accompanies, the "secret." "For it is in ritual," Clifford Geertz wrote, "—that is, in consecrated behavior—that the conviction that religious concepts are veridical and that religious directives are sound is somehow generated." Somehow: there is always this stop in the argument.

It stops at the division of languages, at the tabernacle door, watching the people streaming forward and not knowing what to say.

"There is no criterion," Paul Tillich wrote, "by which faith can be judged from the outside." The question of whether "religious concepts are veridical" will have to be asked by the faithful themselves, who "can say," Tillich went on, ". . . whether the medium through which [they experience] ultimate concern expresses real ultimacy." Then Tillich vacillated: or someone else can say. But how? The truth is that religious believers are always asking themselves this question, though not in Tillich's language, and that if there is a subjective answer in devotion, the objective evidence is the persistence of the community that believes.

For it is finally a matter of how belief is born in the new believer. That it occurs is plain; how it occurs may be told, and the narratives can, within a given community, be formalized, but finally we will have no evidence but the narrative. *I once was lost, but now am found.* Found where? In the place that faith has changed. In that place you meet others whose stories may be radically different from yours; but all of you recognize the place. In the tabernacle most of the young people eventually yielded to the magnetism of the altar and stepped, or were carried, across the threshold. Others went away, up the aisle, hostile and embittered. Their narrative was often political: the service was an exercise of unrationalized authority, an imposition. But they had misread the event; it had shrunk to the size of the preacher's mouth. They had lost track of most of the facts—the singing, the yellow light, the concrete floor so cold through the strip of carpet, the grove outside, where it was so dark. That wasn't where they wanted to be found.

In both worlds it is getting late. The sweetness of the grove rides in the open door on an occasional puff of cool wind. Inside the tabernacle it is warm, almost hot, in the yellow light, and the air has its own stuffy sweetness—perfume, hymnal paper, the dusty plushiness of the old seats. The sermon is almost done. Now it is done, and the altar call begins. If the altar is not barren, as we say, many will kneel there, and your private prayer will be buoyed, or will have to struggle, on the tide of many public ones.

How they swarm up out of my memory, the voices of those altar calls: "Come home!" the melody rises like a question, "come home," the question is answered by deeper voices in harmony, "come home!" the melody sweeps back down and then begins a stepwise climb, "Ye who are weary, come home!" Then the calmer prose—"Softly and tenderly, Jesus is calling. . . ."

When we get to the high note, the minister is waiting for us. It has been all the verses and four choruses, and the aisles are full of people slipping out and going forward in a broken stream, but the minister knows there are more to be persuaded. He has been beating time with his Bible in both hands, not singing, but seeming to soak up the music, to become charged with its electricity, and now as we climb to the song's highest pitch, he calls out, "Softly and tenderly," and then we sing, back and forth, "Softly and tenderly," "Jesus is calling," "Jesus is calling," and when we near the end of the chorus, he says to the song leader, always the attentive lieutenant at his right shoulder, "Brother Mitchell, could we sing just one more verse?" And we do.

All around me the song whelms. I am standing on an inside aisle, sharing a songbook and singing in a choked, subdued voice. I study the ridges and pits and welts in the concrete floor, just feet away. My heart is yanking in my chest like a trigger; I am trembling and cannot move.

Now the minister stops the singing. He tells us how it will be with him in an hour, after the service is done and the last opportunity is gone, when he kneels in his room and the Lord asks him,

"Roy, did you give it to them straight?" He is making us responsible for the agony of self-examination he will have to endure. Eventually he comes to the inescapable, mythical story about the young person who resisted the call and that very night, going home from the meeting, was killed by a tractor trailer, trampled into eternity by the screaming tires. The effect of the story is to make you afraid to step out of the tabernacle; but the child had been afraid to come in. There is, he sees, no escaping; now is the day, the hour, the moment.

There is a woman kneeling at the altar not far from the child. She is a regular, the wife of a minister—a small, energetic, kittenish woman who wears bolero skirts and, instead of braiding her hair and hiding it, lets it cascade, black and prematurely graying and full of ringlets, down her back. She kneels beside her husband, a strikingly handsome man. We know why they are there. They do not need the grace of the altar themselves, though they would not say so; they are praying for others. But her concern has an edge. She is full of spontaneous resentment—she would probably call it righteous anger—against those who would challenge her place in her understanding of things. She is a small, delicate person, but I cannot remember ever seeing her smile. And now, somehow, she lifts her head and turns from the altar rail to look straight at me. The look—which I remember now, forty years later, with perfect lucidity, as if she were looking straight through time—is as flat and cruel as a lynx's stare.

I do not go to the altar—I cannot move—and eventually the meeting ends. I am still afraid but at the same time intensely relieved, as if after months of testing and suspense I have been told that I have a fatal illness and nothing can be done, and I can set about reconciling myself to it. We are near the door and slip out into the darkness throbbing with crickets. The two worlds resolve into one. But it feels flat, one-dimensional. I have lost something.

So the account ends there. The innocent, vacant self is compelled, or required at least, to buckle to the unintelligible, authoritarian demand.

I have told that story to fine, liberal-minded religious people, and they have been shocked. "How did you survive?" The question shows a misunderstanding, though, and in a modern way, by assuming that the self is self-ordaining and that any contribution to its options that is larger than the self is an imposition and therefore a cruelty. But this is not the meaning of the experience.

The question is, have you met whatever you take to be non-negotiable—God, the divine, death, the ultimate ground of being—and held the encounter until the other declared its name? "Those who are awakened to the light," Tillich wrote, "ask passionately the question of ultimate reality. They are different from those who do not." The awakening and then the question. Whatever interior movement it is that occurs in conversion, that small, deeply cut turning of a corner, it is a moment when one has no choice and one's choice is free.

Other nights, other moments. We are singing, many have gone forward, the altar is not barren. Then one of the seekers stands and walks back up the aisle toward me. He passes my right shoulder, and, as he does, he looks me in the face and smiles.

I know him slightly. He is someone caught up and bewildered by religion, someone who lacks the emotional sturdiness, perhaps, to stand in the beating of that relentless surf. He is odd. He buttonholes people on Wednesday mornings and demands, "Is there an angel in that tree? *Right there.* Do you believe that?" Angels are as palpable to him as bathtubs.

Anyhow, he passes me and smiles. Something happens to me, more in my face than in my mind. "You were radiant," my girl-friend says. She also is one of us and knows what it means. It is an evidence, a mark in the flesh.

Another service. The sermon ends, the singing begins. An elderly man, dressed in the flat brown gabardine typical of fifties Sunday best, steps out of his row. But he doesn't go to the altar. Instead he stands in the aisle, facing the front, and then raises his right hand above his head. He says nothing, doesn't sing, gesticulate, or look around. But the aisles are suddenly thronged.

Of course he may be a plant, a charlatan, one more device. But the more likely possibility is that he has absorbed the power of that gesture, distilled and intensified, from a lifetime of such services. He has raised Moses' hand above the Red Sea. He might even say it that way. It is like the gesture of a great actress who has moved all her life in the literature of her roles, and no longer invents anything, but moves with the authority of her whole community and tradition.

In any case, it is a manifestation. What was hidden has been shouted from the rooftop. That conductivity of looks and gestures, that radiance passed from face to face as a flame is dipped out of one candle by another, is the unofficial sacrament of the whole enterprise.

I remember wandering past the east wall of the tabernacle one evening and finding, to my surprise, that the door was unlocked. I hauled it barely open on its grating track and edged through. It was late summer, the sun was already down, and while under the trees the air was still light, inside it was dim. The hundreds of seats overlapped up the gentle rake of the floor like the ghosts of shells. I sighed harshly, too deeply, I don't know why. Or I do. I had been afraid here—not the needle panic at human violence, but the larger fear that makes the floor shake and your tongue cleave to the roof of your mouth. The tabernacle's air was sweet with the smell of dusty hymnbook paper. There was something in it, though, of Ezekiel's salt-waste valley where the bones stood up. I walked to the center of the altar rail and knelt. But the people had gone for the season, the meeting had left with them, and the tabernacle was silent at my back.

Where does the power of the religious claim come from? *From something having happened.* The event is the source and the subject of ritual. Yet we can idolize events. "What did you come out to see?" Jesus asked the crowd, with his familiar unsettling irony. "A reed shaken by the wind?" They were expecting too little: a newsworthy occurrence, one more in a series, trivial no matter what—not a change of world. What happened to me was a long cumulative event, a location, an opening. I knew the tabernacle for what it was—a tent in the wilderness, a *sukkah,* the proper home for a journey, for a setting-out-one-knows-not-where, for confidence in things summoned by hope.

This is perhaps the place to say that I am a Christian. If you take as a rule James's divergence of languages, you will find it hard to imagine that the camp meeting carried me beyond its terrors, that I learned—I am indebted to the lynx for this—that I was dealing not with one tainted mind but with ultimate concern. The truth is that I never wholly belonged to the camp-meeting people and cannot easily say why. But I had been enclosed, very young, in very old circumstances—the tabernacle and the wilderness. The believer learns to sit in two worlds at once. What a training for a writer!

And fear had its place in this, along with radiance and longing. "Thanks to its tenderness, its joys and fears," Wordsworth wrote of the heart—and the heart must have places to be afraid in, as Wordsworth knew, and to acknowledge that the fear is not petty or vestigial but called for and warranted. We must know when and how to acknowledge, in the company of others, that our explanations, our myths, and our practical uses for things thin out quite close to us, and that then we must simply wait for meanings that come to us from outside.

We stood, sang, knelt, prayed in the tabernacle on late July nights and waited there together. In their prayer caps and wide, garish ties, these people had made a cultural triumph by paying attention first of all to other things. They had built according to an ideal of plainness—light, dark, the wooden roof, the grove. What the plainness meant was: the intention to *be plain,* with yourself and others; directness of purpose; the long establishment of languages in which spiritual things could be spoken of directly, plainly, in which spiritual business could be done. I would go back and sit there again, if I could—if the tabernacle had not been torn down and the people gone elsewhere—and absorb the preacher's words, the songs, watch the night and the rain wait on the threshold, smell the dense unflowered sweetness of the northern woods. I know that place for what it was: Immanuel's ground.

WENDELL BERRY

The Failure of War

from *Shambhala Sun*

If you know even as little history as I do, it is hard not to doubt the efficacy of modern war as a solution to any problem except that of retribution—the "justice" of exchanging one damage for another.

Apologists for war will insist that war answers the problem of national self-defense. But the doubter, in reply, will ask to what extent the cost even of a successful war of national defense—in life, money, material, foods, health, and (inevitably) freedom—may amount to a national defeat. National defense through war always involves some degree of national defeat. This paradox has been with us from the very beginning of our republic. Militarization in defense of freedom reduces the freedom of the defenders. There is a fundamental inconsistency between war and freedom.

In a modern war, fought with modern weapons and on the modern scale, neither side can limit to "the enemy" the damage that it does. These wars damage the world. We know enough by now to know that you cannot damage a part of the world without damaging all of it. Modern war has not only made it impossible to kill "combatants" without killing "noncombatants," it has made it impossible to damage your enemy without damaging yourself.

That many have considered the increasing unacceptability of modern warfare is shown by the language of the propaganda surrounding it. Modern wars have characteristically been fought to end war; they have been fought in the name of peace. Our most terrible weapons have been made, ostensibly, to preserve and assure the peace of the world. "All we want is peace," we say as we increase relentlessly our capacity to make war.

Yet at the end of a century in which we have fought two wars to end war and several more to prevent war and preserve peace, and in which scientific and technological progress has made war ever more terrible and less controllable, we still, by policy, give no consideration to non-violent means of national defense. We do indeed make much of diplomacy and diplomatic relations but by diplomacy we mean invariably ultimatums for peace backed by the threat of war. It is always understood that we stand ready to kill those with whom we are "peacefully negotiating."

Our century of war, militarism and political terror has produced great—and successful—advocates of true peace, among whom Mohandas Gandhi and Martin Luther King are the paramount examples. The considerable success that they achieved testifies to the presence, in the midst of violence, of an authentic and powerful desire for peace and, more important, of the proven will to make the necessary sacrifices. But so far as our government is concerned, these men and their great and authenticating accomplishments might as well never have existed. To achieve peace by peaceable means is not yet our goal. We cling to the hopeless paradox of making peace by making war.

Which is to say that we cling in our public life to a brutal hypocrisy. In our century of almost universal violence of humans against fellow humans, and against our natural and cultural commonwealth, hypocrisy has been inescapable because our opposition to violence has been selective or merely fashionable. Some of us who approve of our monstrous military budget and our peace-keeping wars nonetheless deplore "domestic violence" and think that our society can be pacified by "gun control." Some of us are against capital punishment but for abortion. Some of us are against abortion but for capital punishment.

One does not have to know very much or think very far in order to see the moral absurdity upon which we have erected our sanctioned enterprises of violence. Abortion-as-birth-control is justified as a "right," which can establish itself only by denying all the rights of another person, which is the most primitive intent of warfare. Capital punishment sinks us all to the same level of primal belligerence, at which an act of violence is avenged by another act of violence.

What the justifiers of these acts ignore is the fact—well-established by the history of feuds, let alone the history of war—that violence breeds violence. Acts of violence committed in "justice" or in affirmation of "rights" or in defense of "peace" do not end violence. They prepare and justify its continuation.

The most dangerous superstition of the parties of violence is the idea that sanctioned violence can prevent or control unsanctioned violence. But if violence is "just" in one instance, as determined by the state, why might it not also be "just" in another instance, as determined by an individual? How can a society that justifies capital punishment and warfare prevent its justifications from being extended to assassination and terrorism? If a government perceives that some causes are so important as to justify the killing of children, how can it hope to prevent the contagion of its logic spreading to its citizens—or to its citizens' children?

If we give to these small absurdities the magnitude of international relations, we produce, unsurprisingly, some much larger absurdities. What could be more absurd, to begin with, than our attitude of high moral outrage against other nations for manufacturing the selfsame weapons that we manufacture? The difference, as our leaders say, is that we will use these weapons virtuously, whereas our enemies will use them maliciously—a proposition that too readily conforms to a proposition of much less dignity: we will use them in our interest, whereas our enemies will use them in theirs.

Or we must say, at least, that the issue of virtue in war is as obscure, ambiguous, and troubling as Abraham Lincoln found to be the issue of prayer in war: "Both [the North and the South] read the same Bible, and pray to the same God, and each invokes his aid against the other. . . . The prayers of both could not be answered—that of neither could be answered fully."

Recent American wars, having been both "foreign" and "limited," have been fought under the assumption that little or no personal sacrifice is required. In "foreign" wars, we do not directly experience the damage that we inflict upon the enemy. We hear and see this damage reported in the news, but we are not affected. These limited, "foreign" wars require that some of our young people should be killed or crippled, and that some families should grieve, but these "casualties" are so widely distributed among our population as hardly to be noticed.

Otherwise, we do not feel ourselves to be involved. We pay taxes to support the war, but that is nothing new, for we pay war taxes also in time of "peace." We experience no shortages, we suffer no rationing, we endure no limitations. We earn, borrow, spend and consume in wartime as in peacetime.

And of course no sacrifice is required of those large economic interests that now principally constitute our economy. No corporation will be required to submit to any limitation or to sacrifice a dollar. On the contrary, war is the great cure-all and opportunity of our corporate economy, which subsists and thrives upon war. War ended the Great Depression of the 1930s, and we have maintained a war economy—an economy, one might justly say, of general violence—ever since, sacrificing to it an enormous economic and ecological wealth, including, as designated victims, the farmers and the industrial working class.

And so great costs are involved in our fixation on war, but the costs are "externalized" as "acceptable losses." And here we see how progress in war, progress in technology, and progress in the industrial economy are parallel to one another—or, very often, are merely identical.

Romantic nationalists, which is to say most apologists for war, always imply in their public speeches a mathematics or an accounting of war. Thus by its suffering in the Civil War, the North is said to have "paid for" the emancipation of the slaves and the preservation of the Union. Thus we may speak of our liberty as having been "bought" by the bloodshed of patriots. I am fully aware of the truth in such statements. I know that I am one of many who have benefited from painful sacrifices made by other people, and I would not like to be ungrateful. Moreover, I am a patriot myself and I know that the time may come for any of us when we must make extreme sacrifices for the sake of liberty—a fact confirmed by the fates of Gandhi and King.

But still I am suspicious of this kind of accounting. For one reason, it is necessarily done by the living on behalf of the dead. And I think we must be careful about too easily accepting, or being too easily grateful for, sacrifices made by others, especially if we have made none ourselves. For another reason, though our leaders in war always assume that there is an acceptable price, there is never a previously stated level of acceptability. The acceptable price, finally, is whatever is paid.

It is easy to see the similarity between this accounting of the price of war and our usual accounting of "the price of progress." We seem to have agreed that whatever has been (or will be) paid for so-called progress is an acceptable price. If that price includes the diminishment of privacy and the increase of government secrecy, so be it. If it means a radical reduction in the number of small businesses and the virtual destruction of the farm population, so be it. If it means cultural and ecological impoverishment, so be it. If it means the devastation of whole regions by extractive industries, so be it. If it means that a mere handful of people should own more billions of wealth than is owned by all of the world's poor, so be it.

But let us have the candor to acknowledge that what we call "the economy" or "the free market" is less and less distinguishable from warfare. For about half of this century, we worried about world conquest by international communism. Now with less worry (so far) we are witnessing world conquest by international capitalism. Though its political means are milder (so far) than those of communism, this newly internationalized capitalism may prove even more destructive of human cultures and communities, of freedom and of nature. Its tendency is just as much toward total dominance and control. Confronting this conquest, ratified and licensed by the new international trade agreements, no place and no community in the world may consider itself safe from some form of plunder. More and more people all over the world are recognizing that this is so, and they are saying that world conquest of any kind is wrong, period.

They are doing more than that. They are saying that local conquest also is wrong, and wherever it is taking place local people are joining together to oppose it. All over my own state of Kentucky this opposition is growing—from the west, where the exiled people of the Land Between the Lakes are struggling to save their homeland from bureaucratic depredation, to the east, where the native people of the mountains are still struggling to preserve their land from destruction by absentee corporations.

To have an economy that is warlike, that aims at conquest and that destroys virtually everything that it is dependent on, placing no value on the health of nature or of human communities, is absurd enough. It is even more absurd that this economy, that in some respects is so much at one with our military industries and programs, is in other respects directly in conflict with our professed aim of national defense.

It seems only reasonable, only sane, to suppose that a gigantic program of preparedness for national defense should be founded first of all, upon a principle of national and even regional economic independence. A nation determined to defend itself and its freedoms should be prepared, and always preparing, to live from its own resources and from the work and the skills of its own people. But that is not what we are doing in the United States today. What we are doing is squandering in the most prodigal manner the natural and human resources of the nation.

At present, in the face of declining finite sources of fossil fuel energies, we have virtually no energy policy, either for conservation or for the development of safe and clean alternative sources. At present, our energy policy simply is to use all that we have. Moreover, in the face of a growing population needing to be fed, we have virtually no policy for land conservation and no policy of just compensation to the primary producers of food. Our agricultural policy is to use up everything that we have, while depending increasingly on imported food, energy, technology and labor.

Those are just two examples of our general indifference to our own needs. We thus are elaborating a surely dangerous contradiction between our militant nationalism and our espousal of the international "free market" ideology. How do we escape from this absurdity?

I don't think there is an easy answer. Obviously, we would be less absurd if we took better care of things. We would be less absurd if we founded our public policies upon an honest description of our needs and our predicament, rather than upon fantastical descriptions of our wishes. We would be less absurd if our leaders would consider in good faith the proven alternatives to violence.

Such things are easy to say, but we are disposed, somewhat by culture and somewhat by nature, to solve our problems by violence, and even to enjoy doing so. And yet by now all of us must at least have suspected that our right to live, to be free, and to be at peace is not guaranteed by any act of violence. It can be guaranteed only by our willingness that all other persons should live, be free, and be at peace—and by our willingness to use or give our own lives to make that possible. To be incapable of such willingness is merely to resign ourselves to the absurdity we are in; and yet, if you are like me, you are unsure to what extent you are capable of it.

Here is the other question that I have been leading toward, one that the predicament of modern warfare forces upon us: How many deaths of other people's children by bombing or starvation are we willing to accept in order that we may be free, affluent and (supposedly) at peace? To that question I answer: None. Please, no children. Don't kill any children for my benefit.

If that is your answer too, then you must know that we have not come to rest, far from it. For surely we must feel ourselves swarmed about with more questions that are urgent, personal and intimidating. But perhaps also we feel ourselves beginning to be free, facing at last in our own selves the greatest challenge ever laid before us, the most comprehensive vision of human progress, the best advice, and the least obeyed:

> *"Love your enemies, bless them that curse you, do good to them that hate you, and pray for them which despitefully use you and persecute you;*
>
> *"That ye may be the children of your Father which is in heaven: for he maketh his sun to rise on the evil and the good, and sendeth rain on the just and on the unjust."*

Apocatastasis

from *Spirituality & Health*

Among obscurer heresies, the dearest rests
within a special class of gross immoderaton,
the heart of which reveals what proves these days to be
a refreshing degree of filial regard.

Specifically, the word is how we apprehend
one giddy, largely Syriac belief that all
and everyone will be redeemed—or, more nearly,
have been redeemed—always—, have only to notice.

You may have marked by now how late Semitic habits
are seldom quite so neighborly, but this ancient one
looks so downright cordial I shouldn't be surprised
if it proved genesis for the numbing vision

Abba Isaac Luria glimpsed in his spinning
permutations of The Word: Namely, everything
we know as well as everything we don't in all
creation came to be in that brief, abysmal

vacuum The Holy One first opened in Himself.
So it's not so far a stretch from *that* Divine Excess
to advocate the sacred possibility
that in some final, graceful *metanoia* He

will mend that ancient wound completely, and for all.

A Conversation with Jimmy Carter

from *Image*

This interview with Jimmy Carter, the thirty-ninth president of the United States, was conducted by Miller Williams, who is one of America's most distinguished poets. A long-time friend of President Carter, Williams has served as one of Carter's poetry mentors. Williams delivered the inaugural poem at President Clinton's second inauguration and is the author, editor, or translator of thirty books, including Some Jazz a While: Collected Poems.

Image: Preparing for this dialogue has sent me back to your books, and that's been a joy.

Jimmy Carter: Thank you.

Image: After the best-selling collection *Always a Reckoning,* no one will have to be told that you're a poet, but some won't know that you're also a children's book author, and probably few know that you're a painter. Can you say something about your interests in the arts and letters, how they became important to you?

JC: Even as a child and student, I had an intense interest in the arts and letters. Though my formal education was in engineering and science, I was an avid reader, and took correspondence courses in art appreciation and oil painting while I was in the Navy. My roommate at Annapolis was a classical pianist, and we bought and analyzed a large collection of music during our time together. We drew straws on graduation, and I won the records. He got the turntable.

Image: What drew you to writing?

JC: My first two books were written for specific purposes. *Why Not the Best?* was an autobiography that I hoped would introduce me to the people of America as I began my presidential campaign in 1975. The book was quite successful, selling more than a million copies as I began to win primaries and people wanted to learn more about me. *Keeping Faith* was a memoir of my years in the White House, written to fulfill a political obligation and to help pay off the great debt that had accumulated from our days in politics.

By then, I had learned to enjoy writing, and I began a series of quite diverse books on history, political science, health, religion, conflict resolution, nature, and aging. The most challenging— and gratifying—was the collection of poems, and the most enjoyable was a children's story illustrated by my daughter. Helped, of course, by my having been president, all the books have been quite successful and our major source of income.

Image: When an experience moves you to capture it in a poem or prose or a painting, is there a clear difference in the impulses? Do you know which form is calling to you?

JC: I haven't had much experience in painting, but I've worked in oils enough to know that I'm eager to get back to it in the years ahead. I can express myself fairly well in prose, but I have to turn to poetry when I want to be more self-revealing. My feelings about southern racism, unpleasant memories of relations with my father, my intense love for Rosalynn, or the killing of a beloved dog are examples of this need, as in my poem "Sport."

Yesterday I killed him. I had known
for months I could not let him live. I might

have paid someone to end it, but I knew
that after fifteen years of sharing life
the bullet ending his must be my own.

Alone, I dug the grave, grieving, knowing
that until the last he trusted me.
I placed him as he'd been some years ago
when, lost, he stayed in place until I came
and found him shaking, belly on the ground,
his legs too sapped of strength to hold him up,
but nose and eyes still holding on the point.
I knelt beside him then to stroke his head—
as I had done so much the last few days.

He couldn't feel the tears and sweat that fell
with shovelfuls of earth. And then a cross—
a cross, I guess, so when I pass that way
I'll breathe his name,
and think of him alive,
and somehow not remember yesterday.

Image: What sort of music do you prefer? Does it depend on the time of day or what you're doing or where you are?

JC: When I was in my small private study adjoining the Oval Office, my secretary played classical music throughout the day. She knew my favorites, but she also introduced me to new works, placing three-by-five cards on my desk with the names of compositions and composers.

At home, I have an excellent CD player and a tuner that's usually set on National Public Radio. On Saturday mornings I listen to the top country favorites. In addition to my classical CDs, I also have a good selection of more popular music by Bob Dylan,

Willie Nelson, Paul Simon, the Allman Brothers, John Denver, Shania Twain, James Taylor, Lucinda Williams, and many others. Several of these have been personal friends.

Image: Who among painters, sculptors, composers, poets, fiction writers, and playwrights past and present have been most important to you?

JC: It's not possible to have just one composer, artist, or author who is always preferred, but I've always said that El Greco was my favorite artist, and that I liked James Agee's *Let Us Now Praise Famous Men* best of the books I've read. The text and Walker Evans's photographs touched me deeply because they described so vividly many of the scenes of my boyhood life. I've always had a tendency to concentrate on a particular author's works, often reading everything the author has written, along with any biography, before shifting my attention to other writers.

Image: You've said that Dylan Thomas stands out for you as a giant among poets. Can you say what it is about his work that speaks to you so compellingly?

JC: I've just counted thirty-eight books on my shelf by or about Dylan Thomas. I still listen to his recordings, and I've been to his home community in Wales to understand the environment within which he worked. Since I first read a poem of his, "A Refusal to Mourn the Death, by Fire, of a Child in London," I've been fascinated with his poems, but I've never tried to emulate his style.

Image: Would you tell again, for those who haven't heard it, the story of your involvement in his belated recognition by the British establishment?

JC: When I made my official state visit to Great Britain in 1977 and went to the poets' corner in Westminster Abbey, my request of the archbishop was to see Dylan Thomas's commemorative stone. He expressed both displeasure at my request and distaste for the poet, stating that neither his works nor his moral character would justify his being honored. I pointed to the markers for drug addicts and other artists who were social outcasts, and argued that I considered Dylan Thomas to be a truly great poet. I had the usual entourage of White House reporters with me, and some of them mentioned the confrontation briefly in their news articles. Dylan's wife Caitlin wrote me a thank-you note, and I submitted my thoughts to the official screening committee from the abbey.

As I was leaving the White House in early 1981, this group finally announced that Dylan had been approved for a memorial stone, and asked me to speak at the ceremony. I couldn't go, but I did a long interview with a skeptical BBC reporter, who was finally convinced of my sincerity when I quoted some of Dylan's poems and answered detailed questions about the poet's life. Later a delegation from Laugharne came to present a duplicate stone to me. I summarized this episode in one of the poems I later included in *Always a Reckoning,* "A President Expresses Concern on a Visit to Westminster Abbey."

Poet's Corner had no epitaph
to mark the Welshman's
sullen art or craft
because, they said,
his morals were below
the standards there.
I mentioned the ways of Poe
and Byron,
and the censored Joyce's works;
at least the newsmen listened,
noted my remarks,
and his wife, Caitlin, wrote.
We launched a clumsy, weak campaign,

the bishops met
and listened to the lilting lines again.
Later, some Welshmen brought to me
a copy of the stone
that honors now the beauty he set free
from a godhead of his own.

Image: Three times in your book *Living Faith* and twice, I believe, in *Sources of Strength,* you turn to your own poems to express your feelings and thoughts, saying in one instance that you found it impossible to express them otherwise. How is it that poetry can say what prose cannot?

JC: My wife and I have a very close relationship and a gratifying ease of communication with each other, but I've found that I can express my most private thoughts only through the lines of a poem. When she's read some of them, Rosalynn has said, "Jimmy, I never knew you felt this way." I'm sure there are other, more experienced poets who could explain this better, but there are two things I've considered as explanations for this. One is the element of aloofness between a poet and the lines written, so that the casual reader can assume that the thoughts come from an imaginary person. You and other advisors have said that literal accuracy in a poem is not at all necessary, and is often an obstacle to quality, but I haven't yet reached the point of separating myself from the thoughts expressed.

The other possible reason that poetry can say for me what prose cannot is that when I've written poetry I've deliberately tried to open thought processes that had been buried in my subconscious because they might have been painful or perhaps embarrassing.

Image: The point about the factual in poetry, of course, is that a work of art need not be an entry in a diary, but ought to be free—as John Ciardi put it—to lie its way to the truth; that the truth in a poem rests in the insight to which a reader comes, and not in the poem's biographical details. Your poems lead unfailingly to such insights, and apparently without the facts behind the poem being bent for the sake of sound, pacing, or the rhetorical shape of the poem. That's a remarkable achievement, but would it bother you if you should learn that the dead child in Dylan Thomas's "A Refusal to Mourn . . ." had in fact been a boy but was made a girl because "daughter" rhymes with "water"? Would the poem be less meaningful, less "true"?

JC: I understand what you and Ciardi have to say about accuracy in poetry texts, and I don't disagree. I was pointing out my lingering reluctance to depart from the literal truth to indicate my lack of maturity as a poet. In fact, I'm not absolutely certain that there were thirty-seven Harleys in my sister's funeral procession, as I have it in "A Motorcycling Sister."

Her lives were always, simply said, her own,
So no one ever knew which one we'd come
To find—a charming southern lady who
Was dressed for tea, or one who made her home

A pad for biker gangs, Daytona bound,
Who'd stop and sometimes stay a week, as though
They'd found a mother—one who rode with them
On many trips. Once, down in Mexico,

She broke her leg, which kept her home awhile
But gave her extra time to freeze and can
Her garden's harvest for the crowds that came,
And ate, and slept on floors, then rode again.

Her final illness filled our town with men,
Leather-jacketed, with beards, who stayed
In shifts, uneasy, in her darkened room.
Telegrams were sent. The hearse was led

To graveside by those friends, two by two,
With one ahead: in all by thirty-seven
Large and noisy bikes. And on her tomb
They had inscribed SHE RIDES IN HARLEY HEAVEN.

Image: Any number of convincing poems in *Always a Reckoning* deal with love, resentment, fear, loneliness, and need in human-to-human relationships, but only three, as I read them, deal directly, overtly, with matters of faith. Do you see a possible contemporary role for the arts in witnessing to faith, as poets did in the psalms, as many painters and composers did in the past?

JC: It's not an attractive or profitable custom anymore for visual artists or poets to express religious themes in their work. Although *Living Faith* and *Sources of Strength* are about my personal faith and though I've written several poems on the subject, I've decided to publish only a very few of them.

Image: Apart from the life of Jesus itself, what story in the Bible do you find most intriguing, as a story?

JC: It's difficult to choose a favorite biblical story or person. Peter is the most intriguing, but I've found that my classes respond, often with surprise, when they learn more about "Doubting" Thomas. He was a remarkable man, a real hero, who clearly committed himself to be killed with Jesus: "Then said Thomas. . . . Let us also go, that we may die with him." And he was the first and only disciple to refer to Christ as "My Lord and my God." I use Thomas to illustrate our tendency to underestimate others or to characterize a complicated character with a catch phrase.

Another intriguing story is when the Corinthians asked Peter, in effect, what were the most important or lasting attributes of life, and he responded, "Those you cannot see." This somewhat mysterious answer derogates the ambitions we have for wealth, prestige, security, and such and reminds us that the simple things needed for success are available to anyone: commitments to peace, justice, humility, service, forgiveness, compassion, love.

Image: Your creative interests and talents go even beyond what we've mentioned, if—as I understand it—you made the furniture shown in your painting entitled *Our Mountain Home.* Did you build the cabin itself?

JC: I didn't construct the log cabin, but I did help design it, and then I made all the furniture in it—beds, tables, chairs, stools, chifforobes, benches, swings, and so forth. This was done while I was writing *Keeping Faith,* the memoirs, and when I'm home I still do woodworking after I'm exhausted at the word processor.

Image: Probably no one on earth knows as much about as many lands, the people of those lands, as Jimmy Carter. What have you gleaned from this?

JC: Let me come at that by summarizing a question I was asked after a speech in Destin, Florida, recently: "What has been the most difficult and interesting lesson you've learned in your adult life?" After some hesitation, I finally responded that it was the realization that all people are really equal in the eyes of God. I went on to explain that Rosalynn and I have visited more than 110 nations since leaving the White House, working with some of the most unfortunate and often despised people in the world, and have had to admit, reluctantly, that their moral values, intelligence, ambitions, and family values are equal to our own. There are obvious individual exceptions, but they are present, too, in all societies.

Image: What questions would you like to answer that I haven't asked?

JC: I'm now embarked on a major project—a long historical novel about the Revolutionary War in the Deep South. As usual, I have had to do this kind of work very early in the morning and on my all-too-rare days at home. I'll soon be celebrating my seventy-fifth birthday, and I look forward to having more uninterrupted time to write and paint.

Image: What drew you to long fiction? And why the Revolutionary War?

JC: I decided to work on a novel because I like to learn and study new things. Dealing with the creative writing of prose has been a new experience that's demanded a study of technique, and it's an interesting challenge when I'm not busy with other things. As I did with you in learning to write poetry, I've met with about a half-dozen professors who've given me reading assignments, which I've enjoyed, and advice on textbooks. I have admonitions taped to my computer, such as: "Only trouble is interesting!" "Characters must want something," "Particulars, not generalities," "Keep it vivid and continuous."

The choice of a novel about the Revolutionary War gives me a long text that requires research about history and lets me insert some of the information I've accumulated about my own family and a few other interesting, actual people. Also, I've long felt that most historians have ignored the later war years in the South, usually concentrating on early events in Massachusetts, New York, and Canada and then skipping almost three years to Yorktown.

Writing prose of this kind seems quite different from my limited experience with poetry, which for me was deeply self-analytical and tightly constrained to precise word-meanings and their interrelationships and sounds. My prose, at least, is more loosely structured, like non-fiction, with the added element of imagination and the creation of characters. I've found to my surprise that these characters take on lives of their own as they encounter circumstances and other characters.

Image: Looking back over the past seventy-five years, if you could change something in your own personal history with a wave of your hand, what would it be?

JC: I wouldn't want to change the careers I've had as a submariner, a farmer and businessman, and in politics, but it would have been helpful if I could have had a better academic foundation for the small portion of my life devoted to the liberal arts.

Image: Thank you for your time. I have some intimation of what a scarce commodity it is in your life.

JC: Some of my most pleasant times are when I discuss poetry and the other arts with you.

DAVID CHADWICK

Crooked Cucumber

from *Tricycle*

*The following is a collection of anecdotes about
and teachings by Shunryu Suzuki, a Japanese
teacher in the Soto school of Zen, who came to
San Francisco in 1959 to minister to a small
Japanese American congregation. He came with
no plan, but with the confidence that some
Westerners would embrace the essential practice of
Buddhism as he had learned it from his teachers.
He had a way with things—plants, rocks, robes,
furniture, walking, sitting—that gave a hint of
how to be comfortable in the world. He had a
way with people that drew them to him, a way
with words that made people listen, a genius that
seemed to work especially in America and
especially in English.*

Zen Mind, Beginner's Mind, *a skillfully
edited compilation of his lectures published in
1970, has sold over a million copies in a dozen
languages. It's a reflection of where Suzuki put his
passion: in the ongoing practice of Zen with others.
He did not wish to be remembered or to have
anything named after him. He wanted to pass on
what he had learned to others, and he hoped that
they in turn would help to invigorate Buddhism in
America and reinvigorate it in Japan.*

I moved to San Francisco in the winter of 1966 and began attending morning zazen at the San Francisco Zen Center. Suzuki Roshi had been away in Japan during my initial visit to the Center, but, despite having been told very little about zazen and Zen, and with very little encouragement from anyone, I resolved to come to zazen every morning and every afternoon for one year.

My first encounter with Suzuki was when I bowed to him after zazen upon his return to the U.S. I could barely see him through the million thoughts that raced through my mind. A moment later, I was in the hall putting on my sandals. I could see Suzuki in his office, behind the crowd of people on their way out. Still my mind was bubbling. He turned, caught my eye, and smiled, and for the tiniest increment of time everything stopped, and I saw him. It was in small, seemingly insignificant, nonverbal exchanges like this one that Suzuki established contact with students and guided us along our invisible paths. We were almost entirely on our own.

One night in February of 1968, I sat among fifty black-robed fellow students, mostly young Americans, at Zen Mountain Center, Tassajara Springs, ten miles inland from Big Sur, California, deep in the mountain wilderness. The kerosene lamplight illuminated our breath in the winter air of the unheated room.

Suzuki had just concluded a lecture from his seat on the altar platform. "Thank you very much," he said softly, with a genuine feeling of gratitude. He took a sip of water, cleared his throat, and looked around at his students. "Is there some question?" he asked, just loud enough to be heard above the sound of the creek gushing by in the darkness outside.

I bowed, hands together, and caught his eye.

"Hai?" he said, meaning yes.

"Suzuki Roshi, I've been listening to your lectures for years," I said, "and I really love them, and they're very inspiring, and I know that what you're talking about is actually very clear and simple. But I must admit I just don't understand. I love it, but I feel like I could listen to you for a thousand years and still not get it. Could you just please put it in a nutshell? Can you reduce Buddhism to one phrase?"

Everyone laughed. He laughed. What a ludicrous question. I don't think any of us expected him to answer it. He was not a man you could pin down, and he didn't like to give his students something definite to cling to. He had often said not to have "some idea of what Buddhism was."

But Suzuki did answer. He looked at me and said, "Everything changes." Then he asked for another question.

As a child, Shunryu Suzuki was small yet strong, eager to learn, impatient to do things before he was old enough, sensitive, and kind but prone to quick bursts of anger. And his most notorious weakness was absentmindedness. He couldn't keep track of anything. Schoolwork and books, caps and coins—whatever it was, he'd leave it at home or at school, wherever he wasn't.

> *My habit is absentmindedness. I am naturally very forgetful. I worked on it pretty hard but could not do anything about it. I started to work on it when I went to my master at twelve. Even then I was very forgetful. But by working on it steadily, I found I could get rid of my selfish way of doing things. If the purpose of practice and training is just to correct your weak point, I think it is almost impossible to change your habits. Even so, it is necessary to work on them, because as you do so, your character will be trained and your ego will be reduced.*

At the age of eleven, a year earlier than most other boys and against his parents' best wishes, Suzuki decided to train with his first master, Gyokujun So-on Suzuki, the abbot of Zoun-in, the temple at which his father trained as a boy.

When my master and I were walking in the rain, he would say, "Do not walk so fast, the rain is everywhere."

Suzuki's favorite story about his novice days with his teacher, So-on, was a cautionary tale not of selfishness but of discrimination, and of pickles gone bad. At the temple Zoun-in, pickles were made to eat year-round but especially in the winter, when there were few fresh vegetables. There were pickles made from cucumbers, carrots, eggplants, cabbage, and *daikon,* the giant white radishes. A batch of *takuan,* daikon pickles, had been undersalted and had gone bad. So-on was told about it. He wouldn't throw it out. "Serve it anyway!" he ordered. So for meal after meal decomposing daikon was served, and the pickles were getting worse with the passage of time. One night when they could take it no more, after they were sure So-on was asleep, Suzuki and a couple of cohorts took the pickles out to the garden and buried them.

The boys were pleased with themselves, thinking they had gotten away with their prank. But a few days later when they sat down for breakfast at the low wooden table, So-on brought in a special dish—the rotten pickles back from the dead! So-on ate the pickles with them. Suzuki gathered the courage and took the first bite, then the next. He found that he could do it if he didn't think about it. He said it was his first experience of nondiscriminating consciousness.

Sometimes it is better for your teacher to be mean, so you don't attach to him. . . . If we have surrendered to our master, we employ all our effort to control our mind so that we may exist under all conditions, extraordinary and ordinary.

When Suzuki had arrived at Zoun-in there were eight boys studying with his master, So-on. After the first year there were only four, and midway through the second year they too had gone. So-on was not just hard on Suzuki; one by one the boys had been driven away by his imperious manner and the privations they had to endure with him. Now it was just Suzuki and So-on. He had a lot of responsibility for a fourteen-year-old. Suzuki was lonely without his friends, but he was getting lots of personal attention. That often didn't work out the way he wanted it to, however.

A hard part of being alone with So-on was that now Suzuki had to carry everything when they went places. One day there was a service in the next valley, a few miles away, and So-on sent Suzuki ahead with a small trunk and a bag of scrolls. At one point along his journey, Suzuki stopped to rest his feet on the way and went down to a riverbank to catch frogs and let them go. Enjoying himself, he forgot the time till he saw So-on crossing a bridge. Suzuki hid till So-on had passed, then took the shortcut over the hill. He arrived huffing and puffing just before his master.

"I saw you under the bridge playing," So-on said, wagging a finger at Suzuki. "You crooked cucumber. You're sticking with it but I feel sorry for you. You're such a dimwit."

My master always called me "You crooked cucumber!" I understand pretty well that I am not so sharp. I was the last disciple, but I became the first one because all the good cucumbers ran away. Maybe they were too smart. Anyway, I was not smart enough to run away, so I was caught. For studying Buddhism my dullness was an advantage. A smart person doesn't always have the advantage, and a dull person is sometimes good because he is dull. Actually there is no dull or smart person. They are the same.

"Not always so" was never far away in Suzuki's teaching. He prefaced much of what he said with the word "maybe," and yet he did not seem at all unsure of himself. When he said this sort of thing, it seemed to come from a deeply rooted strength. He did speak of the absolute, but in enigmatic terms: "There is nothing absolute for us, but when nothing is absolute, that is absolute."

He talked about the Buddha's teaching as something fluid and living. "To accord with circumstances, the teaching should have an infinite number of forms."

He talked about enlightenment, but said, "Enlightenment is not any particular stage that you attain."

The secret of Soto Zen is just two words: not always so. . . . Not always so. In Japanese it's two words, three words in English. This is the secret of our teaching. If you understand things in this way, without being caught by words or rules, without too much of a preconceived idea, then you can actually do something, and in doing something, you can apply this teaching which has been handed down from the ancient masters. When you apply it, it will help.

It couldn't be grasped. It was a paradox, he said, that could only be understood through sincere practice and zazen. The point of his talks wasn't to tell the truth as he saw it, but to free minds from obstacles so they might include contradictions.

Suzuki thought it was a frequent weakness of Buddhist teachers to cling to a fixed understanding; it was not a weakness of the great Zen master Dogen.

Usually a Zen master will give you: "Practice zazen so that you will attain enlightenment. If you attain enlightenment, you will be detached from everything and you will see 'things as it is.'" But our way is not always so. What the Zen master says is of course true. But what Dogen-zenji told us was how to adjust the flame of our lamp back and forth. The point of Dogen's zazen is to live each moment in total combustion, like a kerosene lamp or candle.

"Buddhism is a two-edged sword," Suzuki said, pretending to swing a sword, turning his wrist, a mischievous smile on his face. "Back and forth, back and forth. Sometimes I strike you with this side and sometimes with that." He often spoke of the dual nature of reality, but what the two sides were was not so easy to understand. It wasn't just oneness and duality, but "the duality of oneness and the oneness of duality." He said one couldn't speak the whole truth, that there was always another side created by whatever was said, and if his students didn't get it on their own, they'd get it by the sword that cuts away the side they're attached to.

We should understand everything both ways, not just from one standpoint. We call someone who understands things from just one side a tambankan. *This means a "man who carries a board on his shoulder." Because he carries a big board on his shoulder, he cannot see the other side.*

Often he said, "Just keep sitting." Very often. Sitting would loosen the grip of what seemed to be reality. But then the idea of sitting or zazen might grip the sitter. Zazen was the first thing he taught, but if it became something too special he'd pull out the rug. Someone would ask for more periods of zazen, and he'd say the schedule was fine as it was. Someone would speak of pain in their legs, and he'd say sit more.

Even "Not always so" was not always so. It wasn't offered as a formula to cling to.

"There is no question," a student said, "because there is no answer. Whatever you say will not always be so. So I will just sit."

Suzuki shook his head.

"No?" the student said. "But you said . . ."

"When I said it, it was true. When you said it, it was false."

If there is always another side in Suzuki's teaching, what's the other side of "not always so"? To look for that, you must take the board off your shoulder.

Almost all people are carrying a big board, so they cannot see the other side. They think they are just the ordinary mind, but if they take the board off they will understand, "Oh, I am Buddha, too. How can I be both Buddha and ordinary mind? It is amazing!" That is enlightenment.

Suzuki talked about the first principle and the second principle from his early days in San Francisco. He said the first principle had many names: Buddha-nature, emptiness, reality, truth, the Tao, the absolute, God. The second principle is what is said about the first and the way to realize it—rules, teaching, morality, forms. All those things change according to the person, time, and place—and they are not always so. Suzuki said that talking about Buddhism was not truth, but mercy, skillful means, encouragement. "There is no particular teaching or way, but the Buddha-nature of all is the same, what we find is the same."

The first principle is not something that the Buddha or other people came up with. Suzuki spoke about Buddha's sermons in the woods, where he "proclaimed the first principle, the Royal Law." And he added, "If you think what Buddha proclaimed is the Royal Law, that is not right. The Royal Law was already there before he was on the pulpit."

Suzuki taught that Buddhism is not the first principle, but is a way to know and express the first principle. Buddha's teaching can only be thought of as the first principle in "its pure and formless form."

If you have a preconceived idea of the first principle, that idea is topsy-turvy, and as long as you seek a first principle which is something that can be applied in one way to every occasion, you will have topsy-turvy ideas. Such ideas are not necessary. Buddha's great light shines forth from everything, each moment.

Suzuki always made clear that the first principle is beyond discrimination or knowing in the ordinary sense, in the way that relative truth is known.

Bodhidharma said, "I don't know." "I don't know" is the first principle. Do you understand? The first principle cannot be known in terms of good or bad, right or wrong, because it is both right and wrong.

Once Suzuki divided up the zendo: those on the right were to ask questions about the first principle and those on the left about the second. If someone asked about the wrong principle, they'd have to move to the other side of the zendo. Nobody actually changed sides, though they had a good time trying to present their understanding of the first principle. In the end it seemed like there was nothing at all to say.

ROBERT CORDING

Kafka and the Rabbi of Belz

from *Green Mountains Review*

Rain for days and rain again tonight,
but the Rabbi's followers have taken to heart
a moment three days back when the Rabbi
emerged for his daily exercise and the rain halted
and the sun, as stories already have it, blazed again.
Kafka has tagged along, invited by a friend
who has told him how, when the Rabbi speaks,
everyday objects take on subtler forms.

By the swollen river, the Rabbi stares
so intently at the moving water, Kafka's friend
feels the Rabbi is transferring the world into himself.
Kafka watches a swan that never once turns
its head, the bird utterly complete in itself,
inconvertible. It glitters in a circle of lamplight
then disappears under a stone bridge, an interval
passing so quickly it might never have been.

Gusts of wind make the flames in the gaslights
spurt and sputter as if any one of them, or all,
might break into speech. Piles of dead leaves stir
and are lifted up, weightless and figured
for a moment, before dropping to the rain-pocked
street. Above, the trees gesture mutely. The Rabbi

invokes Ezekiel, God's breath entering the bones
of the dead so that they stand up, alive again.

Kafka tells his friend the leaves are just leaves,
and this is quite enough for him.
On the walk back, Kafka sickens himself
with thoughts of work he should be doing,
has not done. When he looks down
the empty streets smeared with rain, the city
appears, as if through the wrong end
of a telescope, to be shrunken and abandoned.

A few days later, to his friend's bewilderment
and surprise, Kafka returns to follow behind
the Rabbi and his students. As they walk,
the sun dissolving over the city grants
the streets and buildings another, brighter life,
every edge gleaming. The Rabbi is talking
of what is sacred in every human being—
the sense, despite all odds, that life itself is good.

Kafka finds himself recalling a single paragraph
he wrote over and over, how it shone
unexpectedly with what he could not say,
the words enlarged, it seemed, by what was
uninterpretable, defiantly other, yet
requiring words. When his friend asks why
he has come, Kafka shakes his head and says,
there is always something unaccounted for.

ALFRED CORN

Jerusalem

from *Image*

> *"Then keep thy heart. . . ."*
>
> Melville, *Clarel*

They will lift up their heads:
the Lion Gate, St. Stephen's, the New,
Jaffa, and, last, the Gate of Dung.
The gates will lift up their heads
that the King of Glory may come in.

As Judah means "Praised," its chief city will be
more highly praised, the ramparts and the towers
of David's citadel praised and exalted.

Come this far, how close the door on what
not even they had strength enough to bar?
The Rock, where Isaac, his wrists bound tight,
saw above him a face clench in agony
moments before an angel dove down to stay
Abraham's hand is now perpetual,
preserved in the furnace of tradition
along with that ram whose horn became the *shofar.*

—Or is it rock as fact, one of the sights,
coated with dust and roofed with a golden dome
reverberant with a murmured *sura*
expanding on the Prophet's airborne nocturnal
journey, which fixed him like a star
on the cusp of the crescent moon?

Just as the present-day pilgrim goes from station
to station in a loud array of discount tours,
tenants have reconstrued the basilica
of the Holy Sepulcher as real estate
for hereditary zeal to balkanize
among several sects. Each has its sharply
defended square yardage of theology, but none
equals that stone niche off to one side where an oil lamp's
starred wick baffles the sway of archaic shadows.

The Temple abides in its myth
but also in limestone fact, at least the part
Roman demolition experts failed
to pound into undatable rubble.
Foundation Wall, you won't be alone again,
alive with the *Shekhinah's* quiet thunder,
bloodwarm dovecote of fissured building blocks
into which ten thousand hand-written
praises or lamentations have flown.

And Via Dolorosa toils south from Gabbatha's
courtyard, where a few detached centurions
gave their charge the prescribed flogging

before sending him on his forced march.
A path useless to retrace without spiriting away
two millennia or any obstacle
to contemplation of punished flesh at ground zero
staggering forward under a massive wooden T,
palm fronds still underfoot, but dry and broken,
whispering hosannas no one hears.

Because a Procurator exercised available
options, the name "Pilate" survives globally
on the lips of millions when the Credo's recited
tenets descend into history and make it faith.

What was truth? What will it be?
For the condemned whose breath comes shorter and shorter,
"Even death may prove unreal at last"—unreal,
like the sound of a tree fallen to earth
far from any ear, or any human ear.
When the body atoned to its trunk and limbs toppled
out of time, did it finally become audible
to his listeners? To some. To Clarel, and for later
pilgrims who risked as much as one step beyond doubt.

No other dispatch could outdistance the silence
following on that farewell to his friend—
who, standing at the Place of the Skull,
heard him say, "Woman, behold thy son,"
as prelude to, "Behold thy mother."
Seeing where sons of earth were bound to go,
from that day forth he housed a second mother under his roof.

Lift up your heads.

HARVEY COX

The Market as God

from *The Atlantic Monthly*

A few years ago a friend advised me that if I wanted to know what was going on in the real world, I should read the business pages. Although my lifelong interest has been in the study of religion, I am always willing to expand my horizons; so I took the advice, vaguely fearful that I would have to cope with a new and baffling vocabulary. Instead I was surprised to discover that most of the concepts I ran across were quite familiar.

Expecting a *terra incognita,* I found myself instead in the land of *déjà vu.* The lexicon of *The Wall Street Journal* and the business sections of *Time* and *Newsweek* turned out to bear a striking resemblance to Genesis, the Epistle to the Romans, and Saint Augustine's City of God. Behind descriptions of market reforms, monetary policy, and the convolutions of the Dow, I gradually made out the pieces of a grand narrative about the inner meaning of human history, why things had gone wrong, and how to put them right. Theologians call these myths of origin, legends of the fall, and doctrines of sin and redemption. But here they were again, and in only thin disguise: chronicles about the creation of wealth, the seductive temptations of statism, captivity to faceless economic cycles, and, ultimately, salvation through the advent of free markets, with a small dose of ascetic belt tightening along the way, especially for the East Asian economies.

The East Asians' troubles, votaries argue, derive from their heretical deviation from free-market orthodoxy—they were practitioners of "crony capitalism," of "ethnocapitalism," of "statist capitalism," not of the one true faith. The East Asian financial panics, the Russian debt repudiations, the Brazilian economic turmoil, and the U.S. stock market's $1.5 trillion "correction" momentarily shook belief in the new dispensation. But faith is strengthened by adversity, and the Market God is emerging renewed from its trial by financial "contagion." Since the argument from design no longer proves its existence, it is fast becoming a postmodern deity—believed in despite the evidence. Alan Greenspan vindicated this tempered faith in testimony before Congress last October. A leading hedge fund had just lost billions of dollars, shaking market confidence and precipitating calls for new federal regulation. Greenspan, usually Delphic in his comments, was decisive. He believed that regulation would only impede these markets, and that they should continue to be self-regulated. True faith, Saint Paul tells us, is the evidence of things unseen.

Soon I began to marvel at just how comprehensive the business theology is. There were even sacraments to convey salvific power to the lost, a calendar of entrepreneurial saints, and what theologians call an "eschatology"—a teaching about the "end of history." My curiosity was piqued. I began cataloguing these strangely familiar doctrines, and I saw that in fact there lies embedded in the business pages an entire theology, which is comparable in scope if not in profundity to that of Thomas Aquinas or Karl Barth. It needed only to be systematized for a whole new *Summa* to take shape.

At the apex of any theological system, of course, is its doctrine of God. In the new theology this celestial pinnacle is occupied by The Market, which I capitalize to signify both the mystery that enshrouds it and the reverence it inspires in business folk. Different faiths have, of course, different views of the divine attributes. In Christianity, God has sometimes been defined as omnipotent (possessing all power), omniscient (having all knowledge), and omnipresent (existing everywhere). Most Christian theologies, it is true, hedge a bit. They teach that these qualities of the divinity are indeed *there,* but are hidden from human eyes both by human sin and by the transcendence of the divine itself. In "light inaccessible" they are, as the old hymn puts it, "hid from our eyes." Likewise, although The Market, we are assured, possesses these divine attributes, they are not always completely evident to mortals but must be trusted and affirmed by faith. "Further along," as another old gospel song says, "we'll understand why."

As I tried to follow the arguments and explanations of the economist-theologians who justify The Market's ways to men, I spotted the same dialectics I have grown fond of in the many years I have pondered the Thomists, the Calvinists, and the various schools of modern religious thought. In particular, the econologians' rhetoric resembles what is sometimes called "process theology," a relatively contemporary trend influenced by the philosophy of Alfred North Whitehead. In this school although God *wills* to possess the classic attributes, He does not yet possess them in full, but is definitely moving in that direction. This conjecture is of immense help to theologians for obvious reasons. It answers the bothersome puzzle of theodicy: why a lot of bad things happen that an omnipotent, omnipresent, and omniscient God— especially a benevolent one—would not countenance. Process theology also seems to offer considerable comfort to the theologians of The Market. It helps to explain the dislocation, pain, and disorientation that are the result of transitions from economic heterodoxy to free markets.

Since the earliest stages of human history, of course, there have been bazaars, rialtos, and trading posts—all markets. But The Market was never God, because there were other centers of value and meaning, other "gods." The Market operated within a plethora of other institutions that restrained it. As Karl Polanyi has demonstrated in his classic work *The Great Transformation,* only in the past two centuries has The Market risen above these demigods and chthonic spirits to become today's First Cause.

Initially The Market's rise to Olympic supremacy replicated the gradual ascent of Zeus above all the other divinities of the ancient Greek pantheon, an ascent that was never quite secure. Zeus, it will be recalled, had to keep storming down from Olympus to quell this or that threat to his sovereignty. Recently, however, The Market is becoming more like the Yahweh of the Old Testament—not just one superior deity contending with others but the Supreme Deity, the only true God, whose reign must now be universally accepted and who allows for no rivals.

Divine *omnipotence* means the capacity to define what is real. It is the power to make something out of nothing and nothing out of something. The willed-but-not-yet-achieved omnipotence of The Market means that there is no conceivable limit to its inexorable ability to convert creation into commodities. But again, this is hardly a new idea, though it has a new twist. In Catholic theology, through what is called "transubstantiation," ordinary bread and wine become vehicles of the holy. In the mass of The Market a reverse process occurs. Things that have been held sacred transmute into interchangeable items for sale. Land is a good example. For millennia it has held various meanings, many of them numinous. It has been Mother Earth, ancestral resting place, holy mountain, enchanted forest, tribal homeland, aesthetic inspiration, sacred turf, and much more. But when The Market's Sanctus bell rings and the elements are elevated, all these complex meanings of land melt into one: real estate. At the right price no land is not for sale, and this includes everything from burial grounds to the cove of the local fertility sprite. This radical desacralization dramatically alters the human relationship to land; the same happens with water, air, space, and soon (it is predicted) the heavenly bodies.

At the high moment of the mass the priest says, "This is my body," meaning the body of Christ and, by extension, the bodies of all the faithful people. Christianity and Judaism both teach that the human body is made "in the image of God." Now, however, in a dazzling display of reverse transubstantiation, the human body has become the latest sacred vessel to be converted into a commodity. The process began, fittingly enough, with blood. But now, or soon, all bodily organs—kidneys, skin, bone marrow, sperm, the heart itself—will be miraculously changed into purchasable items.

Still, the liturgy of The Market is not proceeding without some opposition from the pews. A considerable battle is shaping up in the United States, for example, over the attempt to merchandise human genes. A few years ago, banding together for the first time in memory, virtually all the religious institutions in the country, from the liberal National Council of Churches to the Catholic bishops to the Christian Coalition, opposed the gene mart, the newest theophany of The Market. But these critics are followers of what are now "old religions," which, like the goddess cults that were thriving when the worship of the vigorous young Apollo began sweeping ancient Greece, may not have the strength to slow the spread of the new devotion.

Occasionally backsliders try to bite the Invisible Hand that feeds them. On October 26, 1996, the German government ran an ad offering the entire village of Liebenberg, in what used to be East Germany, for sale—with no previous notice to its some 350 residents. Liebenberg's citizens, many of them elderly or unemployed, stared at the notice in disbelief. They had certainly loathed communism, but when they opted for the market economy that reunification promised, they hardly expected this. Liebenberg includes a thirteenth-century church, a Baroque castle, a lake, a hunting lodge, two restaurants, and 3,000 acres of meadow and forest. Once a favorite site for boar hunting by the old German nobility, it was obviously entirely too valuable a parcel of real estate to overlook. Besides, having been expropriated by the East German Communist government, it was now legally eligible for sale under the terms of German reunification. Overnight Liebenberg became a living parable, providing an invaluable glimpse of the Kingdom in which The Market's will is indeed done. But the outraged burghers of the town did not feel particularly blessed. They complained loudly, and the sale was finally postponed. Everyone in town realized, however, that it was not really a victory. The Market, like Yahweh, may lose a skirmish, but in a war of attrition it will always win in the end.

Of course, religion in the past has not been reluctant to charge for its services. Prayers, masses, blessings, healings, baptisms, funerals, and amulets have been hawked, and still are. Nor has religion always been sensitive to what the traffic would bear. When, in the early sixteenth century, Johann Tetzel jacked up the price of indulgences and even had one of the first singing commercials composed to push sales ("When the coin into the platter pings, the soul out of purgatory springs"), he failed to realize that he was overreaching. The customers balked, and a young Augustinian monk brought the traffic to a standstill with a placard tacked to a church door.

It would be a lot harder for a Luther to interrupt sales of The Market's amulets today. As the people of Liebenberg discovered, everything can now be bought. Lakes, meadows, church buildings—everything carries a sticker price. But this practice itself exacts a cost. As everything in what used to be called creation becomes a commodity, human beings begin to look at one another, and at themselves, in a funny way, and they see colored price tags. There was a time when people spoke, at least occasionally, of "inherent worth"—if not of things, then at least of persons. The Liebenberg principle changes all that. One wonders what would become of a modern Luther who tried to post his theses on the church door, only to find that the whole edifice had been bought by an American billionaire who reckoned it might look nicer on his estate.

It is comforting to note that the *citizens* of Liebenberg, at least, were not put on the block. But that raises a good question. What *is* the value of a human life in the theology of The Market? Here the new deity pauses, but not for long. The computation may be complex, but it is not impossible. We should not believe, for example, that if a child is born severely handicapped, unable to be "productive," The Market will decree its death. One must remember that the profits derived from medications, leg braces, and CAT-scan equipment should also be figured into the equation. Such a cost analysis might result in a close call—but the inherent worth of the child's life, since it cannot be quantified, would be hard to include in the calculation.

It is sometimes said that since everything is for sale under the rule of The Market, nothing is sacred. But this is not quite true. About three years ago a nasty controversy erupted in Great Britain when a railway pension fund that owned the small jeweled casket in which the remains of Saint Thomas à Becket are said to have rested decided to auction it off through Sotheby's. The casket dates from the twelfth century and is revered as both a sacred relic and a national treasure. The British Museum made an effort to buy it but lacked the funds, so the casket was sold to a Canadian. Only last-minute measures by the British government prevented removal of the casket from the United Kingdom. In principle, however, in the theology of The Market, there is no reason why any relic, coffin, body, or national monument—including the Statue of Liberty and Westminster Abbey—should not be listed. Does anyone doubt that if the True Cross were ever really discovered, it would eventually find its way to Sotheby's? The Market is not omnipotent—yet. But the process is under way and it is gaining momentum.

Omniscience is a little harder to gauge than omnipotence. Maybe The Market has already achieved it but is unable—temporarily—to apply its gnosis until its Kingdom and Power come in their fullness. Nonetheless, current thinking already assigns to The Market a comprehensive wisdom that in the past only the gods have known. The Market, we are taught, is able to determine what human needs are, what copper and capital should cost, how much barbers and CEOs should be paid, and how much jet planes, running shoes, and hysterectomies should sell for. But how do we know The Market's will?

In days of old, seers entered a trance state and then informed anxious seekers what kind of mood the gods were in, and whether this was an auspicious time to begin a journey, get married, or start a war. The prophets of Israel repaired to the desert and then returned to announce whether Yahweh was feeling benevolent or wrathful. Today The Market's fickle will is clarified by daily reports from Wall Street and other sensory organs of finance. Thus we can learn on a day-to-day basis that The Market is "apprehensive," "relieved," "nervous," or even at times "jubilant." On the basis of this revelation awed adepts make critical decisions about whether to buy or sell. Like one of the devouring gods of old, The Market—aptly embodied in a bull or a bear—must be fed and kept happy under all circumstances. True, at times its appetite may seem excessive—a $35 billion bailout here, a $50 billion one there—but the alternative to assuaging its hunger is too terrible to contemplate.

The diviners and seers of The Market's moods are the high priests of its mysteries. To act against their admonitions is to risk excommunication and possibly damnation. Today, for example, if any government's policy vexes The Market, those responsible for the irreverence will be made to suffer. That The Market is not at all displeased by downsizing or a growing income gap, or can be gleeful about the expansion of cigarette sales to Asian young people, should not cause anyone to question its ultimate omniscience. Like Calvin's inscrutable deity, The Market may work in mysterious ways, "hid from our eyes," but ultimately it knows best.

Omniscience can sometimes seem a bit intrusive. The traditional God of the Episcopal Book of Common Prayer is invoked as one "unto whom all hearts are open, all desires known, and from whom no secrets are hid." Like Him, The Market already knows the deepest secrets and darkest desires of our hearts—or at least would like to know them. But one suspects that divine motivation differs in these two cases. Clearly The Market wants this kind of x-ray omniscience because by probing our inmost fears and desires and then dispensing across-the-board solutions, it can further extend its reach. Like the gods of the past, whose priests offered up the fervent prayers and petitions of the people, The Market relies on its own intermediaries: motivational researchers. Trained in the advanced art of psychology, which has long since replaced theology as the true "science of the soul," the modern heirs of the medieval confessors delve into the hidden fantasies, insecurities, and hopes of the populace.

One sometimes wonders, in this era of Market religion, where the skeptics and freethinkers have gone. What has happened to the Voltaires who once exposed bogus miracles, and the

H. L. Menckens who blew shrill whistles on pious humbuggery? Such is the grip of current orthodoxy that to question the omniscience of The Market is to question the inscrutable wisdom of Providence. The metaphysical principle is obvious: If you *say* it's the real thing, then it must *be* the real thing. As the early Christian theologian Tertullian once remarked, *"Credo quia absurdum est"* ("I believe because it is absurd").

Finally, there is the divinity's will to be *omnipresent.* Virtually every religion teaches this idea in one way or another, and the new religion is no exception. The latest trend in economic theory is the attempt to apply market calculations to areas that once appeared to be exempt, such as dating, family life, marital relations, and child-rearing. Henri Lepage, an enthusiastic advocate of globalization, now speaks about a "total market." Saint Paul reminded the Athenians that their own poets sang of a God "in whom we live and move and have our being"; so now The Market is not only around us but inside us, informing our senses and our feelings. There seems to be nowhere left to flee from its untiring quest. Like the Hound of Heaven, it pursues us home from the mall and into the nursery and the bedroom.

It used to be thought—mistakenly, as it turns out—that at least the innermost, or "spiritual," dimension of life was resistant to The Market. It seemed unlikely that the interior castle would ever be listed by Century 21. But as the markets for material goods become increasingly glutted, such previously unmarketable states of grace as serenity and tranquillity are now appearing in the catalogues. Your personal vision quest can take place in unspoiled wildernesses that are pictured as virtually unreachable—except, presumably, by the other people who read the same catalogue. Furthermore, ecstasy and spirituality are now offered in a convenient generic form. Thus The Market makes available the religious benefits that once required prayer and fasting, without the awkwardness of denominational commitment or the tedious ascetic discipline that once limited their accessibility. All can now handily be bought without an unrealistic demand on one's time, in a weekend workshop at a Caribbean resort with a sensitive psychological consultant replacing the crotchety retreat master.

Discovering the theology of The Market made me begin to think in a different way about the conflict among religions. Violence between Catholics and Protestants in Ulster or Hindus and Muslims in India often dominates the headlines. But I have come to wonder whether the real clash of religions (or even of civilizations) may be going unnoticed. I am beginning to think that for all the religions of the world, however they may differ from one another, the religion of The Market has become the most formidable rival, the more so because it is rarely recognized as a religion. The traditional religions and the religion of the global market, as we have seen, hold radically different views of nature. In Christianity and Judaism, for example, "the earth is the Lord's and the fullness thereof, the world and all that dwell therein." The Creator appoints human beings as stewards and gardeners but, as it were, retains title to the earth. Other faiths have similar ideas. In the Market religion, however, human beings, more particularly those with money, own anything they buy and—within certain limits—can dispose of anything as they choose. Other contradictions can be seen in ideas about the human body, the nature of human community, and the purpose of life. The older religions encourage archaic attachments to particular places. But in The Market's eyes all places are interchangeable. The Market prefers a homogenized world culture with as few inconvenient particularities as possible.

Disagreements among the traditional religions become picayune in comparison with the fundamental differences they all have with the religion of The Market. Will this lead to a new jihad or crusade? I doubt it. It seems unlikely that traditional religions will rise to the occasion and challenge the doctrines of the new dispensation. Most of them seem content to become its acolytes or to be absorbed into its pantheon, much as the old Nordic deities, after putting up a game fight, eventually settled for a diminished but secure status as Christian saints. I am usually a keen supporter of ecumenism. But the contradictions between the world views of the traditional religions on the one hand and the world view of the Market religion on the other are so basic that no compromise seems possible, and I am secretly hoping for a rebirth of polemics.

No religion, new or old, is subject to empirical proof, so what we have is a contest between faiths. Much is at stake. The Market, for example, strongly prefers individualism and mobility. Since it needs to shift people to wherever production requires them, it becomes wrathful when people cling to local traditions. These belong to the older dispensations and—like the high places of the Baalim—should be plowed under. But maybe not. Like previous religions, the new one has ingenious ways of incorporating preexisting ones. Hindu temples, Buddhist festivals, and Catholic saints' shrines can look forward to new incarnations. Along with native costumes and spicy food, they will be allowed to provide local color and authenticity in what could otherwise turn out to be an extremely bland Beulah Land.

There is, however, one contradiction between the religion of The Market and the traditional religions that seems to be insurmountable. All of the traditional religions teach that human beings are finite creatures and that there are limits to any earthly enterprise. A Japanese Zen master once said to his disciples as he was dying, "I have learned only one thing in life: how much is enough." He would find no niche in the chapel of The Market, for whom the First Commandment is "There is *never* enough." Like the proverbial shark that stops moving, The Market that stops expanding dies. That could happen. If it does, then Nietzsche will have been right after all. He will just have had the wrong God in mind.

Holy Sparks:
A Prayer for the Silent God

from *Notre Dame Magazine*

In 135 C.E., Romans killed Rabbi Akiva for teaching Torah. They killed him by flaying his skin and stripping his bones with currycombs. He was 85 years old. A Roman currycomb in those days was an iron scraper; its blunt teeth combed mud and burrs from horsehair. To flay someone—an unusual torture—the wielder had to bear down. Perhaps the skin and muscles of an old scholar are comparatively loose.

"All depends on the preponderance of good deeds," Rabbi Akiva said. The weight of good deeds bears down on the balance scales. Paul Tillich also held this view. If the man who stripped Rabbi Akiva's bones with a currycomb bore down with a weight of, say 200 psi, how many pounds of good deeds tip the balance to the good?

"Are we only talking to ourselves in an empty universe?" a 20th century novelist asked. "The silence is often so emphatic. And we have prayed so much already."

Akiva Ben Joseph was born in the Judean lowlands in 50 C.E. He was illiterate and despised scholarship; he worked herding sheep. Then he fell in love with a rich man's daughter. She agreed to marry him only when he vowed to devote his life to studying Torah. So he did. He learned to read along with their son.

Rabbi Akiva systematized, codified, explained, analyzed, and amplified the traditional religious laws and practices in his painstaking Mishnah and Midrash. Because of Akiva, Mishnah and

Midrash joined scripture itself in Judaism's canon. His interpretations separated Judaism from both Christian and Greek influence.

His contemporaries prized him for his tireless interpretation of each holy detail of Torah. They cherished him for his optimism, his modesty, his universalism (which included tolerance of, and intermarriage with, Samaritans), and his devotion to *Eretz Yisrael,* the land of Israel. He taught that "Thou shalt love thy neighbor as thyself" is the key idea in Torah.

Nelly Sachs wrote, "Who is like you, O Lord, among the silent, remaining silent through the suffering of His children?"

Emperor Hadrian of Rome had condemned Rabbi Akiva to his henchman and executioner Rufus. Rufus was present in the prison cell as the currycombs separated the man's skin and muscles from his bones. Some of Rabbi Akiva's disciples were there, too, likely on the street, watching and listening at the cell window.

Rabbi Akiva had taught his disciples to say, "Whatever the all-merciful does he does for the good"—the sentiment Voltaire ridiculed. During Akiva's innovative execution he was reciting the Shema, because this was the time of day for reciting the Shema. It was then his disciples remonstrated with him, saying, "Our master, to such an extent?"

Spooked that the dwindling rabbi continued to say prayers, Rufus asked him, conversationally, if he was a sorcerer. Rabbi Akiva replied that he was happy to die for God. He said he worshiped the Lord with all his heart, and with all his mind, and now he could add, "with all my soul."

When Rabbi Akiva died, Moses was watching from heaven. Moses saw the torture and martyrdom, and complained to God about it. Why did God let the Romans flay an 85-year-old Torah scholar? Moses' question—the tough one about God's allowing human, moral evil—is reasonable only if we believe that a good God either causes or at any rate allows everything that happens, and that it's all for the best. (This is the doctrine Voltaire, and many another thinker before and since, questioned—or in Voltaire's case mocked.)

God told Moses, "*Shtok,* keep quiet. *Kakh ala bemakhshava lefanai,* this is how I see things." In another version of the same story, God replied to Moses, "Silence! This is how it is in the highest thought."

Rabbi Akiva taught a curious solution to the ever-galling problem that many good people and their children suffer enormously, while many louses and their children prosper and thrive in the pink of health. God punishes the good, he proposed, in this short life, for their few sins, and rewards them eternally in the world to come. Similarly, God rewards the evil-doers in this short life for their few good deeds, and punishes them eternally in the world to come. I do not know how that sat with people. It is, like every ingenious, God-fearing explanation of natural calamity, harsh all around.

Is it not late? A late time to be living? Are not our generations the important ones? For we have changed the world. Are not our heightened times the important ones? For we have nuclear bombs. Are we not especially significant because our century is?—our century and its unique Holocaust, its refugee populations, its serial totalitarian exterminations, our century and its antibiotics, silicon chips, men on the moon, and spliced genes? No, we are not and it is not. These times of ours are ordinary times, a slice of life like any other. Who can bear to hear this, or who will consider it? Though perhaps we are the last generation—now there is a comfort. Take the bomb threat away and what are we? We are ordinary beads on a never-ending string. Our time is a routine twist of an improbable yarn.

We have no chance of being here when the sun burns out. There must be something heroic about our time, something that lifts it above all those other times. Plague? Funny weather? Dire things are happening. People have made great strides at obliterating other people, but that has been the human effort all along and our cohort has only enlarged the means, as have people in every century. Why are we watching the news, reading the news, keeping up with the news? Only to enforce our fancy—probably a necessary lie—that these are crucial times, and we are in on them. Newly revealed, and we are in the know: crazy people, bunches of them. New diseases, shifts in power, floods! Can the news from dynastic Egypt have been any different?

In the beginning, according to Rabbi Isaac Luria, God contracted himself—*zimzum*. The divine essence withdrew into itself to make room for a finite world. Evil became possible: those genetic defects that dog cellular life, those clashing forces which erupt in natural catastrophes, and those sins human minds invent and human hands perform.

Luria's Kabbalist creation story, however baroque, accounts boldly for both moral evil and natural calamity. The creator meant his light to emanate, ultimately, to man. Grace would flow downward through 10 holy vessels, like water cascading. Cataclysm—some say creation itself—disrupted this orderly progression. The holy light burst the vessels. The vessels splintered and scattered. Sparks of holiness fell to the depths, and the opaque shards of the broken vessels *(gelippot)* imprisoned them. This is our bleak world. We see only the demonic shells of things. It is literally sensible to deny that God exists. In fact, God is hidden, exiled, in the sparks of divine light the shells entrap. So evil can exist, can continue to live: the spark of goodness within things, the Gnostic-like spark that even the most evil tendency encloses, lends evil its being.

"The sparks scatter everywhere," Martin Buber said. "They cling to material things as in sealed-up wells, they crouch in substances as in caves that have been bricked up, they inhale darkness and breathe out fear; they flutter about in the movements of the world, searching where they can lodge to be free."

The Jews in 16th century Palestine were in exile—"a most cruel exile," Gershom Scholem called it. They had lived in Muslim Spain a thousand years—far longer than any Europeans have lived in the Americas. In 1492, Christians expelled Muslims and Jews. About 10,000 Spanish Jews moved to Palestine. In Safad they formed the core of the community of the devout. Here unmolested, they contemplated their exile which they understood as symbolizing the world's exile from God. Even the divine is estranged from itself; its essence scatters in sparks. *The Shekinah*—the Divine Presence—is in exile from *Elohim,* the being of God, just as the Jews were in exile in Palestine.

Only redemption—restoration, *tikkun*—can return the sparks of light to their source in the primeval soul; only redemption can restore God's exiled presence to his being in eternity. Only redemption can reunite an exiled soul with its root. The holy person, however, can hasten redemption and help mend heaven and earth.

The presenting face of any religion is its mass of popular superstitions. It seems to take all the keenest thinkers of every religion in every generation to fend off this clamoring pack. In New Mexico in 1978, the face of Jesus arose in a tortilla. "I was just rolling out my husband's burrito . . ." the witness began her account. An auto-parts store in Progresso, Texas, attracted crowds when an oil stain on its floor resembled the Virgin Mary. Another virgin appeared in 1998 in Colma, California, in hardened sap on a pine trunk. At a Nashville coffee shop named Bongo Java, a cinnamon bun came out of the oven looking like Mother Teresa—the nun bun, papers called it. In 1996 in Leicester, England, the name of Allah appeared in a halved eggplant. Several cities—Kandy, Sri

Lanka, is one—claim to own a tooth from the jaw of Buddha. A taxonomist who saw one of these said it belonged to a crocodile.

When he leads trips to Israel, Abbot Philip Lawrence of the monastery of Christ in the Desert in Abiquiu, New Mexico, gives only one charge to his flock. "When they show the stone with the footprint of Christ in it," he says, "don't laugh." There is an enormous footprint of Buddha, too, in Luang Prabang, Vietnam.

"Suddenly there is a point where religion becomes laughable," Thomas Merton wrote. "Then you decide that you are nevertheless religious." Suddenly!

One of the queerest spots on earth—I hope—is in Bethlehem. This is the patch of planet where, according to tradition, a cave once stabled animals, and where Mary gave birth to a son whose later preaching—scholars of every stripe agree, with varying enthusiasm—caused the occupying Romans to crucify him. Generations of Christians have churched over the traditional Bethlehem spot to the highest degree. Centuries of additions have made the architecture peculiar, but no one can see the church anyway, because many monasteries clamp onto it in clusters like barnacles. The Greek Orthodox Church owns the grotto site now, in the form of the Church of the Nativity.

There, in the Church of the Nativity, I took worn stone stairways to descend to levels of dark rooms, chapels, and dungeonlike corridors where hushed people passed. The floors were black stone or cracked marble. Dense brocades hung down old stone walls. Oil lamps hung in layers. Each polished silver or brass lamp seemed to absorb more light than its orange flame emitted, so the more lamps shone, the darker the space.

Packed into a tiny, domed upper chamber, Norwegians sang, as every other group did in turn, a Christmas carol. The stone dome bounced the sound around. The people sounded like seraphs singing inside a bell, sore amazed.

Descending once more I passed several monks, narrow men, fine-faced and black, who wore tall black hats and long black robes. Ethiopians, they use the oldest Christian rite. At a lower level, in a small room, I peered over half a stone wall and saw Europeans below; they whispered in a language I could not identify.

Distant music sounded deep, as if from within my ribs. The music was, in fact, people from all over the world in the upper chamber singing harmonies in their various tongues. The music threaded the vaults.

Now I climbed down innumerable dark stone stairs to the main part, the deepest basement: the Grotto of the Nativity. The grotto was down yet another smoky stairway at the back of a stone cave far beneath street level. This was the place. It smelled of wet sand. It was a narrow cave about 10 feet wide; cracked marble paved it. Bunched tapers, bending grotesque in the heat, lighted a corner of floor. People had to kneel, one by one, under arches of brocade hangings, and stretch into a crouch down among dozens of gaudy hanging lamps, to see it.

A 14-pointed silver star, two feet in diameter, covered a raised bit of marble floor at the cave wall. This silver star was the X that marked the spot: here, just here, the infant got born. Two thousand years of Christianity began here, where God emptied himself into man. Actually, many Christian scholars think "Jesus of Nazareth" was likely born in Nazareth. Early writers hooked his birth to Bethlehem to fit a prophecy. Here, now, the burning oils smelled heavy. It must have struck many people that we were competing with these lamps for oxygen.

In the center of the silver star was a circular hole. That was the bull's-eye, God's quondam target.

Crouching people leaned forward to wipe their fingers across the hole's flat bottom. When it was my turn, I knelt, bent under a fringed satin drape, reached across half the silver star, and touched its hole. I could feel some sort of soft wax in it. The hole was a quarter inch deep and six inches across, like a wide petri dish. A newborn's head would be too small for it; a newborn's body would be too big. I have never read any theologian who claims that God is particularly interested in religion, anyway.

Any patch of ground anywhere smacks more of God's presence on earth, to me, than did this marble grotto. The ugliness of the blunt and bumpy silver star impressed me. The bathetic pomp of the heavy, tasseled brocades, the marble, the censers hanging from chains, the embroidered antependium, the aspergillum, the crosiers, the ornate lamps—some humans' idea of elegance—bespoke grand comedy, too, that God put up with it. And why should he not? Things here on earth get a whole lot worse than bad taste.

"Everyday," said Rabbi Nachman of Bratslav, "the glory is ready to emerge from its debasement."

It is "fatal," Teilhard said of the old belief that we suffer at the hands of God omnipotent. It is fatal to reason. It does not work. The omnipotence of God makes no sense if it requires the all-causingness of God. Good people quit God altogether at this point, and throw out the baby with the bath, perhaps because they last looked into God in their childhoods, and have not changed their views of divinity since. It is not the tooth fairy. In fact, even Aquinas dissolved the fatal problem of natural, physical evil by tinkering with God's omnipotence. As Baron von Hugel noted, Aquinas said that "the Divine Omnipotence must not be taken as the power to effect any imaginable thing, but only the power to effect what is within the nature of things."

Similarly, Teilhard called the explanation that God hides himself deliberately to test our love, "hateful"; it is "mental gymnastics." Here: "The doctors of the church explain that the Lord deliberately hides himself from us in order to test our love. One would have to be irretrievably committed to mental gymnastics . . . not to feel the hatefulness of this solution."

Many times in Christian churches I have heard the pastor say to God, "All your actions show your wisdom and love." Each time I reach in vain for the courage to rise and shout, "That's a lie!"— just to put things on a solid footing.

"He has cast down the mighty from their thrones, and has lifted up the lowly.

"He has filled the hungry with good things, and the rich he has sent away empty." Again, Paul writes to the Christians in Rome, "In all things God works for the good of those who love him."

When was that? I missed it. In China, in Israel, in the Yemen, in the Ecuadorean Andes and the Amazon basin, in Greenland, Iceland, and Baffin Island, in Europe, on the shore of the Beaufort Sea inside the Arctic Circle, and in Costa Rica, in the Marquesan Islands and the Tuamotus, and in the United States, I have seen the rich sit secure on their thrones and send the hungry away empty. If God's escape clause is that he gives only spiritual things, then we might hope that the poor and suffering are rich in spiritual gifts, as some certainly are, but as some of the comfortable are too. In a soup kitchen, I see suffering. *Deus Otiosus*—do-nothing God, who, if he has power, abuses it.

Of course God wrote no scriptures, neither chapter nor verse. It is foolish to blame or quit him for his admirer's claims superstitious or otherwise. "God is not on trial," I read somewhere. "We are not jurors but suppliants."

Maybe "all your actions show your wisdom and love" means that the precious few things we know that God did, and does, are in fact unambiguous in wisdom and love, and all other events derive not from God but only from blind chance, just as they seem to.

The Baal Shem Tov, by his own account, ascended to heaven many times. During these ascents, his friends said, he stood bent for many hours while his soul rose. He himself related in a letter on his return from two such vertical expeditions that he could not, much as he tried, deflect either moral evils or natural calamities. He could, however, report how God explained his actions. At that time Polish Christians were already killing Jews. On Rosh Hashanah (September 15, 1746) during an ascent to heaven, the Baal Shem Tov complained about the killings to God. He knew that some Jews apostasized, and they died along with the devout. Why—why any of it? God's answer: "So that no son of Israel would convert." (It would not even save their lives.) Later, an epidemic was scourging Poland. Again on Rosh Hashanah the Baal Shem Tov's soul climbed to heaven. Why the epidemic? The epidemic, God gave him to understand, came because he himself, the Baal Shem Tov, had prayed, "Let us fall into the hands of the Lord but let us not fall into the hands of man." Now God, into whose plaguey hands they had fallen, asked him on the spot, "Why do you want to cancel?"—to cancel, that is, your earlier prayer. Now you want the Christian Poles instead of the epidemic? The best bargain the Baal Shem Tov could strike was to keep the epidemic from his town.

In other words, the Baal Shem Tov, who was not a theologian, believed that God caused evil events—both moral evil (the Jew-killing Poles) and natural evil (the epidemic)—to teach or punish. The Baal Shem Tov learned much about God, but theodicy was not his bailiwick, and he did not shed the old "fatal" explanation that we suffer at the hands of God omnipotent.

In 1976 an earthquake in Tangshan killed 750,000 people. Before it quaked, many survivors reported, the earth shone with an incandescent light.

"Your fathers did eat manna and are dead," Jesus told people—one of his cruelest remarks. Trafficking directly with the divine, as the manna-eating wilderness generation did, and as Jesus did, confers no immunity to death or hazard. You can live as a particle crashing about and colliding in a welter of materials with God, or you can live as a particle crashing about and colliding in a welter of materials without God. But you cannot live outside the welter of colliding materials.

Are we ready to think of all humanity as a living tree, carrying on splendidly without us? We easily regard a bee hive or an ant colony as a single organism, and even a school of fish, a flock of dunlin, a herd of elk. And we easily and correctly regard an aggregate of individuals, a sponge or coral or lichen or slime mold, as one creature—but us? When we people differ, and know our consciousness, and love? Even lovers, even twins, are strangers who will love and die alone. And we like it this way, at least in the West; we prefer to endure any agony of isolation than to merge and extinguish our selves in an abstract "humanity" whose fate we should hold dearer than our own. Who could say, I'm in agony because my child died, but that's all right, mankind as a whole has abundant children? The religious idea sooner or later challenges the notion of the individual. The Buddha taught each disciple to vanquish his fancy that he possessed an individual self. Huston Smith suggests that our individuality resembles a snowflake's: the seas evaporate water, clouds build and loose water in snowflakes which dissolve and go to sea. This simile galls. What have I to do with the ocean, I with my unique and novel hexagons and spikes? Is my very mind a wave in the ocean, a wave the wind flattens, a flaw the wind draws like a finger?

We know we must yield, if only intellectually. Okay, we're a lousy snowflake. Okay, we're a tree. These dead loved ones we mourn were only those brown lower branches a tree shades and kills as it grows; the tree itself is thriving. But what kind of tree are we growing here, that could be worth such waste and pain? For each of us loses all we love, everyone we love. We grieve and leave. What marvels shall these future whizzes, damn their eyes, accomplish?

"How can evil exist in a world created by God, the Beneficent One? It can exist, because entrapped deep inside the force of evil there is a spark of goodness. This spark is the source of life of the evil tendency. . . . Now, it is the specific mission of the Jew to free the entrapped holy sparks from the grip of the forces of evil by means of Torah study and prayer. Once the holy sparks are released, evil, having lost its life-giving core, will cease to exist." So wrote Rabbi Yehuda Aryeh Leib Alter of Ger, in 19th century Poland. It was the Baal Shem Tov who taught this vital idea.

God is spirit, spirit expressed infinitely in the universe, who does not give as the world gives. His home is absence, and there he finds us. In the coils of absence we meet him by seeking him. God lifts our souls to their roots in his silence. Natural materials clash and replicate, shaping our fates. We lose the people we love, we lose our vigor, and we lose our lives. Perhaps, and at best, God knows nothing of these temporal accidents, but knows souls only. This God does not direct the universe, he underlies it. Or he "prolongs himself" into it, in Teilhard's terms. Or in dear nutcase Joel Goldsmith's terms, God is the universe's consciousness. The consciousness of divinity is divinity itself. The more we wake to holiness, the more of it we give birth to, the more we introduce, expand, and multiply it on earth, the more God is "on the field."

God is—for the most part—out of the physical loop of the fallen world he created, let us say. Or God is the loop, or pervades the loop, or the loop runs in God like a hole in his side he never fingers. Certainly God is not a member of the loop like the rest of us, passing the bucket to splash the fire, kicking the bucket, passing the buck. After all, the semipotent God has one hand tied behind his back. (I cannot prove that with the other hand he wipes and stirs our souls from time to time; he spins like a fireball through our skulls, and knocks open our eyes so we see flaming skies and fall to the ground and say "Abba!")

A man who struggles long to pray and study Torah will be able to discover the sparks of divine light in all of creation, in each solitary bush and grain and woman and man. And when he cleaves strenuously to God for many years he will be able to release the sparks, to unwrap and lift these particular shreds of holiness, and return them to God. This is the human task: to direct and channel the sparks' return. This is *tikkun,* restoration.

Yours is a holy work on earth right now, they say, whatever that work is, if you tie your love and desire to God. You do not deny or flee the world, but redeem it, all of it—just as it is.

Who is dead? The Newtonian God, some call that tasking and antiquated figure who haunts children and repels strays, who sits on the throne of judgment frowning and figuring, and who with the strength of his arm dishes out human fates, in the form of cancer or cash, to 5.9 billion people—to teach, dazzle, rebuke, or try us, one by one, and to punish or reward us, day by day, for our thoughts, words, and deeds.

"The great Neolithic proprietor," Teilhard called him, the God of the old cosmos, who was not yet known as the soul of the world but as its mage. History, then, was a fix.

People once held a "Deuteronomic" idea of God, says Rabbi Lawrence Kushner. God intervened in human affairs "without human agency." He was a Lego lord.

The first theological task, Paul Tillich said 50 years ago, by which time it was already commonplace, is to remove absurdities in interpretation.

It is an old idea, that God is not omnipotent. Seven centuries have passed since Aquinas wrote that God has power to effect only what is in the nature of things. Leibnitz also implied it; working within the "possible world" limits God's doings. Now the notion of God the Semipotent has trickled down to the theologian in the street. Teilhard in his day called the belief that we suffer at the hands of an omnipotent God "fatal," remember, and indicated only one escape: to recognize that if God allows us both to suffer and to sin it is "because he cannot here and now cure us and show himself to us"—because we ourselves have not yet evolved enough. Paul Tillich said in the 1940s that "omnipotence" symbolizes Being's power to overcome finitude and anxiety in the long run, while never being able to eliminate them.

God is no more blinding people with glaucoma, or testing them with diabetes, or purifying them with spinal pain, or choreographing the seeding of tumor cells through lymph, or fiddling with chromosomes, than he is jimmying floodwaters or pitching tornadoes at towns. God is no more cogitating which among us he plans to be born as bird-headed dwarfs or elephant men—or to kill by AIDS or kidney failure, heart disease, childhood leukemia or sudden infant death syndrome—than he is pitching lightning bolts at pedestrians, triggering rock slides, or setting fires. The very least likely things for which God might be responsible are what insurers call "acts of God."

Then what, if anything, does he do? If God does not cause everything that happens, does God cause anything that happens? Is God completely out of the loop?

Sometimes God moves loudly, as if spinning to another place like ball lightning. God is, oddly, personal; this God knows. Sometimes en route, dazzlingly or dimly, he shows an edge of himself to souls who seek him, and the people who bear those souls, marveling, know it, and see the skies carousing around them, and watch cells stream and multiply in green leaves. He does not give as the world gives; he leads invisibly over many years, or he wallops for 30 seconds at a time. He may touch a mind, too, making a loud sound, or a mind may feel the rim of his mind as he nears. Such experiences are gifts to beginners. "Later on," a Hasid master said, "you don't see these things anymore." (Having seen, people of varying cultures turn—for reasons unknown, and by a mechanism unimaginable—to aiding and serving the poor and afflicted.)

Mostly God is out of the physical loop. Or the loop is a spinning hole in his side. Simone Weil takes a notion from Rabbi Isaac Luria to acknowledge that God's hands are tied. To create, God did not extend himself but withdrew himself; he humbled and obliterated himself, and left outside himself the domain of necessity, in which he does not intervene. Even in the domain of souls, he intervenes only "under certain conditions."

Does God stick a finger in, if only now and then? Does God budge, nudge, hear, twitch, help? Is heaven pliable? Or is praying eudaemonistically—praying for things and events, for rain and healing—delusional? Physicians agree that prayer for healing can work what they routinely call miracles, but of course the mechanism could be self-hypnosis. Paul Tillich devoted only two paragraphs in his three-volume systematic theology to prayer. Those two startling paragraphs suggest, without describing, another mechanism. To entreat and to intercede is to transform situations powerfully. God participates in bad conditions here by including them in his being and ultimately overcoming them. True prayer surrenders to God; that willing surrender itself changes the situation a jot or two by adding power which God can use. Since God works in and through existing conditions, I take this to mean that when the situation is close, when your friend might die or might live, then your prayer's surrender can add enough power—mechanism unknown—to tilt the balance. Though it won't still earthquakes or halt troops, it might quiet cancer or quell pneumonia.

For Tillich, God's activity is by no means interference, but instead divine creativity—the ongoing creation of life with all its greatness and danger. I don't know. I don't know beans about God.

Nature works out its complexities. God suffers the world's necessities along with us, and suffers our turning away, and joins us in exile. Christians might add that Christ hangs, as it were, on the cross forever, always incarnate, and always nailed.

"Spiritual path" is the hilarious popular term for those nightblind mesas and flayed hills in which people grope, for decades on end, with the goal of knowing the absolute. They discover others spread under the stars and encamped here and there by watchfires, in groups or alone, in the open landscape; they stop for a sleep, or for several years, and move along without knowing toward what or why. They leave whatever they find, picking up each stone, carrying it a while, and dropping it gratefully and without regret, for it is not the absolute, though they cannot say what it is. Their life's fine, impossible goal justifies the term "spiritual." Nothing, however, can justify the term "path" for their bewildered and empty stumbling, this blackened vagabondage—except one thing: they don't quit. They stick with it. Year after year they put one foot in front of the other, though they fare nowhere. Year after year they find themselves still feeling with their fingers for lumps in the dark.

The planet turns under their steps like a water wheel rolling; constellations shift without anyone's gaining ground. They are presenting themselves to the unseen gaze of emptiness. Why do they want to do this? They hope to learn how to be useful.

Their feet catch in nets; they untangle them when they notice, and keep moving. They hope to learn where they came from. "The soul teaches incessantly," said Rabbi Pinhas, "but it never repeats." Decade after decade they see no progress. But they do notice, if they look, that they have left doubt behind. Decades ago they left behind doubt about this or that doctrine, abandoning the issues as unimportant. Now, I mean, they have left behind the early doubt that this feckless prospecting in the dark for the unseen is a reasonable way to pass one's life.

"Plunge into matter," Teilhard said—and at another time, "Plunge into God." And he said this fine thing: "By means of all created things, without exception, the divine assails us, penetrates us, and molds us. We imagine it as distant and inaccessible, whereas in fact we live steeped in its burning layers."

Only by living completely in the world can one learn to believe. One must abandon every attempt to make something of one-self—even to make of oneself a righteous person. Dietrich Bonhoeffer wrote this in a letter from prison a year before the Nazis hanged him for resisting Nazism and plotting to assassinate Hitler.

"I can and must throw myself into the thick of human endeavor, and with no stopping for breath," said Teilhard, who by no means stopped for breath. But what distinguishes oneself "completely in the world" (Bonhoeffer) or throwing oneself "into the thick of human endeavor" (Teilhard) as these two prayerful men did, from any other life lived in the thick of things? A secular broker's life, a shoe salesman's life, a mechanic's, a writer's, a farmer's? Where else is there? The world and human endeavor catch and hold everyone alive but a handful of hobos, nuns, and monks. Were these two men especially dense, that they spent years learning what every kid already knows, that life here is all there is? Authorities in Rome or the Gestapo forbade them each to teach (as secular Rome had forbidden Rabbi Akiva to teach). One of them in his density went to prison and died on a scaffold. The other in his density kept his vows despite Rome's stubborn ignorance and righteous cruelty and despite the importunings of a woman he loved. No.

We live in all we seek. The hidden shows up in too-plain sight. It lives captive on the face of the obvious—the people, events, and things of the day—to which we as sophisticated children have long since become oblivious. What a hideout: holiness lies spread and borne over the surface of time and stuff like color.

What to do? There is only matter, Teilhard said; there is only spirit, the kabbalists and gnostics said. These are essentially identical views. Each impels an individual soul to undertake to divinize, transform, and complete the world, to—as these thinkers say quite as if there were both matter and spirit—"subject a little more matter to spirit," to "lift up the fallen and to free the imprisoned," to "establish in this our place a dwelling place of the Divine Presence," to "work for the redemption of the world," to "extract spiritual power without letting any of it be lost," to "help the holy spiritual substance to accomplish itself in that section of Creation in which we are living," to "mend the shattered unity of the diving worlds," to "force the gates of the spirit," and cry, "'Let me come by.'"

Our lives come free; they're on the house to all comers, like the shopkeeper's wine. God decants the universe of time in a stream, and our best hope is to, by our own awareness, step into the steam and serve, empty as flumes, to keep it moving.

The birds were mating all over Galilee. I saw swifts mate in mid-air. At Kibbutz Lavi, in the wide-open hills above the Sea of Galilee, 300 feet above me under the sky, the two swifts flew together in swoops, falling and catching. These alpine swifts were large, white below. How do birds mate in mid-air? They start high. Their beating wings tilt them awkwardly sometimes and part those tiny places where they join; often one of the pair stops flying and they lose altitude. They separate, rest in a tree for a minute, and fly again. Alone they rise fast, tensely, until you see only motes that chase, meet—you, there, here, out of all this air!—and spiral down; breaks your heart. At dusk, I learned later, they climb so high that at night they actually sleep in the air.

Rabbi Menachem Nahum of Chernobyl: "All being itself is derived from God and the presence of the Creator is in each created thing." This double notion is pan-entheism—a word to which I add a hyphen to emphasize its difference from pantheism. Pan-entheism, according to David Tracy, theologian at the University of Chicago, is the private view of most Christian intellectuals today. Not only is God immanent in everything, as plain old pantheists hold, however loosely, but more profoundly everything is simultaneously in God, within God the transcendent. There is a divine, not just bushes.

I saw doves mate on sand. It was early morning. The male dove trod the female on a hilltop path. Beyond them in blue haze lay the Sea of Galilee, and to the north Mount Meron and the town of Safad traversing the mountain Jebel Kan'an. Other doves were calling from nearby snags. To writer Florida Scott Maxwell, doves say, "Too true, dear love, too true." But to poet Margaret Gibson, doves in Mexico say, "No hope, no hope." An observant Jew recites a grateful prayer at seeing landscape—mountains, hills, seas, rivers, and deserts, which are, one would have thought, pretty much unavoidable sights. "Blessed art Thou, O Lord, our God, King of the Universe, THE MAKER OF ALL CREATION." One utters this blessing also when he meets the sea again—at seeing the Mediterranean Sea, say, after an interval of 30 days.

All the religions of Abraham deny that the world, the colorful array that surrounds and grips us, is illusion, even though from time to time anyone may see the vivid veil part. But no one can deny that God *per se* is wholly invisible, or deny that his voice is very still, very small, or explain why.

That night there was a full moon. I saw it rise over a caperbush, a still grove of terebinths, and a myrtle. According to the Talmud, when a person is afraid to walk at night, a burning torch is worth two companions, and a full moon is worth three. Blessed are Thou, O Lord our God, creator of the universe, who brings on evening; whose power and might fills the world; who did a miracle for me in this place; WHO HAS KEPT US IN LIFE AND BROUGHT US TO THIS TIME.

GRETEL EHRLICH

On the Road with God's Fool

from *The New York Times Magazine*

The road from Assisi to Gubbio is sometimes a footpath, a horse track, a Roman street and now, a gravel road that winds through a roller-coaster landscape of treeless peaks and deep stream-cut valleys all dotted with tiny farms and fortresslike monasteries where 13th-century travelers could spend the night. It is called the Sentiero Francescano della Pace because it is the path that Francesco di Bernardone—better known as St. Francis— is believed to have taken after he stood naked in Assisi's central piazza, renounced family and friends and set out on the journey that effectively defined the rest of his life as wanderer, seeker, ultimately saint.

As I shouldered my rucksack on a cold March morning, preparing to follow his footsteps almost 800 years later, the Piazza del Comune in Assisi and the streets leading to it, lined with religious souvenir shops and bars, were empty except for pigeons and dogs. Bells chimed the hours and robins sang wake-up songs. All over town, Franciscan monks—the order of mendicants that is St. Francis' legacy—were praying. Soon the roar of cement trucks and rubble pouring from the blank windows of buildings under repair filled the town. Since a series of earthquakes in the fall of 1997, all of Assisi is being restored.

"Take nothing for your journey, no staff, nor bag, nor bread, nor money." That verse from Luke 9:3 spurred St. Francis on. In similar (if involuntary) spirit, I found that all my money had been stolen—not in Italy, but on the airplane from New York, and though I tried to entertain the joys of disburdenment, I failed. Three runners in Lycra sped by, and a nun talked vigorously into a cell phone clutched to her ear. With my companion, Tony, an Australian with a Franciscan's hard-won sense of joy, I ambled up the street to the gate that would lead us out of the walled city.

At Porta Giacomo a blind man stood in the shadows. His eyes were blue oceans, and under his feet the cobblestones shone, still wet from the previous night's rain. A hand-carved cane hung from his folded arms. I stood for a moment, thinking of how St. Francis passed here on just such a freezing spring day, spiritually blind as he began his long journey, and literally blind 22 years later when he was carried back through the gate to die.

The blind man began singing and talking as we passed by, the two sounds rolling together into squeaks, grunts and held notes. Then he stamped his feet in place as if he, too, had decided to walk along.

Blind or sighted, it is impossible to know one's direction. The path is a place where going never ends, where arriving is always happening. It is a wavering that receives our falls, a gash in geology's stacked floor where our uncertain feet break through to another level.

By the time St. Francis set out for Gubbio, he was beginning to understand that renunciation means giving up habitual thought. Conversion was "a turning around," implying as well an engagement, a *conversation* with the world. He had already torn away so much, but there was more to come, and the open road would be his teacher.

He was not handsome, but said to be beautiful with joy. Long-faced, sweet-voiced, with large sparkling eyes, Francesco di Bernardone had oversize ears and eyebrows that drew a line straight across his forehead. Fun-loving and charismatic, he wooed women with the troubadour songs of Provence, spending each year's 150 religious holidays sauntering through the Umbrian countryside on foot and horseback. He was a libertine with an unaffected generosity and an affinity for nature.

What is it in a life that leads a medieval playboy to sainthood, and where does the path begin? That's what I wondered as I stepped onto the Sentiero and followed Francesco's footsteps out of Assisi. I had been attracted to St. Francis because I'm a walker myself and have walked away from a life-threatening encounter with lightning into health. I've lived with the herds and now share a house with wild birds—a family of canyon wrens was born in my bedroom, and a sparrow often perches on a rafter watching me write. I've loved St. Francis for his unmediated kinship with animals as well as for his modernity. He could well have been a 60's radical, casting off convention and everything money can buy, yet every action had something to teach: he was radical without bitterness, vital yet gentle, dramatic—even outrageous at times—without narcissism.

Most likely, he stepped onto the path out of despair—a sense that something was wrong, though he didn't know quite what. His father, Pietro, was a wealthy cloth merchant who traveled between Italy and France, and because of his love for things French, he changed his son's name from Giovanni to Francesco. In training for the clothier guild of Assisi, the young Francesco was a charming gadabout, often more elegantly dressed than his clients, and given to lavish spending when it came to banquets.

Every time Francesco started off on a trip, something happened—bad weather, bandits, illness, visions, even revelation—to alter the meaning of the journey. Sometimes the shortest walk brought the biggest change.

When Francesco went to San Damiano, a quiet hermitage just below Assisi's walls, during vespers one day, the crucifix lighted up and a voice spoke: "Francis, do you not see how my house is falling into ruin? Go and repair it for me!" Francis took the words literally, thinking he was to repair the crumbling walls of the church. To help with reconstruction, he stole a horse and bolts of precious fabric from his father's store and sold them, then offered the money to the priest at San Damiano, who refused the donation.

When Francis' father discovered the theft, he came after his son. Francis hid in a cave on Mount Subasio, a mountain that rises almost straight up behind Assisi and is pocked with limestone caves known as the *Eremo delle Carceri* (hermitage cells). Many times, Francesco took up residence in those frigid grottoes to pray. Finally regaining his courage, he walked back down. He was no longer Assisi's man about town but a footsore dharma bum who had traded in his dandy's silk-and-velvet breeches and capes for a sackcloth tunic in the sign of the cross, held in place by a three-knot cord representing his vow of poverty, chastity and obedience. Once the most popular man in town, he was now viewed as a madman, as "God's fool." *"Pazzo, pazzo,"* his friends yelled. Stones were thrown. His father seized him, dragged him to the house, tied him in chains and beat him. When no one was looking, Francis' gentle mother, Pica, a deeply religious Catholic who believed her son was on the path to sainthood, set him free.

It was not long before Francis' father caught up with his son and brought him before the Bishop of Assisi in the Piazza del Comune to be tried as a thief. There, father renounced son, and Francis in turn famously renounced his father. "Our father who art in heaven. . . ." he began. "I am the son of God, not of man." He stripped off all his clothes. Standing naked, he handed his garments and the purse full of money to his father, then began to walk north to the walled city of Gubbio, where he planned to stay with a friend.

. . .

The road to Gubbio is cobblestone, pavement and gravel that gives onto a path through what were once forests and are now open fields. The A.D. 1371 statutes of the Eugubine Comune, now called Gubbio, state that the road that St. Francis took, *"qua itur Valfabbrica,"* followed the river Tescio downstream to the village of Campolongo, then on to a nearby Benedictine monastery, where he stayed the night. In the morning, he discovered a waterfall, where he washed his body clean of worldly concerns. Refreshed, he left the river and walked cross-country over snowy mountaintops.

Each step he took represented an inward peregrination. Walking and giving, walking and singing, walking and praying: the path was the proving ground for sainthood, and walking was an ambulation of heart and mind. Just after the village of Pioppo and before reaching Valfabbrica, bandits jumped St. Francis, but he had nothing to give—only his poverty. For the bandits to possess his poverty, they would have had to go naked and divest themselves of all they had previously stolen. Disgusted, the robbers threw St. Francis into a snowy ditch and ran off. Francis emerged singing.

Penniless, sick, frail, he had no address. He had never been ordained. His self-styled vocation, shaky as it seemed at first, was for redemption and liberation, not the medieval alchemy of secrecy and poison, and his natural radiance magnetized those near him. Instead of taking on the monastic rule of the church, he abandoned himself to God and the road. He was God's vagabond and "geography's ant." With unimaginable self-discipline, he kept adjusting to the difficulty of the path, learning to live each moment in total combustion.

Winter snows lay draped in lazy drifts across the Sentiero. I took off my shoes and plunged into the snow. The arches of my feet ached with the cold. After a few moments I put my socks and shoes back on and, with tingling feet, kept walking. Behind me, to the south, Mount Subasio showed its back. It was a black wall crowned with sun-glinting silver.

To walk is to unbalance oneself. Between one step and the next we become lost. Balance is regained as the foot touches earth, then it goes as the foot lifts. A path is made of dirt and rock; it is also a swath of light cut through all that appears to be solid and unchanging. It is a flesh wound that opens deep in the foot of the walker, so that what we are, and where we are going, and the way we've chosen to get there, remains directionless; the traveler is forever wounded and lost. Pain, discomfort and groundlessness are the seeker's friends. Being lost turns into a state of awakeness; it is the same as being found.

As I walked, I tried to feel his path: how the Sentiero had opened him; how the Umbrian landscape became the font of inspiration into which he dipped. As we trekked out of a deep valley between patches of snow, the path was lined with blackberry bushes, *ginestra* (Scotch broom) and wild iris. Hayfields were thick with bunch grass and clover, interspersed with wheat, corn, sunflowers, grapes, figs, apples, plums and walnuts.

I tried to imagine the animals darting out from forest cover to amble at his side or flutter around his head, but there were no animals anywhere. So much of this landscape had been changed and desecrated since St. Francis walked here: mountains have been denuded of trees and almost all the animals and birds shot. In the distance we saw cranes—what Tony referred to as "Italy's national bird." Not the avian kind but the mechanical cranes with which tumbled farmhouses are now being restored. Bereft of life and diversity, the Umbrian beauty seemed surprisingly shabby.

We passed neat-as-a-pin subsistence farms whose vineyards were so old as to look like groves of thick-trunked trees. We walked

uphill through Pian della Pieve, then down again toward a waterfall. Somewhere between San Presto and Collemincio, a farmer
invited us in for coffee. He was small and wiry with huge dirt-
stained hands. Renato had been born in the house and his wife,
Teresa, came from a farm just up the road. She had recently suffered bouts of angina and had cut down on the number of cows
she milked every day. Her wide, coarse face opened in a beatific
smile as she offered us *pane di San Francesco*—bread with nuts
and fruit—and assured us that St. Francis had once passed
this way.

The house was a series of small rooms connected by a hallway.
Only the kitchen and eating room were heated. Near the fireplace
two large hams hung from the rafters. Every once in a while there
was a thud and the wall shook. *Terremoto?* I asked. They shook
their heads, no, no earthquake. "It is the cows. They live on the
first floor."

To embrace poverty meant more than going without. It demanded a way of living that was all-accommodating. St. Francis
disproved the apparent contradiction that you could spend your
life giving when you possessed nothing. Poverty meant materializ-
ing riches from emptiness. St. Francis' sick body humbled him
whenever prayer failed, enabling him to welcome the disinherited
and the sick, and share their lives with a pure heart because it was
his life too. Between walkabouts he helped care for the lepers, the
poor, the homeless. From emptiness came compassion.

We continued up the road. Farmers pruned grapevines and
olive trees. Stacks of firewood gave way to stacks of roof tiles drying. A blue tent, distributed after the earthquakes, was still pitched
in one of the yards—just in case. Not far from there, a whole village had collapsed during the October earthquake. The yearly
custom of baking a certain kind of bread as an offering against
natural disaster was overlooked in 1997. Now the villagers, all

living in tents and containers, attributed their tragedy to that single lapse. The earthquakes were a result of "things that we have done that are bad," one resident told us. Who can say?

We walked a ridge line, dipped into a valley then trudged uphill again. The air was cold but we were sweating. Farm implements—a hay rake and a horse-drawn ditcher—were 19th century; no sign of the upcoming millennium here. The week before, we had visited the Basilica di San Francesco, which was severely shaken by the earthquakes. The three-story complex sits like a sore thumb at the west end of Assisi, once a place of execution called the Hill of Hell. Now it is referred to as the Hill of Paradise. Deep inside, St. Francis' bones are locked away in a sepulcher, the immense weight of the basilica—a place he would have hated—weighing down on top of him.

Four people, including two engineers, were killed when portions of the vaulted ceiling fell on them during the second of two earthquakes on September 26. "A few minutes more and the whole thing would have come down," an injured bystander said. Brother Daniel, a Franciscan friar from Buffalo, told us the earthquake was "a call for us to return to rebuilding our church, as St. Francis did, a spiritual rebuilding in a time of greed and battling." As we walked under what remained of the Giotto and Cimabue frescoes, Brother Daniel reminded us that the root word for obedience means "to listen." As we listened, military planes flew overhead in the direction of Yugoslavia.

The walled cities of medieval Italy were fixed universes, bastions of defense, outlets for commerce, built out of fear. By turning his back on the religious status quo, St. Francis began to take the roof off 13th-century superstition and violence by sticking to the open road and welcoming whatever came his way. His previous enthusiasms for war, wine, women and song transmigrated into a divine intoxication with the natural world.

Hunted animals sought refuge at his side. Fish refused to die in his hands. A pheasant and a rabbit followed him like dogs, as well as a goat and a hawk. During cold snaps he set out honey for bees to eat. He talked to flowers when they came into bloom. Sparrows rode his body like a moving tree, catching rides up and down mountains. Followers said they saw light wherever he went, that sometimes his body was lifted up in a silver cloud. By seeing into the essential nature of things, St. Francis opened the door for animals to see into him. No skin, no feather, no blood barriers existed. He used mountains and rivers for words and owl songs and bear grunts for prayers.

It would be a mistake to think that St. Francis lived a life of solitude. Quite the opposite. Bernard, Giles, Sylvester, Juniper, Leo and Elias all joined St. Francis, and together they formed a brotherhood, walking two by two around Italy, Spain, France and Switzerland, preaching and praying, meditating in the *carceri* on Mount Subasio, living together in the little shacks beside the chapel at the Porziuncola in the Spoleto Valley. Francis forbade sadness in his presence, urging laughter and singing, along with a hefty dose of discipline and a stricture to keep their vows. Walking tirelessly, they kicked discursive thought aside (books were forbidden) and lived wide awake.

We walked higher and higher. The Apennine Mountains glistened in the northeast. Under melting snow, green grass showed through, and sun came as bright darts stabbing clouds. On a north-facing slope, waist-high snowbanks stretched across the road: our footsteps through them left black holes, like eyes, looking for the next season.

If St. Francis was hard on himself, he was kind to others. He refused to shake off the icicles that hung from his robes in the winter and cut his legs. Yet when one young follower cried of hunger in the middle of the night, St. Francis didn't reprimand him for lack of discipline but instead woke the others and prepared a feast, which they spent the rest of the night eating.

Rain came in heavy curtains and undulated across stippled peaks. The pencil-point cypresses were stirred by gusts of wind that bent their tips and straightened them again. If they could write something, what would they say? Two cars whizzed by, then the woodcutter's truck passed, laden with dried branches for cooking fires. The sky brightened and the sun was suddenly hot. Four gray and black birds the size of ravens took turns flying across a hayfield then returning. Rainwater washed back and forth between gathering clouds, then dropped as snow. A chill ran down my back. I pulled my hood up, clasped my hands together and kept going.

We crossed the roiling Chiascio river on a high bridge and walked north. When St. Francis reached this point, he had to knock on the doors of the Benedictine monastery at Santa Maria di Valfabbrica because the flooding river was impassable. The monks, known to be aggressive and rude, grudgingly let him stay. He was lucky that his rapture was not seen as dangerous or delusional; the time had not yet come when the Inquisitors were burning heretics at the stake. A few days later, St. Francis walked north to La Barcaccia, where he crossed the river by pole barge, then continued on toward Gubbio.

Pine wind roared. We were on pavement now. Following a steep mountain road, sheep parted, letting us pass. At Casa Castalda, we turned left and took the gravel road north-west to Colpalombo. The hayfields were steep. They looked like green cloths pinned to a blackboard. What was left of the oak forest was still brown leafed, dormant, hiding patches of snow that had not yet seen the sun. Under my feet the flinty soil shattered into a thousand arrows pointing a hundred different ways.

St. Francis' feet must have been calloused and torn. The thousands of miles he walked came to stand for the unending inward journey he was making. He believed that physical suffering would bring redemption. He called his own body "Ass" and the donkey that sometimes accompanied him "Brother." His tireless exertion propelled him toward the truth of the human condition, which is suffering. Each footstep and heartbeat enlarged his capacity to understand.

As we climbed higher, the temperature dropped. We took a shortcut through hayfields and trees, then came into a clearing: shoals of clouds shifted among reefs of light; the sky was an ocean and the storms came in waves. I thought of the blind man's eyes, then of the earthquakes of 1997: of the basilica's roof sections that fell, the frescoes of Giotto and Cimabue shaken into colored dust, and how this high spine of central Italy kept wiggling its back as if trying to shake something off—a blindness perhaps—to make room for a renewed Franciscan simplicity. I looked up. My mouth must have gone slack: a snow-flake alighted on my tongue. *Take. Eat. This is my blood. . . .*

We stayed the night in a castle that had once given St. Francis sanctuary. The old peasant who greeted us was corpulent and, at 9 A.M., red-faced with wine. He was splitting wood with a dull ax. The interior was frigid. We were taken up three flights of stairs by a young woman who spoke a bit of English. The room's two immense arched windows faced north toward Gubbio. Had St. Francis plotted his trail from this aerie?

In the middle of the night a wheel of thunder threw hail at the window. Lightning showed the peaks of the Apennines one by one. Far to the north was La Verna, the mountain where the wounds that Jesus suffered on the cross—the stigmata—appeared on St. Francis' body. Was his experience an agony or did the wounds simply appear? And how are we to think of them? Are they real or the result of a collective hallucination?

Three brothers had gone with St. Francis to La Verna, where they lived in solitude in the caves and said their matins on a rocky ledge overlooking the valley. On Sept. 17, 1224, Brother Leo later reported, rays of light fell down on St. Francis' head, and after, the marks of the crucifying nails in the hands and feet and the lance that pierced Christ's side showed on St. Francis' body. I imagine all of La Verna enveloped with light. If Brother Leo told me this story, I'd say St. Francis had been hit by lightning.

The next day I walked in blackness. Storms lifted like hats, then slammed down again. Later, the mountains shone with a strange radiance. We walked into a valley and crossed a frothing stream whose hoarse voice cried out, "This way, he went this way." We tumbled down, down. Sometimes the river shimmered on our right and our left—a brown god—churning chocolate, white and red. Gubbio was just ahead. In the valley a chemical factory stood on the bank. Pavement began. The way to the walled city took us past more factories, then into suburbs.

Somewhere on this road St. Francis encountered the legendary wolf that had been killing people in Gubbio. When beckoned, the wolf sat at the saint's feet, lowered his head and wagged his tail. Francis implored the wolf to stop eating people; when he entered Gubbio with the wolf, the towns-people were astonished. Everyone fed him, and the wolf never ate a human again.

Approaching Gubbio, we lost our way. A man with a wolfish face gave us directions. We stayed in a 13th-century hotel near the top of town, from which everything flowed downhill like lava. Some days I thought of St. Francis as a living ember plucked from one of Italy's volcanoes. These mountains were places of retreat for him: Gubbio, Cortona, Le Celle and La Verna, where his pet hawk woke him for matins. Wandering from mountain to mountain, I began to feel his presence everywhere—bringing alive the dormant forests and stone cities that seemed so dead.

Sleep didn't come easily that night. I was perched on the head of a pin at century's end and didn't know how to proceed. The medieval European mind was fixated on eternity and driven by notions of sin and mystery. Now, at the end of the 20th century, we have traded in linear time for the ever-present Einsteinian time. Our weak link is not a Christian tragedy we are powerless to escape but the nihilism of living in the ever-present Present. To find the path through a continuum takes another kind of imagination and tenacity.

All I knew was that the path moved. It was not a solid place but a continuous unfolding. It could be described as a road where everything changes and is made of dirt, stone, space, light, twigs broken by hard winds, indentations where hailstones hit earth, hoof prints, bird tracks and litter from humans passing.

If the path represents the intrinsic poverty and humbleness of all things, it is also a richness, functioning as a lens through which we can see things as they really are, without the embellishment of our ideas about them.

By the end of the week the temperature soared, and a blue haze rose up from the valley, where the farmers were burning pruned branches from vineyards and olive trees. A friend came for us and drove us back to the center of Assisi.

A woman in dark glasses, high heels and a mink coat walked her whippet. Two men, both tipsy, their car doors opened wide, stood listening to a CD of Frank Sinatra. (His real name, of course, was Francis.) In the Piazza del Comune, the Irish setter that always lay in front of the confectionery store was gone. Teen-agers lounged on the steps of the Temple of Minerva.

By the time St. Francis reached his mid-40's, his pace had slowed. For the last two years of his life, the stigmata were oozing sores, compounding a frailty already complicated with malaria, malnutrition, tuberculosis, rheumatism and what was probably glaucoma, which made it impossible for him to tolerate light. Brother Elias predicted that he would soon die. The people of Assisi sent knights to Nocera Umbra to bring St. Francis back on the eve of his death. His final ride through Porta Perlici was on a palanquin because he was too weak to walk or ride. After blessing the town that had earlier repudiated him, he begged to be taken down into the valley to his beloved chapel at Porziuncola.

There, his friends came and said goodbye. Ignoring his own ban on being in the presence of women, his last visitor was a woman. Her name was Giacoba dei Settesoli, and she had brought his favorite food: an almond frangipani, which he ate with pleasure. After, his final request was honored: he was laid naked on the cold floor of the Porziuncola to die.

Assisi had originally been called Asceti, which means "a place of rising." St. Francis died on Oct. 3, 1226. At the moment of death, light shone from his body and the bells at San Stefano began ringing spontaneously. The oak forests in the mountains where he loved to walk were dormant then, as now. I stared up at the endless series of peaks. The white eyelash on Mount Subasio—all that was left of the previous week's snow—had almost melted. Down in the valleys the fruit trees stood white with blossoms.

Spring weather is capricious, not unlike the way death comes. I thought of the pleasure St. Francis must have felt each time he hit the open road. As it was with Jesus and the Gautama Buddha, the poet Matsuo Basho and the great Ch'an masters of China and Japan, all teachings were given on the move, under an open sky. "We are not so much traveling as just stopping here and there,"

Matsuo Basho said. The divinity of a place rose up through the soles of their feet and went everywhere with them.

Walking back to our rooms on a narrow street, Tony and I heard a roar. For a moment we thought it might be an earthquake—the day before there had been a tremor in the nearby town of Gualdo Tadino—but it was only distant thunder, another spring storm passing by.

I paused at the bottom of the stairs. Two parakeets were feeding each other water. Pots of primroses had been set out. The qualities I most cherished about St. Francis were these: inexhaustible tenderness. Unconditional living.

A raindrop came out of the dark and hit my forehead—just one. An opening in the clouds revealed stars. I climbed the stairs to my room, cracked the window wide and went to bed.

FRANK X. GASPAR

A Field Guide to the Heavens

from *The Kenyon Review*

Tonight I am speaking in tongues again.
Listen to all the stars with names as old as Mesopotamia:
Rukbat Arkab, Nunki, Lesath, Shaula. They are shining forth
in the Archer and the Scorpion. They are ablaze in the
    southern sky.
The Scorpion rests his tail on some trees and a streetlight.
    Now and then
when I go inside to warm some coffee or toast some bread,
    I read
a few snatches of Milton, who laments death as the loss of
    intellect,
who says, *Are not the towers of heaven filled with armed watch?*
I am looking for certain signs, certain deliriums. This
    Scorpion
is the same that stung mighty Orion to death. This Archer
pursues him for all eternity, in his left hand the bow, in his
    right,
the flaming arrow. This region is rich and manifold. In this
    direction
lies the center of our galaxy, a holy fire. *Aloof the vulgar
constellations thick,*
says Milton, and I walk outside again. The ducks over in the
    park
are raving mad. Their sounds float on the nightwind. The
    neighbors sleep

in one another's arms. Listen: *Dschubba, Antares, Acrab.* What
are they saying in the aisles and naves of the light years? What
is the sacred word on the street? What celestial music am I
so afraid to miss? In my right hand there is nothing. In my left
hand there is a cup. In my short chair in the shadows I am
    invisible.
This is how I know my street is a garden and my yard is a
    bower.
My coffee cools in the slow breeze. Someone's cat circles,
curious, lets me touch the scruff of its neck before it goes off to
    hunt
for meat or sex. The shrubs and trees and flowers all become
one another's equals in the slow eyes of darkness. *Sing,*
heavenly Muse, says Milton. *Geidi, Nashira, Dabih.* Eat
every fruit, sleep soundly: surely, verily, nothing will be lost.

WILLIAM H. GASS

In Defense of the Book

from *Harper's Magazine*

When Ben Jonson was a small boy, his tutor, William Camden, persuaded him of the virtue of keeping a commonplace book: pages where an ardent reader might copy down passages that especially pleased him, preserving sentences that seemed particularly apt or wise or rightly formed and that would, because they were written afresh in a new place, and in a context of favor, be better remembered, as if they were being set down at the same time in the memory of the mind. Here were more than turns of phrase that could brighten an otherwise gloomy page. Here were statements that seemed so directly truthful they might straighten a warped soul on seeing them again, inscribed, as they were, in a child's wide round trusting hand, to be read and reread like the propositions of a primer, they were so bottomed and basic.

Jonson translated or rewrote the quotes and connected them with fresh reflections until their substance seemed his own, and seamlessly woven together, too, which is how the work reads today, even though it is but a collection of loose pages taken, after his death, from the defenseless drawers of his desk. The title, extended in the manner of the period into an explanation, reads, *Timber: or, Discoveries; Made upon Men and Matter: as they have flow'd out of his daily Readings; or had their refluxe to his peculiar Notion of the Times;* and it is followed by an epigraph taken from Persius' *Satires:* "To your own breast in quest of worth repair, and blush to find how poor a stock is there." With a flourish whose elegance is lost on our illiterate era, Jonson fills his succeeding page, headed *Sylva,* with a justification of his title in learned Latin, which can be translated as follows:

> *(here are) the raw material of facts and thoughts, wood, as it were, so called from the multiplicity and variety of the matter contained therein. For just as we are commonly wont to call a vast number of trees growing indiscriminately "a wood," so also did the ancients call those of their books, in which were collected at random articles upon various and diverse topics, a wood, or timber trees.*

My copy of *Discoveries* has its own history. It came from the library of Edwin Nungezer (Catalogue #297), whose habit it was to write his name and the date of his acquisition on the title page (2/22/26), and his name, date, and place, again, at the end of the text, when he had finished reading it (Edwin Nungezer, Ithaca, New York, October 17, 1926). He underlined and annotated the book as a professor might (mostly, with a kind of serene confidence, in ink), translating the Latin as if he knew boobs like me would follow his lead and appreciate his helpful glosses. I have already quoted one of his interlineations. My marginalia, in a more cautious pencil, are there now too, so that Ben Jonson's text, itself a pastiche drawn from the writings of others, has leaped, by the serendipitous assistance of The Bodley Head's reprint, across the years between 1641 to 1923, not surely in a single bound but by means of a few big hops nevertheless, into the professor's pasture a few years after, and then into mine in 1950, upon the sale of his estate, whereupon my name, with stiff and self-conscious formality, was also placed on its title page: William H. Gass, Cornell, '50. Even so, the book belongs to its scholarly first owner; I have only come into its possession. I hold it in my hand now, in 1999.

Another book, which is also a library but in a different way, George Saintsbury's *A History of English Prose Rhythm,* provides testimony concerning what happens when the guest is taken to a hostelry of transformatory power such as Ben Jonson's inn is:

> . . . *the selection, coadaptation, and application of the borrowed phrases to express Ben's views constitute a work more really original than most utterances that are guiltless of literature.*

In setting down the provenance of my copy of *Discoveries* I have also done the same for the following sentence, which I put a faint marginal line beside while researching opinions about metaphor for my dissertation (now, thank God, a distant memory); it is a sentence that (having served in several capacities since) I know quite by heart, and treasure, inasmuch as it is as personal and particular to me now as its book is, having absorbed so much of myself, like the paper wrapped around fish and chips.

> *What a deale of cold busines doth a man mis-spend the better part of life in! in scattering complements, tendring visits, gathering and venting newes, following Feasts and Playes, making a little winter-love in a darke corner.*

We shall not understand what a book is, and why a book has the value many persons have, and is even less replaceable than a person, if we forget how important to it is its body, the building that has been built to hold its lines of language safely together through many adventures and a long time. Words on a screen have visual qualities, to be sure, and these darkly limn their shape, but they have no materiality, they are only shadows, and when the light shifts they'll be gone. Off the screen they do not exist as words. They do not wait to be reseen, reread; they only wait to be remade, relit. I cannot carry them beneath a tree or onto a side porch; I cannot argue in *their* margins; I cannot enjoy the memory of my dismay when, perhaps after years, I return to my treasured copy of *Treasure Island* to find the jam I inadvertently smeared there still spotting a page precisely at the place where Billy Bones chases Black Dog out of the Admiral Benbow with a volley of oaths and where his cutlass misses its mark to notch the inn's wide sign instead.

My copy, which I still possess, was of the cheapest. Published by M. A. Donohue & Co. of Chicago, it bears no date, and its coarse pages are jaundiced and brittle, yet they've outlived their manufacturer; they will outlive their reader—always comforting yet a bit sad. The pages, in fact, smell their age, their decrepitude, and the jam smear is like an ancient bruise; but as well as Marcel did by means of his madeleine, like a scar recalling its accident, I remember the pounding in my chest when the black spot was pressed into Billy Bones's palm and Blind Pew appeared on the road in a passage that I knew even then was a piece of exemplary prose.

That book and I loved each other, and I don't mean just its text: that book, which then was new, its cover slick and shiny, its paper agleam with the tossing sea and armed, as Long John Silver was, for a fight, its binding tight as the elastic of new underwear, not slack as it is now, after so many openings and closings, so many dry years; that book would be borne off to my room, where it lived through my high school miseries in a dime-store bookcase, and it would accompany me to college too, and be packed in the duffel bag I carried as a sailor. Its body may have been cheaply made by machine, and there may have been many copies of this edition printed, but the entire press run has by this time been dispersed, destroyed, the book's function reduced to its role as my old school chum, whom I see at an occasional reunion, along with editions of Malory and Mann, Nietzsche and Schopenhauer, Hardy and Spengler, gloomy friends of my gloomy youth. Each copy went forth into bookstores to seek a purchaser it would make fortunate, and each has had its history of success or failure since, years of standing among rarity and leather, say, when suddenly, after a week of weeping that floods the library, it finds itself in some secondhand ghetto, dumped for a pittance by customarily callous heirs into a crowd of those said, like cars, to have been "previously owned."

We all love the "previously owned." We rescue them like orphans from their Dickensian dismay. I first hold the volume upside down and give its fanned-out pages a good ruffle, as if I were shaking fruit from a tree: out will fall toothpicks and hairpins, calling cards and bits of scrap paper, the well-pressed envelope for a stick of Doublemint gum, a carefully folded obituary of the book's author, the newsprint having acidulously shadowed its containing pages, or, now and then, a message, interred in the text, as I had flutter from a volume once owned by Arthur Holly Compton (and sold to me by the library of his own university). It was the rough draft of a telegram to the U.S. High Commissioner in charge of our occupation troops in Germany requesting the immediate dispatch of Werner Heisenberg to the United States.

Should we put these feelings for the object and its vicissitudes down to simple sentimental nostalgia? to our commonly assumed resistance to change? I think not; but even as a stimulus for reminiscence, a treasured book is more important than a dance card, or the photo that freezes you in mid-teeter at the edge of the Grand Canyon, because such a book can be a significant event in the history of your reading, and your reading (provided *you* are significant) should be an essential segment of your character and your life. Unlike the love we've made or meals we've eaten, books congregate to form a record around us of what they've fed our stomachs or our brains. These are not a hunter's trophies but the living animals themselves.

In the ideal logotopia, every person would possess his own library and add at least weekly if not daily to it. The walls of each home would seem made of books; wherever one looked one would only see spines; because every real book (as opposed to dictionaries, almanacs, and other compilations) is a mind, an imagination, a consciousness. Together they compose a civilization, or even several. Utopias, however, have the bad habit of hiding in their hearts those schemes for success, those requirements of power, rules concerning conduct, which someone will one day have to carry forward, employ and enforce, in order to achieve them, and afterward, to maintain the continued purity of their Being. Books have taught me what true dominion, what right rule, is: it is like the freely given assent and labor of the reader who will dream the dreams of the deserving page and expect no more fee than the reward of its words.

A few of us are fortunate enough to live in Logotopia, to own our own library, but for many this is not possible, and for them we need a free and open public institution with a balanced collection of books that it cares for and loans, with stacks where a visitor may wander, browse, and make discoveries; such an institution empowers its public as few do. In fact, it has no rival, for the books in the public library are the books that may take temporary residence in yours or mine. We share their wealth the way we share the space of a public park. And the benefits include the education of the body politic, an education upon which the success of democracy depends, and one that is largely missing from the thrill-seeking, gossip-mongering, and mindless masses who have been content to place their governing, as well as their values, faiths, and future plans, in the hands of the crudest commercial interests. The myths that moved us to worship in ways preferred and planned by the Church, or to feel about things in a manner that served the interests of the State, have less power over our souls now than the latest sale of shoes, which promise, through the glory of their names, the pleasures of sex and health and social rank, and give new meaning to the old expression "leap of faith."

My high school had no library worthy of the name "book," so I would walk about a mile downtown to the public one to borrow, in almost every case, a new world. That's what a library does for its patrons. It extends the self. It is pure empowerment. I would gather my three or four choices, after deliberations governed by ignorant conjecture, and then, before leaving, I would sit at one of the long wide tables we associate with the institution now and read a page or two farther than I had while standing in the stacks. I scorned the books deemed appropriate for my age and selected only those I wouldn't understand. Reading what I didn't understand was, for one blissful period of my life, the source of a profound if perverse pleasure. I also liked to look at the card pasted in the back of the book to record previous borrowings—a card that is, like so much other information, there no longer or discreetly incomplete. It gave me a good deal of satisfaction to be taking home some rarely read, symbolically dusty, arcane tome. I checked out both my books and my pride at the same desk. See, O world, what I am reading and be amazed: Joyce, Wells, Carlyle. Well, Wells I could understand. That, I would realize later, was what was the matter with him.

And the Saturday that *Ulysses* was denied me because my ears were too young to hear its honesty was a large red-letter day, burned upon my symbolic bosom wherever it was then kept, for on that day I learned what righteous indignation was; I realized what libraries were really for, just in the moment that my own was failing its function.

Public libraries have succumbed to the same pressures that have overwhelmed the basic cultural functions of museums and universities, aims that should remain what they were, not because the old ways are always better but because in this case they were the right ones: the sustaining of standards, the preservation of quality, the conservation of literacy's history, the education of the heart, eye, and mind. Now libraries devote far too much of their restricted space, and their limited budget, to public amusement. It is a fact of philistine life that amusement is where the money is.

Universities attract students by promising them, on behalf of their parents, a happy present and a comfortable future, and these intentions are passed along through the system like salmonella until budgets are cut, research requirements are skimped, and the fundamental formula for academic excellence is ignored if not forgotten. That formula is: a great library will attract a great faculty, and a great faculty will lure good students to its log; good students will go forth and win renown, endowments will increase, and so will the quality of the football team, until original aims are lost sight of, academic efforts slacken, the library stands neglected, the finer faculty slip away, good students no longer seek such an environment, and the team gets even better.

The sciences, it is alleged, no longer use books; neither do the professions, since what everyone needs is data, data day and night, because data, like drugs, soothe the senses and encourage us to think we are, when at the peak of their heap, on top of the world. Of course, libraries contain books, and books contain information, but information has always been of minor importance, except to minor minds. What matters is how the information is arranged, how it is understood, and to what uses it is put. In short, what matters is the book the data's in. I just employed the expression "It is a fact of philistine life . . ." That is exactly what the philistine would like the library to retrieve for it. Just the facts, ma'am. Because facts can be drawn from the jaws of some system like teeth; because facts are goods like shoes and shirts and, well, books. This week the library is having a closeout sale on facts about deserts. Get yours now. Gobi will be gone soon, the Sahara to follow.

Frequently, one comes across comparisons of the electronic revolution with that of writing and printing, and these are usually accompanied by warnings to those suspicious of technology that objections to these forward marches are both fuddy-duddy and futile. But Plato's worries that writing would not reveal the writer the way the soul of a speaker was exposed; that spontaneity would be compromised; that words would be stolen (as Phaedrus is about to steal them in that profound, beautifully written dialogue), and words would be put in other mouths than those of their authors; that writing does not hear its reader's response; that lying, hypocrisy, false borrowing, ghost-writing, would increase so that the hollow heads of state would echo with hired words; and that, oddly, the advantages and powers of the book would give power and advantage to the rich, who would learn to read and would have the funds to acquire and keep such precious volumes safe: these fears were overwhelmingly realized.

The advent of printing was opposed (as writing was) for a number of mean and self-serving reasons, but the fear that it would lead to the making of a million half-baked brains, and cause the illicit turning of a multitude of untrained heads, as a consequence of the unhindered spread of nonsense was a fear that was also well founded. The boast that the placement of books in many hands would finally overthrow superstition was not entirely a hollow hope, however. The gift gave a million minds a chance at independence.

It was the invention of photography, I remember, that was supposed to run painters out of business. What it did, of course, was make artists out of them, not grandiose or sentimental describers. And the pixelation of pictures has rendered their always dubious veracity as unbelievable as any other shill for a system. If blessings are mixed, so are calamities. I note also that although the horse-drawn coach or wagon nowadays carries rubes in a circle around Central Park, there are more horses alive and well in the world than there ever were.

So will there be books. And if readers shut their minds down the better to stare at pictures that rarely explain themselves; and if readers abandon reading to swivel-hip their way through the interbunk, picking up scraps of juicy data here and there and rambling on the e-mail in that new fashion of grammatical decay, the result will be to make real readers, then chief among the last who are left with an ability to reason, rulers. Books made the rich richer. Books will make the smart smarter.

The elevator, at first, seemed merely helpful, and the high-rise splendid against the night sky—what you could see of it. Recordings allow us to hear a few elevating strains from the "Ode to Joy" several times a day, the genius long ago beaten out of it. And those miracles of modern electronics that have allowed us to communicate quickly, easily, cheaply, gracelessly with every part of the world permit us to do so in private and in every remove from face to face. Air travel is comfortable, affordable, and swift (right?) and enables us to ignore geography, just as we ignore climate, because we have HVAC and, in addition, can purchase terrible tomatoes any season of the year from stores that are open all night.

Books in libraries, however awful some of them assuredly are, have been screened by editors who have a stake in their quality and their success. Once on shelves, they may receive from readers the neglect they deserve. But at the end of all those digital delivery channels thrives a multitude of pips whose continuous squeaking has created static both loud and distressing. Amid the sound of a million popoffs, how shall we hear and identify a good thought when it pops *out?*

The library is meant to satisfy the curiosity of the curious, offer to stuff students with facts, provide a place for the lonely where they may enjoy the companionship and warmth of the word. It is supposed to supply handbooks for the handy, novels for insomniacs, scholarship for the scholarly, and make available works of literature to those individuals they will eventually haunt so successfully; these readers, in self-defense, will bring them finally to life.

More important than any of these traditional things, I think, is the environment of books the library puts its visitors in and the opportunity for discovery that open stacks make possible. When I wish to look up a word—"golliwogg," which I've encountered spelled with two *g*'s—or when I wish to plenish my mind with some information, say, about the ill-fated Library at Alexandria, why don't I simply hit the right keys on my machine, where both a dictionary and an encyclopedia are imprisoned? Well, I might, if the spelling of "golliwog" were all I wished to know, if researches, however large or small, were not great pleasures in themselves, full of serendipity; for I have rarely paged through one of my dictionaries (a decent household will have a dozen) without my eye lighting, along the way, on words more beautiful than a found fall leaf, on definitions odder than any uncle, on grotesques such as "gonadotropin-releasing hormone" or, barely above it—what?—

"gombeen," which turns out to be Irish for *usury*. I wonder if Ezra Pound knew that.

Similarly, when I walk through the library stacks in search of a number I have copied from the card catalogue, my eyes are not watching my feet or aimlessly airing themselves; they are intently shelf-shopping, running along all those intriguing spines, all those lovely shapes and colors and sizes. That is how, one day, I stopped before a thick yellow-backed book that gave its name in pale blue letters: *The Sot-Weed Factor*. Although published by Doubleday, so there was probably nothing of value in it, I still pulled the book from its place. What did the title mean? I read the first page, as is my habit. Page 1 and page 99 are my test spots. Then I bore it home, neglecting to retrieve the book for which I had begun my search. Instead, for two days, in a trance of delight and admiration, I read John Barth's novel. That is why I stroll through the encyclopedia, why I browse the shelves.

One does not go to a library once, look around, and leave as if having seen it. Libraries are not monuments or sights or notable piles: churches by Wren, villas by Palladio. Libraries, which acquire the books we cannot afford, retain the many of which we are ignorant, the spate of the new and the detritus of ancient life; libraries, which preserve what we prize and would adore; which harbor the neglected until their time to set forth again is marked, restoring the worn and ignoring fashion and repulsing prejudice. Libraries are for life, centers to which we are recycled, as recursive as reading itself.

If I am speaking to you on the phone, watching your tinted shadows cross the screen, downloading your message from my machine, I am in indirect inspection, in converse, with you; but when I read the book you've written, you are as absent as last year, distant as Caesar's reign. Before my eyes, asking for my comprehension, where I stand in the stacks or sit in the reading room, are your thoughts and feelings, hopes and fears, set down in sentences and paragraphs and pages . . . but in words not yours, meanings not mine, rather words and meanings that are the world's.

Yes, we call it recursive, the act of reading, of looping the loop, of continually returning to an earlier group of words, behaving like Penelope by moving our mind back and forth, forth and back, reweaving what's unwoven, undoing what's been done; and language, which regularly returns us to its origin, which starts us off again on the same journey, older, altered, Columbus one more time but better prepared each later voyage, knowing a bit more, ready for more, equal to a greater range of tasks, calmer, confident. After all, we've come this way before, have habits that help and a favoring wind; language like that is the language that takes us inside, inside the sentence—inside—inside the mind—inside—inside where meanings meet and are modified, reviewed, and revised, where no perception, no need, no feeling or thought, need be scanted or shunted aside.

I read around in this reprinted book I've rescued until I stumble on—I discover—my sentence, my marvel, my new found land.

What a deale of cold busines doth a man mis-spend the better part of life in! in scattering complements, tendring visits, gathering and venting newes, following Feasts and Playes, making a little winter-love in a darke corner.

This sentence is a unit of human consciousness. It disposes its elements like the bits and pieces of a collage, and even if a number of artists were given the same materials: say, a length of ribbon, empty manila folder, cellophane wrapping, sheet of blue paper, postage stamp, shocking-pink crayon; or a number of writers

were allowed a few identical words and asked to form a phrase—
with "was," for instance, out of "that," or "fair," or "then," and
"all"—they'd not arrange them in the same way, make the same
object, or invariably ask, in some wonder, "then was all that fair?"
as if a point were being made in a debate. Among them, only
James Joyce would write of paradise, in *Finnegans Wake*, "then all
that was, was fair."

In this process of constituting a unit of human perception,
thought, and feeling, which will pass like every other phase of consciousness into others—one hopes—still more integrated and interesting, nothing is more frequently overlooked or more vital to
language than its pace and phrasing: factors, if this were ballet, we
would never neglect, because we are well aware how the body of
the dancer comes to a periodic point of poise before beginning
another figure; and how the central movement of the torso is
graced and amplified by the comportment of the arms, the tilt of
the head and smile of the eyes; and how the diagram of one gesture is made to flow into another; and how the dancer must land
from a leap, however wide or high, as if a winged seed; and how
the energy of movement is controlled by the ease of its execution
within the beat and mood and color of the music until we see one
unified flow of expression. So too must the language keep its feet
and move with grace, disclosing one face first before allowing
another, reserving certain signals until the end, when they will re-
verberate through the sentence like a shout down a street, and the
vowels will open and close like held hands, and the consonants
will moan like maybe someone experiencing pleasure, and the
reader will speed along a climbing clause, or sigh into a periodic
stop full of satisfaction at this ultimate release of meaning: a little
winter-love in a dark corner.

Every day, from the library, books are borrowed and taken
away like tubs of chicken to be consumed, though many are also

devoured on the premises, in the Reading Room, where traditionally the librarian, wearing her clichés, shushes an already silent
multitude and glares at the offending air. Yet there, or in someone's rented room, or even by a sunny pool—who can predict the
places where the encounter will occur?—the discovery will be
made. And a finger will find the place and mark it before the
book's covers come closed; or its reader will rise and bear her prize
out of the library into the kitchen, back to her dorm room, or,
along with flowers and candy, to a bedside, in a tote bag onto the
beach; or perhaps a homeless scruffy, who has been huddling near
a radiator, will leave the volume behind him when he finally goes,
as if what his book said had no hold on his heart, because he cannot afford a card. Yet, like Columbus first espying land, each will
have discovered what he or she cares about, will know at last what
it is to love—a commonplace occurrence—for, in the library,
such epiphanies, such enrichments of mind and changes of heart,
are the stuff of every day.

NATALIE GOLDBERG

The Rain and the Temple

from *Shambhala Sun*

I just returned from Japan a week ago. I had never thought of going before. I had my own little Japan when I studied with Katagiri Roshi, a Japanese Zen master, for six years in Minneapolis. But when he died I had a great desire to see where he came from and the country that produced him. I should say, that produced the Japanese Zen that I was studying, but I had a heart to heart connection with him, and that personal connection is really what carried me. So I wanted to go to Japan, but I was scared. They didn't speak English, I didn't know how to get around, and their signs were in *kanji*. I had bought airplane tickets two times in the eight years since he died and then I forfeited them. But this time I decided I had to go. I had a friend who is a good traveler and she said she'd come with me.

Right before we went, I visited Katagiri Roshi's wife, Tomoe, in Minnesota. I asked her for exact directions to his old temple. When his teacher died it became his temple. No one since had been abbot there. When I studied with Roshi I'd heard stories about it all the time. Only he and his teacher practiced in this temple. There were no other students. And so I got the directions, and this is how precise Tomoe was: she not only told me where to get the bus after I took the train, but she then opened up a photo album and showed me photos of the train station, the bus stop where I should get off, the spot where I should turn at the corner. And I thought, oh, Tomoe, you're being silly, I'm quite sophisticated.

And so I arrived in Japan on a Thursday and we went to Kyoto and the following Thursday I got up my courage to go out into the country. It was pouring rain. Pouring may be no big deal to someone who lives in San Francisco, but I live in New Mexico, where rain is an auspicious event. You might want to remember that, next time it rains, wherever you are. But the rain in Kyoto scared me—it was flooding the streets. I thought, should I go today? And then I thought, well, I planned to, okay, I'll go. My friend came with me. We wore our green slickers. The Japanese only carry umbrellas, and they think it's very American and cloddish to wear these big plastic things on public transportation where you have to sit all wet next to someone else.

We traveled first in Kyoto on the subway, climbing four deep flights down. You don't realize how deep someone can dig. Really, when you think about it, it's a tremendous thing—a subway under a city. We took that subway to the train station where we would catch the train to a town called Tsuruga. It was going to leave at 9:31. Well, you'd better believe in Japan it leaves at 9:31. And that was really the only way we knew that it was the right train. It showed up at 9:31 and we jumped on. Then I asked people sitting in their seats with newspapers and box lunches of pickles, rice, sushi and seaweed on their laps, "Tsuruga? Tsuruga?" To get their attention I called out, "Hey!" But it's not "Hey"; it's "Hai!" "Hai!" I corrected myself and tried to act Japanese. Then I'd forget and say "Hey!" again. And they'd say, "Hai! Hai!" "Tsuruga? Tsuruga!" "Hai." Yes, we were on the right train and it was pouring hard and the clouds were dark gray.

In about half an hour we passed a big lake on the right and I heard the conductor announce, "Biwa." I looked harder—that was Lake Biwa, where Ikkyu in a rowboat at twenty-seven years old in the sixteenth century heard a crow caw overhead and became fully enlightened. I touched the window glass for a moment. I knew that lake, and even in the storm it was icy blue.

The train ride was altogether an hour and ten minutes and we got off in a little town. I thought Tsuruga was going to be a big town. We went to the small tourist station, but they didn't speak a drop of English and I didn't speak a speck of Japanese. I had the name for the next destination. I said, "Kitada?" "Kitada," they nodded. "Kitada?" "Kitada." I wanted to ask, "Bus Two? Three? Where?" I held up fingers. They pointed to two. After ten minutes we figured out it was bus two, leaving at 12:25. They wrote down "Kitada" in *kanji* on a slip of paper for us, so we could match it with the sign on the front of the bus. The buses, unlike the trains, don't leave exactly on time—we needed to check that the lettering was the same. We found the bus, but it was 11:25. We had about an hour to walk around.

Usually in the U.S. I don't eat lunch at the Greyhound bus station. But when I'm in other countries I'm suddenly wide open and we were hungry, so after finding the bus, we went into a tiny—I mean tiny, one small table width—restaurant. The waiter stood by us, pen poised to take our order. We pointed to something on the menu—we didn't know what it was. The waiter spoke quickly with hands jerking and we nodded, "Hai! Hai!", and he shook his head and went in the back room. A few other people were there and they were being served noodles, vegetables, pieces of white fish. We weren't served and the time was going by. I whispered to my friend, "I think he was trying to tell us something important and we didn't get it." We had 15 minutes till the bus left. I screwed up my courage and ran into the kitchen and pointed to my watch and held up my hand—I flashed five fingers three times—fifteen minutes till the bus leaves, but what my motions meant to the cook I had no idea. I went back to my seat, and

Michele said, "So it's going to come?" I said, "Oh, yeah, he understood."

Ten minutes before the bus left he placed an omelet before us. We were thrilled it wasn't octopus. We ate it up quickly and ran to the bus. I spoke to the bus driver, "Kitada?" He nodded "Kitada." Again I said "Kitada?" I wanted him to tell us when we got to Kitada. How would we know? But he just said, "Kitada." We sat down hoping that someone would motion when Kitada came, or that I would recognize the bus stop from Tomoe's photo in the album. People on the bus were staring at us—we were further away from the city—these giants in green slickers with no umbrellas. And it was still pouring out, the kind of rain that hits and bounces. The bus was moving through the wet countryside and the road became narrow. People in the bus continued to gawk at us. Several times I ran up to the bus driver, "Kitada?" He nodded "Kitada." Finally everyone on the bus knew, *Kitada,* so when we got there they yelled in unison, "Kitada!"

We stumbled out into the rain, the bus took off, and we were left on the edge of the road next to a Japanese version of a 7–11 and a car mechanic building. Kitada? I looked for the picture that Tomoe had shown me, but there was no picture. We were nervous and then we saw a road. As soon as we turned we were suddenly in the Japanese countryside of rice fields, reeds and ponds. In the distance we could see a village. No shops or bakeries, just little houses and farmed fields. It was beautiful through the slate gray of rain. A heavy, powerful bird swooped down in front of us—a cross between a feathered owl and the royal size of an eagle. I said to Michele, "What kind of bird is that?" It was the only bird out that day because it was raining so hard.

We trudged into the little town and everything was closed down. The intricate flower plots dripped with rain. Over a hill I saw the Japan Sea and I remembered Tomoe saying there was a sea. And so we kept going, and finally there was a marker in *kanji*. I took a chance, "This is it," and I hoped I recalled it from one of Tomoe's photos. Behind it we saw a mud path—the old entryway, Tomoe had told me. We both hesitated. Michele nodded, "Let's follow it," and we stepped off the pavement. The earth was soggy, and we squished with each footstep.

In the distance I see a red tiled roof—I know it is Tasoin temple. There's one person in a paddy field in the rain, working with a hoe. He sees us walk by, and he turns and I wave, and he nods. Maybe other people have come over time to visit Roshi's ashes. The temple is deserted, no one to practice here anymore, once Roshi left for America more than thirty years ago. So it's closed down and the little village takes care of it. They open it, I guess, for burials. I see a little cemetery and I say to Michele, "Can I go by myself. I'll meet you." And it's fine. It is a really ancient cemetery with stone buddhas and other things. I don't know anything, but it is wonderful.

Then I panic. I came all the way to Japan. What if I don't find his tombstone? I walk around lots of old stones and then in the distance I see a clutter of rounded tops. I know the rounded part signifies the gravestones of the teacher lineage for that temple. I hurry over and at the very end is a new tombstone. I know it is Roshi's. It is still pouring but I push off my hood and then throw off my slicker. I prostrate myself three times on the wet earth and then I kneel in front of his stone. Pushing the dripping hair from my face, the rain running down my cheeks, I speak to my old teacher. "I'm here. It took me a while, but I made it," and I cannot say how good I feel to finally be there with him.

I look around. Two rhododendron, then trees I cannot name, but I can see them even now, dark green, tall, with drooping needles. A camellia bush, rice paddies, the Japan Sea, and the village. For years with Roshi I'd hear about this place. It was just him and his teacher practicing together. As a young monk, he thought that it was silly to get up in the morning. Why bother? So his teacher kept a schedule, got up at five, sat zazen, made breakfast, and then he'd go and shake Katagiri. "C'mon, it's time to eat." And Katagiri would say, "Oh, I'll just sleep late." And his teacher would be quiet and say, "It's good to follow the schedule even if no one else is here."

Every day, or every few days, they'd walk into town to formally ask the villagers for food with their begging bowls. And every time it was just the two of them, the teacher in front and the student behind. When the student decided to come to America, he told his teacher. His teacher didn't discourage him, but Roshi told us, "When we walked into town I could tell from his back that he felt lonely."

I remember the two of them as I sit in the rain in the cemetery. I make a vow to him right then and I pick up a single black stone and put it in my pocket. I walk over to the temple, which I had been told was locked, but Michele has found a way to unlock it. We take our shoes off and go in. It is a really old temple with a brick oven for a stove. We slide open paper walls, discovering spaces with tatamis on the floor. The final place we find is formal, with a large altar and a faded picture across the room—it must be Katagiri's teacher—and then a little photo is tucked into the bottom of the frame, very faded. I step closer. I can make out Roshi's profile. He must have sent it from America. I stand in front of it a long time, as the rain thunders down on the roof. I've come a long way to see this, I think to myself.

When we leave, walking down the road, facing the Japan Sea, I know this is the path he took into the village, and suddenly that brown bird swoops down in front of me and flies right back to the eaves of the temple. I follow him with my eyes and turn and watch him open and close his wings, calling to me, as he clutches the edge of the roof with his claws. I swallow, lift my hand, wave good-bye and keep walking.

And that one afternoon was worth my entire trip to Japan, to go and do that.

Prayers

from *The Paris Review*

FOR LIARS

For makers of elaborated worlds, adorned and peopled by the creatures and the furniture of their inventions. For those who live as if the way things are were not enough and mean, by their words, to do something about it. For those who would protect the first beloved from the fresh reality of the second. For fabricators of plausible excuses that will save the fragile hostess's *amour-propre*. For ornamenters who cannot endure a history without clear heroes and sharp villains. For speakers of the phrases "it's a fabulous haircut" or "of course you aren't gaining weight." For forgers of Old Masters and fakers of *petites morts*. For advertisers presenting a Paradise that can be bought or cures passed quick, over the counter, sellers of temporary, unlikely, but not impossible hopes: the Brooklyn Bridge, the golf course in the swamp. Keep them from the terror of the hunted, the ring of hounds barking in the freezing air, "the truth, the truth, why can't you tell the truth for once?" Shelter them in their dream of an earth more various than our own. Preserve them from diseases of the tongue, the mouth, the lips. For Your sake, who have thought of universes not yet made, which rest, like lies, in the Mind of Your Infinite Love.

FOR THOSE WHO HAVE GIVEN UP EVERYTHING FOR SEXUAL LOVE

O Lord, fount of Desire and its source, have mercy on these Thy servants who have followed the words of their flesh in the innocence of its singleness. Who have acted in accordance with its urging and obeyed it in humility, bowing the knee before its strength, knowing it greater than their own. Who have, in unity with its precepts (believing they were spoken in Your voice), turned their backs on the sweetness of habit, lost the regard of their fellows, endured the world's shame, suffered remorse, the abandonment of those by whom they knew and named and recognized themselves. Who have refused the blandishments of prosperity, the comforts of home, the pride of faithfulness, the honor of the law.

Protect the reckless, for they gave everything in Your name, their losses have been great.

Keep them from the plagues that they could understand as punishment.

Vouchsafe that in the light proceeding from Your light, they may reap the rewards of their sacrifice and be repaid a hundredfold.

Grant that we who have lacked their courage may be strengthened by their example to pursue our partial loves with gladness and fullness of heart.

FOR THOSE WHOSE WORK IS INVISIBLE

For those who paint the undersides of boats, makers of ornamental drains on roofs too high to be seen; for cobblers who labor over inner soles; for seamstresses who stitch the wrong sides of linings; for scholars whose research leads to no obvious discovery; for dentists who polish each gold surface of the fillings of upper molars; for sewer engineers and those who repair water mains; for electricians; for artists who suppress what does injustice to their visions; for surgeons whose sutures are things of beauty. For all those whose work is for Your eye only, who labor for Your entertainment or their own, who sleep in peace or do not sleep in peace, knowing that their effects are unknown.

Protect them from downheartedness and from diseases of the eye.

Grant them perseverance, for the sake of Your love which is humble, invisible and heedless of reward.

For Those Who Devote Themselves to Personal Adornment

For office workers who have fallen into debt because they spend their salaries on dresses, for women who require regular appointments with podiatrists to compensate for the ravages of years on high heels, for the victims of disastrous plastic surgery, for those who deprive themselves of sugar, for invalids who rise from bed only to dress and make up and then fall back exhausted, for those who weep in front of mirrors, for those with great legs and bad tempers, for mutton dressed as lamb, for those who sweat and strain their muscles out of fidelity to the illusions of a form.

Spare them diseases of the skin and teeth, for in their sacrifice of time and health and friendship they have given hope to strangers whose hearts have been lifted at the sight of a line that finishes itself finely, of colors undreamed of by nature, of constructions which at once affirm and quite deny the body's range.

Bless them, because a change of fashion can allow us to believe there could just be, for all of us, a change of heart.

Grant this for the sake of Your love, which has adorned the

mountains and created feathers and elaborate tails, O Lord, source of all that exists for delight only, for display only, suggestions, in the joy of their variety, of the ecstasy of light which is eternal, changeless and ever-changing.

For the Wasteful

O God, in Your benevolence look with kindness upon those who travel first class in high season, on those who spend whole afternoons in cafés, those who replay songs on jukeboxes, who engage in trivial conversations, who memorize jokes and card tricks, those who tear open their gifts and will not save the wrapping, who hate leftovers and love room service, who do not wait for sales. For all foolish virgins, for those who knowingly give their hearts to worthless charmers, for collectors of snowman paperweights, memorial cups and souvenir pens. For those who take the long way home.

We pray to You, whose love is prodigal, who multiplied the loaves and fishes so that there were baskets upon baskets left, who turned plain water into wine of a quality no one required, who gave Your life when You need only have lifted a finger, protect these, Your servants, from afflictions of the hand, cover their foolish bets and greet them with that mercy whose greatness is unearnable by calculation or by thrift.

For Those Who Misuse or Do Not Use or Cannot Use Their Gifts

For conservatory-trained composers of incidental music, for beauties run to fat, for the patrons of charlatans, for athletes who watch television, for poets who write commercials, for mathematicians turned card-sharks, for Legal Aid lawyers turned corporate counsel, for actors who are waiters, for wives who do not wish to stay at home, for cat-lovers afraid of mess, for paramours who fear transmittable diseases, for those who no longer go to auditions, for blacksmiths and letterpress printers.

Lord who created manna in the desert and who caused to flow the living springs, who made disciples of fishermen and tax collectors, and a king of a shepherd boy, grant these Thy servants the gift of new enthusiasms, protect them from diseases of the spine, so that they may turn and bend to glimpse Your Hand at the fork of roads not taken, at the tunnel's end.

Twice Woods Hebrew

from *Forward*

For Shirley Gladstone

The antique woods, if they spoke, would speak Hebrew,
don't you think? Not Greek or Latin,
the language of luna moths or stones, but guttural sounds
that issue from the bronchial branches.
For that matter, the trees, in their winter state,
even look like Hebrew, since against the sky all the
    ramifying twigs
jumble as the letters printed in a prayer book:
broken ט Tet, twisty ל Lamed, the ש Shin
    candelabrum,
and so on down the gnarly alphabet.

Leafless, the words keep their bound counsel,
reticent growths almost like code,
slow to reveal their meaning (or at least their vowel sounds).
So hard to find your place in them:
filigree of letters in the Torah scroll,
when read aloud weirdly rise and fall,
trip trap of trop, Billy Goats Gruff, in these dense offshoots.
We have only one season to speak.
When the sun returns, and the leaves at last
    express themselves,

the trees no longer seem Hebrew.
In this conversion to light, we tongue another God,
where the words are foppish and lush,
romance us in Spanish or Italian.

From a cantorial family, five generations back,
I sing the Hebrew syllables I read transliterated,
am in awe when my own alto, near bass for a woman's,
chants the *Baruch,* in that minor keyed music of trees.
Grown in intricate sorrow, these arboreal ventriloquists,
throw their voices through me, an Hasidic Lambchop,
or a kind of spooky karaoke.
A force draws my chest voice like water
studded with minerals and light flecks,
sucks it upward against gravity
step by cellular step, rung round by bark,
as one mounts spiral stairs, the Statue of Liberty.
At the same time, my voice is pulled down
through the litter of leaves,
into soil. At once, head to foot,
even farther, I resonate, a reverse Orpheus,
and I reach both ways, nets of roots and twigs
like needlepoints stitch sky and dirt.
Hebrew warms me twice, in my longing for
the blue fire at earth's magnetic core,
and the distant white radiance.

JEANINE HATHAWAY

The Left Hand Is Complement

from *Image*

Praise to my elders who are my left hand.
My awkward hinge, my elders-hand, the hand
that holds the wallet while the quick one
spends, the hand that hugs the bowl
as the adept stirs the dough, the hand
at the end of the bat for stable opposition.
The hand that wears the ring, my elders,
that says until death, that says
I do (I did); the ring I don't wear any more,
that says this hand has a chance at wisdom
if not dexterity. The hand that, when I am
seated at God's right, will be closest,
will brush against the hand of God
as we pass around desserts.

The Great Without

from *Parabola*

In European natural histories, human imagination was most often projected onto the outside world. Pliny's *Natural History*, for instance, was an errant map of a true world. There were dog-headed humans who could only bark, men with heads in their chests, and people with only one foot but with the ability to leap powerfully and to use the foot as a shade tree. There were mermaids, springs believed to grant eternal life, and islands where demons or angels lived. At one time the Egyptians thought that people on the other side of the world walked upside down. Bestiaries included the phoenix, griffins, and unicorns. Unshaped by fact, knowledge, or even observation, these fantasy worlds became the world as seen by the human mind.

Even in later times, the relationship between nature and humanity posed a dilemma. Once it was thought that the world entered the human eye, and that only through our seeing of it did it exist. There was much discussion about how a mountain could fit into the human eye. This difficulty with perspective pushed humans toward other conclusions just as erroneous as believing foremost in the eye of the beholder. Euclid thought the eye was the point of origin for all things. Plato believed the world emanated from the eye, while others thought that there was something given off from objects by which we perceived them. In any case, most of the theories made nature smaller than it is and made the human larger. Vision was about the seer only, not the seen.

Nothing could be more different from how tribal people on all continents have seen the world. From the perspectives of those who have remained in their own terrain for thousands of years, there were—and are—other points of view. For tribal thinkers, the outside world creates the human: we are alive to processes within and without the self. It is a more humble way to view the world, and far more steady. Nature is the creator, not the created.

There exists, too, a geography of spirit that is tied to and comes from the larger geography of nature. It offers to humans the bounty and richness of the world. Father Berard Haile, a priest traveling among the Navajo in the 1930s, was in awe of the complexity of their knowledge, one that exists within the context of what we now call an ecosystem. In the Upward Moving Way, for example, the ceremony brings in all aspects of the growth of plants: the movement upward as the roots deepen, the insects beneath and above the ground, the species of birds which come to this plant. All aspects of the ceremony reveal a wide knowledge of the world. In order to heal, this outside life and world must be taken in and "seen" by the patient as being part of one working system.

Laurens van der Post, a writer, naturalist, and psychologist who grew up in Africa, wrote in his essay "The Great Uprooter" about how his son's illness was announced by a dream. In the dream, the young man stood on a beach, unable to move, watching a great tidal wave of water bearing down on him. From out of the swell of the wave, a large black elephant walked toward him. It was this dream, van der Post was certain, that announced his son's cancer, the first point of cellular change. Van der Post called the dream something that came from "the great without": such an experience seemed to encompass, he said, all the withouts and withins a human could experience.

Nature is now too often defined by people who are fragmented from the land. Such a world is seldom one that carries and creates the human spirit. Too rarely is it understood that the soul lies at all points of intersection between human consciousness and the rest of nature. Skin is hardly a container. Our boundaries are not solid; we are permeable, and even when we are solitary dreamers we are rooted in the soul outside. If we are open enough, strong enough to connect with the world, we become something greater than we are.

Turn-of-the-century Lakota writer Zitkala Sa (Gertrud Simmons Bonnin) wrote of the separation between humankind and the natural world as a great loss to her. In her autobiography, she said that nature was what would have helped her to survive her forced removal to Indian boarding school.

> *I was ready to curse men of small capacity for being the dwarfs their God had made them. In the process of my education I had lost all consciousness of the nature world about me. Thus, when a hidden rage took me to the small, white-walled prison which I then called my room, I unknowingly turned away from my own salvation. For the white man's papers I had given up my faith in the Great Spirit. For these same papers I had forgotten the healing in trees and brooks. Like a slender tree, I had been uprooted from my mother, nature, and God.*

Zitkala Sa might have agreed with Pliny that there were dog-headed, barking men, and men with heads, not hearts, in their chests.

Soul loss is what happens as the world around us disappears. In contemporary North American Hispanic communities, soul loss is called *susto*. It is a common condition in the modern world. Susto probably began when the soul was banished from nature, when humanity withdrew from the world, when there became only two things—human and nature, animate and inanimate, sentient and not. This was when the soul first began to slip away and crumble.

In the reversal and healing of soul loss, Brazilian tribal members who tragically lost their land and place in the world visit or reimagine nature in order to become well again. Anthropologist Michael Harner wrote about healing methods among Indian people relocated to an urban slum of Peru. The healing takes place in the forest at night, as the person is returned for a while to the land he or she once knew. Such people are often cured through their renewed connections, their "visions of the river forest world, including visions of animals, snakes, and plants." Unfortunately, these places are now only ghosts of what they once were.

The cure for *susto,* soul sickness, is not in books. It is written in the bark of a tree, in the moonlit silence of night, in the bank of a river and the water's motion. The cure is outside ourselves.

In the 1500s, Paracelsus, considered by many to be a father of modern medicine, was greatly disliked by his contemporaries. For a while, though, he almost returned the practice of medicine to its wider place of relationships by emphasizing the importance of harmony between man and nature. His view of healing was in keeping with the one that tribal elders still hold, that a human being is a small model of the world and the universe. Vast spaces stretch inside us, he thought, an inner firmament, large as the outer world.

The world inside the mind is lovely sometimes, and large. Its existence is why a person can recall the mist of morning clouds on a hill, the fern forest, and the black skies of night that the Luiseno call their spirit, acknowledging that the soul of the world is great within the human soul. It is an enlarged and generous sense of self, life, and being, as if not only the body is a creation of the world elements, but air and light and night sky have created an inner vision that some have called a map of the cosmos. In Lakota astronomy, the stars are called the breath of the Great Spirit. It is as if the old Lakota foresaw physics and modern astronomy, sciences that now tell us we are the transformed matter of stars, that the human body is a kind of cosmology.

The inward may have been, all along, the wrong direction to seek. A person seems so little and small, and without is the river, the mountain, the forest of fern and tree, the desert with its lizards, the glacial meltings and freezings and movements of life. The cure for soul loss is in the mist of morning, the grass that grew a little through the night, the first warmth of sunlight, the waking human in a world infused with intelligence and spirit.

In Search of Miracles

from *DoubleTake*

The day my father was diagnosed with inoperable lung cancer, I decided to go and find him a miracle. My family had already spent a good part of that September chasing medical options, and what we discovered was not hopeful. Given the odds, a miracle cure was our best and most reasonable hope. A few weeks earlier, while I lay in a birthing center having my daughter, Grace, my father had been in a hospital across town undergoing biopsies to determine the cause of the spot that had appeared in his mediastinum, which connects the lungs. Eight years before, he'd given up smoking after forty years of two packs a day and had been diagnosed with emphysema. Despite yearly bouts of pneumonia and periodic shortness of breath, he was a robust sixty-seven-year-old, robust enough to take care of my son, Sam, to cook, and to clean the house he and my mother had lived in for their forty-seven years of marriage.

We are a superstitious family, skeptical of medicine and believers in omens, potions, and the power of prayer. The week that the first X ray showed a spot on my father's lung, three of us had dreams that could only be read as portents. I dreamed of my maternal grandmother, Mama Rose. My cousin, whose own father had died when she was only two and who had grown up next door to us with my father stepping in as a surrogate parent for her, dreamed of our great-uncle Rum. My father dreamed of his father for the first time since he'd died in 1957. All of these ghosts had one thing in common—they were happy. A few days later, my father developed a fever as the two of us ate souvlaki at the annual Greek Festival. The X ray they took that night in the emergency room was sent to his regular doctor. Nine months pregnant, I arrived at my parents' house the next morning with a bag of bagels. My father stood at the back door with his news. "The X ray showed something," he said dismissively. "They need to do a few more tests."

For the next month, he underwent CAT scans and -oscopies of all sorts, until, finally, a surgeon we hardly knew shouted across the hospital waiting room: "Where are the Woods?" I stood, cradling my newborn daughter. "Hood," I said. "Over here." He walked over to us and without any hesitation said, "He's got cancer. A fair-sized tumor that's inoperable. We can give him chemo, buy a little time. Your doctor will give you the details." He had taken the time to give my father the same information, even though as he was coming out of anesthesia it had seemed like a nightmare to him.

When someone died in our family, my father pulled out his extra-large bottle of Jack Daniels. It had gotten us through the news of the death of my cousin's young husband, my own brother's accidental death in 1982, and the recent deaths of two of my own forty-something cousins, one from melanoma and one from AIDS. That late September afternoon, my father pulled out the bottle for his own grim prognosis. As the day wore on, we'd gotten more news: only an aggressive course of chemotherapy and radiation could help, and even then the help would be short-lived, if it came at all. "Taxol," the pulmonary specialist had told us, "has given some people up to eighteen months." But the way he bowed his head after he said it made me realize that eighteen months was not only the best we could hope for, but a long shot. My sister-in-law, a doctor, too, was harsher. "Six months after diagnosis is the norm," she'd said.

Sitting in the kitchen that once held my mother and her ten siblings, their parents and grandparents, every day for supper, I did some quick math. Was it possible that the man sitting across from me sipping Jack Daniels would not be alive at Easter? A WASP from Indiana, he had married into a large, loud Italian family and somehow become more Italian than some of his in-laws. At Easter, he was the one who made the dozen loaves of sweetbread, the fresh cheese and frittatas. He shaped wine biscuits into crosses and made pizzelles that were lighter than any my aunts produced. At six-foot-one and over two hundred pounds, cracking jokes about the surgeon, he did not look like someone about to die. He was not someone I was going to let die. If medical science could only give him a year and a half tops, then there was only one real hope for a cure. "There's a place in New Mexico with miracle dirt," I announced. "I'm going to go and get you some." "Well," my father said with typical understatement, "I guess I can use all the help I can get."

A Leap of Faith.

Perhaps for some people the notion of seeking a miracle cure is tomfoolery, futile, or even a sign of pathetic desperation. The simplest definition of a miracle that I know is the one that C. S. Lewis proposes in his book *Miracles:* an interference with nature by supernatural power. But even that definition implies something that many people do not believe—that there is something other than nature, the thing that Lewis calls the supernatural. Without that other power, there can be no miracles. For those who cannot buy into the notion of this other power, miracle healing belongs back in the Dark Ages, or at least in a time before the advent of modern medicine. To believe in miracles, and certainly to go and look for one, you must put aside science and rely only on faith.

For me, that leap was not a difficult one. My great-grandmother, who died when I was six, healed people of a variety of ailments with prayer and household items, such as silver dollars and Mazola oil. The source of a headache was always believed to be the evil eye and was treated by my great-grandmother by pouring water into a soup bowl, adding a few drops of oil, then making circles on the afflicted person's palm while muttering in Italian. Curing nosebleeds involved making the sign of the cross on the person's forehead. Around our hometown of West Warwick, Rhode Island, she was famous for her ability to cure sciatica. In order to do this, my great-grandmother had to go to the person's house on the night of a full moon and spend the night, so she could work her miracle at dawn the next day. There was a time when she had a wait list for her services.

Most miracles occur through the intercession of a saint. If one wants a favor, one prays to a particular saint to act on one's behalf. My great-grandmother was no different. She had prayers to various saints to help find lost objects, answer questions, heal. Her prayers to Saint Anthony could answer important questions, such as, Will I have a baby? Does he love me? Will my mother be all right? The prayer was in Italian. She would go into a room, alone, and ask the question. If she was able to repeat the prayer three times quickly and without hesitation or errors, the answer was a favorable one. But if the prayer "came slow" or she couldn't remember the words, the outlook was dire.

The legend goes that my great-grandmother learned all of these things as a young girl in Italy. She was a shepherdess on the hills of a town outside Naples, near a convent. The nuns took a liking to her and passed on their knowledge. Her faith was sealed years later when my grandmother, her only daughter, was three. On a vacation in Italy from the United States, where they had immigrated, my grandmother came down with scarlet fever. The doctors said she would not live through the night. My great-grandmother bundled up her daughter and walked all the miles to the convent. There, the nuns prayed in earnest to the Virgin Mary to spare this child. By morning, she was completely well except for one thing: her long dark curls fell off at the height of her fever. My great-grandmother took her daughter's hair and gave it as an offering of thanks to the Virgin Mary. When my grandmother's hair grew back, it was red, and it remained red until the day she died, seventy years later.

I grew up with this story, and others like it. I never questioned it. Like the story of the day I was born or the day my parents met, I accepted it as fact. But when I shared the story with a friend recently, he said at its conclusion, "But of course that's not true." Startled, I asked him what he meant. "Why, that never happened," he said, laughing. "It couldn't happen. Maybe her fever simply broke or maybe the doctors thought she was sicker than she was. But she wasn't cured by the Virgin Mary, and her hair probably just turned more red as she got older." Therein lies an important distinction between one who believes in miracles and one who doesn't. A believer accepts the miracle as truth, no questions asked. Although I didn't accept my friend's explanations of our family lore, I also knew I could not dissuade him from believing them.

THE HEALING DIRT.

That was how I came to take my ten-week-old daughter an hour northwest of Santa Fe, New Mexico, up into the Sangre de Cristo Mountains, to the little town of Chimayo and its El Santuario. The area had been a holy ground for the Tewa Indians, a place where they believed fire and water had belched forth and subsided into a sacred pool. Eventually, the water had evaporated, leaving only a puddle of mud. The Tewa went there to eat the mud when they wanted to be cured. Sometime around the year 1810, during Holy Week, a man called Don Bernardo Abeyta is said to have been performing the Stations of the Cross in the hills at Chimayo. Suddenly, he saw light springing up from one of the slopes. As he got close to it, he realized the light was coming from the ground itself. He began to dig with his hands and there he found a crucifix. He ran to the Santa Cruz church, which was in a nearby town, and the priest and parishioners went with him and took the crucifix back to their church. The next morning, the crucifix was missing. Somehow it had returned to the place it was found. The same thing happened two more times, so they decided to build a chapel—El Santuario—at the spot. This chapel contains the hole, called *el pocito* (the well)—with the healing dirt.

Like many sites that claim miracles, Chimayo is difficult to reach. Grace and I flew from Boston to Albuquerque, changing planes en route. There, we met my longtime friend Matt, rented a car, and drove for over an hour to Santa Fe. The next morning we rode into the mountains on what is called the High Road to Taos, along curving roads covered with snow. Signs are few, and even getting to El Santuario requires a certain amount of faith. Along the way, we had to stop more than once so I could breastfeed the baby. Despite all of this, I never once grew discouraged. Before I left, my father had hugged me and said, "Go get that dirt, sweetheart." No matter what, I would get it for him and bring it safely home.

Chimayo is called the Lourdes of America because of all the healings that have been associated with it. When one thinks of miracle healing sites, Lourdes is probably the place that first comes to mind. If I hadn't already taken a serendipitous trip there fifteen years earlier, it is probably where I would have gone. In 1982, when I was working as a flight attendant, I was called to work a trip one day while I was on standby. It wasn't until I hung up that I realized the only destination I had been given was "Europe." This was unusual.

I was twenty-five years old and at a point in my life where I had abandoned many of my childhood ways. I had moved from my small hometown in Rhode Island to live in Manhattan. I was working at a job that was not usually associated with someone who had graduated sixth in her high school class and with high honors from college. Instead of the young lawyers I had been steadily dating, I was now madly in love with an unemployed actor. And, perhaps most important, I had given up not just on the Catholicism with which I was raised, but on religion altogether. Like many people I knew at that time, I liked to say that I believed in God, but not in organized religion. The truth is I didn't really think much about God back then, except in sporadic furtive prayers for my immediate needs: Don't let me be late, Please have him call, Help me decide what to do.

When I arrived at Kennedy Airport and looked at my flight schedule, I was delighted to see that the first part of the trip involved deadheading—flying as a passenger—to Paris that evening and staying overnight. The next day, at Charles de Gaulle Airport, I spotted several other flight attendants waiting for the same Air France flight. They all looked glum. After introductions, I asked if any of them knew where we were headed. "Didn't they tell you?" one of them moaned. "We're going to Lourdes!"

It was Easter week, when upward of a hundred thousand people go to Lourdes, and the streets were clogged with people with varying degrees of illness and deformity, nurses and nuns in starched white uniforms, tourists with cameras snapping pictures of the dying prone on their stretchers, the cripples atrophied in their wheelchairs, the blind with their white canes. But none of this prepared me for what was to come.

It took us almost four hours to board the flight back because of all the wheelchairs, stretchers, and medical equipment. Already the doctor on board had administered emergency care to a dying man. A mother told me that her daughter, seventeen years old and blind, had a rare disease in which her brain was destroying itself. "There's nothing to be done," she whispered. "This was our last chance." The girl sat beside her, staring blankly from eyes the light blue of faded denim. When I placed a meal tray in front of a sixty-year-old man suffering from multiple sclerosis, he grunted, gathered all his strength, and threw it back at me, his eyes ablaze with anger. "It's not you," his wife apologized, her head bent to hide the tears that streamed down her cheeks. "He's angry at everyone."

I sought out the priest who had led a group of a hundred people from Philadelphia. "Do you believe that any of these people will be cured by a miracle?" I demanded. I was young and jaded and arrogant, a stranger to death or illness.

"A miracle," he said, "is usually instantaneous. But some of these people have things that it will take X rays and tests to see if they are cured."

I looked at the young girl with the brain disease. Certainly then she had not had a miracle.

"The church has physicians," he explained, "who study alleged miracles." He told me about the process, how a miracle case must be proved by a medical history and the records and notes of everyone who has treated the person. Scientific evidence such as X rays and biopsies are examined. "And," he added, with what I interpreted as skepticism, "the cure must be a total cure. No relapses or reoccurrences."

"How many of these instantaneous cures have happened at Lourdes?"

He averted my eyes. "I think three," he said. "But you're missing the point," he said. "This is all they have left to do. Miracles come in unexpected ways."

It seemed to me a sad journey. Especially when out of the approximately forty cases a year investigated by the Consulta Medica, only about fifteen are deemed miracles. (The Consulta Medica is the Catholic Church's official body for investigating miracle claims.) Such a statistic in 1982 would have made me even angrier that these people had gone so far, with such hope, only to be disappointed. But by the time I went to Chimayo, I was a different person, and that statistic actually bolstered my belief that the dirt there might cure my father.

I was no longer the skeptical, arrogant young woman who had left Lourdes in a self-righteous huff. Just three months after my trip there, my brother died unexpectedly, and I found myself wanting to find faith somewhere, to believe in something more solid than my fleeting encounters with Buddhism, the Quakers, Ethical Culture, and the Unitarian Church. Over the years between then and my father's illness, I'd been married and divorced, suffered a miscarriage, lost jobs, changed careers, remarried, given birth to two children, and moved back to my home state of Rhode Island. And I'd returned to church, though not the Catholic Church of my childhood.

When I arrived at El Santuario, I had the fear of my father's death to motivate me and an open heart, a willingness to believe that a cure—a miracle—was possible. Matt had come with me to bring back dirt for his friend, who was dying from Hodgkin's disease. Not even the signs posted everywhere—NOT RESPONSIBLE FOR THEFT—could deter us. Here was a small adobe church with a dirt parking lot, a religious gift store, and a burrito stand called Leona's, which was written up as the best burrito place in New Mexico in all of my guidebooks.

We proceeded under an archway and through a courtyard where a wooden crucifix stood, then into the church where the altar was adorned with brightly painted pictures by the artist known as the Chili Painter. But we hadn't come to see folk art. We had come for a miracle. So we quickly went into the low-ceilinged room off the church in search of the *pocito*. What we found first was a testimony to all the cures attributed to this place. The walls were lined with crutches and canes, candles and flowers, statues of saints, all offerings of thanks for healings. Despite the signs asking people not to leave notes because of the fire danger around the lit candles, and not to write on anything except the guest book, the offerings had letters tucked into their corners. One statue had a sonogram picture pinned to the saint's cloak. Another had a letter in Spanish: "Thank you for the recovery of our little Luis. Our baby boy is now well. Mil gracias."

Against one wall of this room sits a shrine to the Santo Niño, who is believed to walk about the country at night healing sick children and wearing out his shoes in the process. As a result, an offering of shoes is given to him whenever a child is healed. The shrine at Chimayo is full of children's shoes, handmade knit booties, delicate silk christening shoes. Roses and letters of thanks adorn the statue, which is seated and holds a basket of food and a gourd to carry water.

In this small room, I began to tremble. I felt I was in a holy place, a place that held possibility. I had not felt that sense of possibility in the hospital and doctors' waiting rooms that had dominated my life these past few months. Even when a surgeon promised to remove my father's tumor if "the sucker will only shrink some," I didn't get the sense of peace I had as I stood surrounded by these testimonies to faith. One, from Ida P. of Chicago, stated that her husband still had six more radiation treatments to go when, on a Sunday, she brought him the dirt. On Monday the tumor was gone.

Ducking our heads, Matt and I entered the even smaller room that housed the *pocito*. It was just a hole in the dirt floor. The walls here were also covered with offerings, including a note that said: "Within this small room resides the stillness of souls that have discovered peace. Listen to their silence. JK, New York." Matt and I kneeled in front of the *pocito* and scooped the dirt with our bare hands into the Ziploc bags we had brought. I cannot say what Matt was thinking as he dug. But I had one prayer that I repeated over and over: Please let my father's tumor go away.

TO TRUST AND LOVE AGAIN.

Unlike other sites attributed to miracle healings, Chimayo is not associated with any particular saint. At Lourdes, people believe that Saint Bernadette intercedes on their behalf. Four years before my visit to Chimayo, I went on a long weekend trip to Montreal, Canada. One of my stops was a visit to Saint Joseph's Basilica, where a priest named Brother André was said to have healed people through prayer and oil from a particular lamp. The cures were frequent and often spontaneous. For the year 1916 alone, 439 cures were recorded. "I do not cure," Brother André said. "Saint Joseph cures."

But I did not visit Saint Joseph's Basilica for a cure. I went because the relic displayed there is a particularly gruesome one: Brother André's heart. I've always attributed my love of the more grotesque aspects of Catholicism to my Italian upbringing. My memories of my first trip to Rome are dominated by the various bones and pieces of cloth that churches display. The notion of viewing a heart was especially appealing. However, once I entered the ornate basilica and viewed the heart in its case, I decided I should also see the place where people go to pray to Brother André for a miracle. The walls of this room, too, were lined with offerings, the canes and braces of those who have been healed.

In many ways, I was even more of a cynic than I had been when I'd visited Lourdes. The death of my brother and the emotional havoc it wreaked on my family had left me in a spiritual vacuum from which I had not yet recovered. More recently, a love affair had gone bad, and I was questioning not just my spiritual beliefs, but also my ability to trust and love again.

That day in Montreal, I was not in need of a physical healing, but I had been in turmoil for several months, a turmoil that it did not seem would have an ending anytime soon. For someone who had entered the basilica on a lark—to view a human heart—I was strangely moved by the place, and by the people around me who knelt and prayed. Their conviction was obvious, and in many ways I envied their ability to believe in the power of prayer, or saints, or miracles. I knelt, too, and thought of all the events that had led me to this dark time I was living. At its core was a betrayal in love, a broken promise, a broken heart. A decision—whether to trust this person again—seemed unreachable. I replayed the past months like someone watching a home movie, and then I asked for resolution.

Resolution came. Not that day, or even that month, but many months later. I would not even now claim that the resolution came from the moments I spent praying in Saint Joseph's Basilica. What I gained there was a peace of mind, a calming of the soul, without which I could not have reached a decision. Perhaps more important is that I also began my journey back to faith through that visit. Although the Catholic Church excludes such healings from consideration for miracles, as they do the cures of any mental disorders or diseases that have a high rate of natural remission,

I believe a healing of some sort began there. Three years later, as I stood in El Santuario de Chimayo hoping for a miracle of the physical sort, I remembered that day in Montreal and the feeling that overtook me there. As WK from California wrote after her own visit to Chimayo: "It didn't cure me, but then it's God's will. Peace of mind is sometimes better."

A GRACED WORLD.

Buoyant from our time spent at El Santuario, Matt and I went off to find one of the weavers that live in and around Chimayo. Carefully following the signs for Ortegas, we ended up at a small store that sold carvings and local folk art, not rugs. "Is this Ortegas?" we asked, confused, when we entered. Matt was as certain as I that we had followed the signs exactly and turned in where they pointed. The ponytailed man behind the counter, Tobias, smiled at us. "You've been to get the dirt," he said. Later, Matt and I would both comment on how gentle his face was. Perhaps it was this gentleness that led me to tell him why I had come and the particulars of my father's disease. He nodded. "He'll be cured," he said. "I've seen it myself, the healings."

He told us the story of a couple who had arrived at his door— "like you two!" The man was grumpy, angry at his wife for insisting they come all this way from Los Angeles when her doctors had told her a cure was hopeless. Sympathetic toward the wife's plight, Tobias invited them to dinner. Reluctantly, the man agreed. As they sat eating on the patio of a nearby restaurant, a strange light began to emit from the woman's breast. Soft at first, it grew brighter and larger until it seemed to encompass her entire chest, like a cocoon. Then it slowly dissipated. It was the skeptical husband who spoke first. "Did anyone else see that?" Each of them had. "My tumor is gone," the wife said confidently.

Although Tobias did not know what kind of cancer the woman was suffering from, he was certain then that it was breast cancer, and that she had been cured. He was right on both accounts. Back in California, baffled doctors pronounced her completely free of breast cancer.

"It works," Tobias said.

Matt asked him how, with thousands of people visiting the *pocito,* the dirt was never depleted.

"Oh," Tobias said, "the caretaker refills it every day. Then the priest blesses it."

This mundane refilling disappointed me. The story I had heard about the dirt was that it replenished itself in some inexplicable way.

"It's not the dirt," Tobias told us. "It's the energy of all the people who come and pray into that *pocito* that makes miracles happen."

Of course, there is no real explanation for what makes miracles happen. But there are plenty of explanations that attempt to disprove them. Just as my friend gave many reasons why my grandmother lived through her bout of scarlet fever, skeptics use scientific, historical, and geographic data to explain away "miracles." Simply put, people either believe or don't. In my own search to understand miracles, I came across books and articles in support of each side.

Joe Nickell, the senior research fellow for the Committee for the Scientific Investigation of Claims of the Paranormal, has written an entire book debunking everything from stigmatas to the Shroud of Turin. On miracle healings, he believes that some serious illnesses, such as cancer and multiple sclerosis, can undergo spontaneous remission, in which they go away completely or abate for long periods of time. Nickell also cites misdiagnoses, misread

CAT scans, and misunderstandings as explanations for miracle healings. He reports that as of 1984, six thousand miracles had been attributed to the water at Lourdes but only sixty-four of those had been authenticated as miraculous. Those sixty-four miracles, he claims, were most likely spontaneous remissions, as in the case of a woman who was "cured" of blindness, only to discover she was suffering from multiple sclerosis and the disease had actually temporarily abated.

In response to such skepticism, Dr. Raffaello Cortesini, a specialist in heart and liver transplants and the president of the Consulta Medica, told Kenneth L. Woodward, the religion editor of *Newsweek* magazine and the author of *Making Saints,* "I myself, if I did not do these consultations, would never believe what I read. You don't understand how fantastic, how incredible—and how well-documented—these cases are. They are more incredible than historical romances. Science fiction is nothing by comparison." Believers in miracles do not even need such substantiation.

Still, advances in medical science have made the number of accredited miracles decrease over the years. Pope John Paul II, in his address to a symposium of members of the Consulta Medica and the Medical Committee of Lourdes in 1988, agreed that medicine has helped to understand some of these miraculous cures, but, he added, "it remains true that numerous healings constitute a fact which has its explanation only in the order of faith . . ." Because proving miracle cures has become so difficult, the church has lightened its requirements on miracles for canonization. It is true that historically, miracles were much more commonplace. In the thirteenth century, Saint Louis of Anjou was responsible for a well-documented sixty-six miracles, including raising twelve people from the dead. Obviously, today's doctors might easily disprove not only many of Louis of Anjou's miracles but also a good number of those that came before and after him. That still leaves us with the ones that no one—not even Joe Nickell—can explain that have occurred since the advent of modern medicine.

Other skeptics point to geography as a factor in alleged miracles. Since many miracles depend on the intervention of saints, and since most saints are European, a higher number of miracles occur there. Certain countries, such as Italy, boast more miracles than others. Physicians from Italy—southern Italy in particular— believe so strongly in miracles that they are more willing to accept a cure as miraculous. The culture there is such that saints and miracles are a part of everyday life. As I drove through southern Italy recently I was struck by how common statues of saints were. They appeared on roadsides, hanging from cliffs, in backyards, on city street corners, virtually everywhere. Almost always there were offerings at the statue's feet, flowers, bread, letters. This was where my own ancestors came from, and I can attest to our family's openness about letting miracles into our lives.

But other cultures share this openness, this willingness to recognize the miraculous. Rather than disproving miracles, I wonder if it doesn't support their existence. It was Augustine who claimed that all natural things were filled with miracles. He referred to the world itself as "the miracle of miracles." I saw this acceptance of daily, small miracles when I visited Mexico City during the Feast of the Virgin of Guadalupe. It was there, in 1531, that a local man named Juan Diego, while walking outdoors, heard birds singing, saw a bright light on top of a hill, and heard someone calling his name. He climbed the hill and saw a young girl, radiant in a golden mist, who claimed to be the Virgin. She told him she wanted a church built on that spot. When Juan Diego told the bishop what he had seen, the bishop asked him to go back and demand a sign as proof that this was really the Virgin. When he returned, the apparition made roses miraculously bloom, even though it was December. Convinced, the bishop allowed a cathedral to be built there. More than ten million people annually visit the shrine in Mexico City, making it the most popular site, after the Vatican, in the Catholic world.

Although it was an impressive sight to behold when I made the walk to the Basilica of the Virgin of Guadalupe along with people, many on their knees, who had come from all over Mexico, that spectacle of adoration was not what struck me about Mexico and its relationship to the miraculous. Rather, it was the way the culture as a whole viewed miracles that impressed me. Street vendors everywhere sold *milagros,* the small silver charms that mean, literally, "little miracles." The charms take the shape of body parts—arms, legs, hearts—and are pinned to saints in churches, to the inside of people's own jackets, everywhere. When I told a vendor that my mother had recently broken her hand, he gave me a *milagro* in the shape of a hand, at no charge.

Throughout Mexico one can also view *retablos,* paintings made on wood or tin that request favors for everything from curing someone of pneumonia to asking that children not fall out of windows or that a woman have a safe childbirth or that a house not catch on fire. Although many churches have glorious collections of *retablos,* these paintings also adorn the walls of shops and homes, humble requests for miracles large and small. "Oh, yes," a friend of mine who lives in San Miguel d'Allende told me, "here in Mexico it is a miracle if someone's oxen do a good job or if it doesn't rain on a special day. Miracles happen every day here."

As if to prove her point, we encountered one such miracle the night before I left Mexico City. Several of us climbed into a cab to go to a restaurant, but the driver was unfamiliar with the address. Everyone studied the map and planned the route, but still we couldn't find the street. Several times we stopped and asked directions. We still couldn't find it. After forty minutes and yet another set of directions, the cab came to a screeching halt. "We're here!" our driver exclaimed happily. "It's a miracle!"

Perhaps, then, part of understanding what a miracle is comes from one's openness to the possibility that they exist and occur regularly. It could be argued that one has to be Catholic to have this ability, since predominantly Catholic countries and cultures claim to have such an attitude. There are many Catholics who would agree that they believe in miracles simply because of their religion. Since I haven't actively participated in Catholicism since I was a young teenager, I would not have credited Catholicism with my own belief in the miraculous. But in retrospect, the roots of that belief must be in my Catholic and Italian upbringing, a combination that certainly indoctrinated me into believing of a general kind.

In fact, the connection between miracles and healing stems largely from the miracles attributed to Jesus. One could, then, broaden the definition of who more readily accepts miracles to include all Christians. Yet I suppose that someone could believe in miracles without believing in the teachings of Christ, or even without believing in God. Conversely, one can believe in God without believing in miracles. What seems most likely is what Kenneth Woodward explains: "To believe in miracles one must be able to accept gifts, freely bestowed and altogether unmerited." Once one has the ability to do that, it is a small leap to then accept that these gifts have come because someone has intervened on your behalf. Woodward goes on to say that "in a graced world, such things happen all the time." If one presumes that the world is without grace then one cannot accept any gifts, especially those that come from prayer.

When I made my pilgrimage to Chimayo, I had reached a point in my life where I believed in a graced world. I believed that the birth of my son was miraculous, that the love I shared with my husband was a gift, as was my ability to shape words into meaningful stories. Of course I credited hard work, talent, and character, too. But I had come to believe in Augustine's view of the world as the "miracle of miracles." When I arrived back in Rhode Island with the dirt from El Santuario, I felt that anything could happen.

Twenty-four hours after my father held the dirt, he was in respiratory failure and was rushed to the hospital by ambulance. It was Christmas Eve, three months after his diagnosis. Although it would have been a perfect time to have a crisis of faith, quite the opposite happened. I simply believed that he would survive. What happened next surprised me more than his bad turn of health.

While he was in the hospital, his recovery from what turned out to be pneumonia deemed unlikely, his doctor performed a CAT scan, assuming the tumor had grown. My father had only had two treatments of chemo and he needed five before there was any hope of the tumor shrinking. Visiting him, I asked if he was prepared for a bad CAT scan.

"Oh, no," he said with great confidence, "the tumor is gone." "Gone?" I said. He nodded. "I sat here and watched as cancer left my body. It was black and evil-looking and came out of my chest like sparks, agitated and angry." I was willing to believe the tumor might disappear, but such a physical manifestation was more than I had considered. True, Tobias had told us of a light enveloping a sick woman's chest, and it had seemed miraculous. But here was my father, a practical, no-nonsense midwesterner, telling me a story that hinted of science fiction.

The next day my mother called me from the hospital. "Ann," she said, awed, "the CAT scan shows that the tumor has completely gone. It's disappeared." In the background I heard my father chuckling, and then my mother made the doctor repeat what he had said when he walked into the room with the results: "It's a miracle."

AN ANSWERED PRAYER.

Here is the part where I would like to say that my father came home, tumor-free, cancer-free, miraculously cured. The part where I would like to tell you that, well again, he traveled with me to New Mexico, to El Santuario de Chimayo, to leave his CAT scan results in the little low-ceilinged room beside the baby shoes and notes of thanks and crutches and braces and statues and candles.

Instead, my father went home, had one more dose of Taxol, and the next day was once again rushed by ambulance to the hospital in respiratory failure. He spent almost two weeks in intensive care, diagnosed with double pneumonia. From there, he was moved onto the cardiac ward for a week and then into rehab. Weakened by his near-death illness, he moved around using a walker and had no memory of his days in the ICU. My family remembered it all too well, however: the all-night vigils by his side, sleeping on chairs, waiting for doctors and tests and change. Once he was in rehab, his doctor repeated the CAT scan, suspecting a recurrence of the tumor. But there was none, and a date for his release was set.

Two days before he was to come home, he spiked a fever and acquired a cough that proved to be the onset of yet another bout of pneumonia, this one a fungal pneumonia common in patients undergoing chemotherapy, and usually fatal. The doctors prepared us for the worst. "He will never leave the hospital," his pulmonary specialist told us. His health failing, my father instructed us on how to prepare the Easter breakfast specialties that he had been in charge of for the last twenty-five years—how to turn a frittata so it doesn't break, the secret to making light pizzeles.

The day before Easter he began to die. His oxygen supply was so low that his legs grew blue and mottled. A priest was called and administered the last rites, now known as the sacrament of the sick. But when the priest walked away, I grabbed my father's hand and sought a miracle yet again: "Daddy," I said, "please come back. For me and Sam and Grace." At the sound of my children's names, my father struggled not only to open his eyes, but to breathe, a deep life-sustaining breath. By that evening, he was sitting up. "I thought I was a goner there," he joked. Easter morning he told my mother that her frittata was too dry. I stayed with him all day. We watched a movie that night, and then he went to sleep.

The doctor suspected the cancer was back and had spread to my father's brain. He did CAT scans on his bones, lungs, and head. But my father remained tumor-free and cancer-free. Despite this, he died a week later, from the pneumonia he'd caught because of a compromised immune system. More than once since then I have found myself wondering not *if* I got a miracle or not, but whether I prayed for the wrong thing. Should I have bent over the *pocito* and asked for my father to live rather than for the tumor to go away? What I am certain of is this: I got exactly what I prayed for on that December afternoon at El Santuario de Chimayo.

Around the world, at Lourdes and Fatima, on the Greek island of Tinos and in a municipality called Esquipulas on the far eastern part of Guatemala, in Montreal and Chimayo, people are making pilgrimages, asking for miracles to save their lives or the lives of their loved ones. At least, that is what they believe they want, and they will settle for nothing less. After my father died, I still wanted to find someone whose miracle had happened, who had prayed for God to spare their loved one, and for God to have answered.

In my search I traveled to the remote Italian town of San Giovanni Rotondo on the Monte Gargano, the "spur" of the Italian boot that divides the plains of Apulia from the Adriatic Sea. There, a Capuchin monk known as Padre Pio is said to have performed miraculous cures, even after his death in 1968. No ordinary man, Padre Pio had the stigmata, the gift of transverberation (a wound in his side like the one Jesus had), and the ability to bilocate—to be in two places at the same time.

On our way from Naples to San Giovanni Rotondo, an all-day car ride through mountains and rugged terrain, I read the story of Padre Pio aloud to my husband and our eight- and four-year-olds. My husband kept rolling his eyes. More than once he whispered to me, "The guy was a kook." But when I'd finished, I asked the children if they believed that Padre Pio was capable of everything the book said. Did they believe he could heal people, too? "Oh, yes!" they both said without hesitation. He was, they concluded, a very special person.

It was a brutally cold March afternoon when we arrived at the cathedral there. The wind blew at over fifty miles an hour. But still the church was packed. I made my way downstairs to Padre Pio's tomb, where the kneelers around it were full of pilgrims with offerings of roses. A father stood beside his young son, who sat hunched and twisted in a wheelchair. As they prayed, the father lovingly stroked the boy's cheek. Watching them, I was convinced that the boy would not walk out of here, leaving his wheelchair behind. I did not believe that the boy would ever walk. But rather than feeling anger at this, as I had years earlier at Lourdes, I felt a sense of peace, a certainty that the boy and his father would leave here spiritually stronger, that they would somehow have the courage to deal with the disease the boy had been given.

True, Padre Pio has been given credit for many miracles. In one, a young girl was born without pupils in her eyes. Her grandmother prayed to Padre Pio without any results. A nun urged her to make a pilgrimage from her small town to San Giovanni Rotondo. There, the monk touched the girl's eyes, and she could see. On their way home, they stopped to visit a doctor who, upon examining the child, was puzzled. The girl could see, but she still had no pupils. As in all places where miracles are said to happen, the legends of the healings are whispered among those who go. They are written about in the small brochures one can buy for a few dollars at the church. But it is only the hopeful, the desperate, who crowd around the water, the dirt, the heart, the tomb.

As I stood to leave Padre Pio's tomb, a middle-aged man and his mother hurried into the room. The woman held a statue of the Virgin Mary, an offering. But what I saw on their faces was a look that I recognized too well, a look I wish I was not familiar with. They wore the shocked and grief-stricken expressions of those who know they are about to lose someone they love. Perhaps they had just received the news. Or perhaps the person had taken a turn for the worse. They had come here because the doctors had told them there was nothing else that could be done. It was a matter of days or weeks or months. The only thing left to do was ask for a miracle.

ANOTHER MIRACLE.

Despite the fact that I am a woman who is firmly rooted in the physical world, practical and realistic and skeptical about many things in life at the end of the twentieth century, I still traveled across the country with my newborn daughter, believing I could bring home a miracle for my dying father. Almost a year to the day that my father died, I went back to El Santuario de Chimayo. Father Roca, who has been the parish priest there for forty years, talked to me in his tiny office inside the church. I had written to him months earlier and told him my story. In person, he is a man who dispenses smiles and stories as easily as holy water; several people came in while I was there and, without missing a beat, he blessed their medals and crucifixes, sprinkling holy water, murmuring prayers.

"I have reread your letter many times," he told me. "I am so happy for your family." Thinking he was confused, I said, "But my father died." Father Roca shrugged. "It was God's will. The tumor went away, yes?" I nodded. "Do you know who came here one month before he died? Cardinal Bernadin. From Chicago. He came here and asked me to take him to where the dirt was. I led him to the *pocito* and then left. Fifteen minutes later he emerged, smiling, at peace. 'I got what I came for,' he said." "He wasn't cured," I said. Father Roca smiled. "I know."

I spent about twenty minutes with Father Roca. He told me about the crucifix that was found here. He told me about the miracles he had personally witnessed: the woman who was so sick that her son had to carry her to the *pocito* but who walked out on her own; the young man who came to pray en route to throwing himself off the mountain in despair, but after praying at the *pocito,* decided to return to his wife and baby. To Father Roca, the miracles of El Santuario de Chimayo are not just physical. Rather, they are miracles of inner transformation. "There is," he told me, "something very special about this place."

Later, I returned to the small room with the offerings, and the smaller room with the *pocito* that the caretaker refilled every day. I prayed there, a prayer of thanks for the miracles that had come my way since I'd last visited Chimayo: good health, the love of my children and my husband, the closeness of my family, and, finally, the courage to accept what had come my way. If someone at the shrine on my first visit had told me the miracle I would receive was peace of mind, I would have been angry. But miracles come in many forms, both physical and spiritual. Before I left El Santuario, I again removed a Ziploc bag from my pocket and filled it with dirt. Back at home, my aunt had recently been diagnosed with lung cancer. She needed a miracle, too.

ANDREW HUDGINS

Blur

from *Image*

The sashes all jump upward and the long sweep
of May wind bellies the curtains, chases
the stale smoke from the farthest corner. Storms
of perfume lift from honeysuckle, lilac,
mown grass, clover—and drift across the threshold,
outside reclaiming inside as its home.
Warm days whirl in an unnumberable blur,
a cup—a grail—brimmed with delirium
and humbling boredom both. I was a boy,
I thought I'd always be a boy, pell mell,
mean, and gaily murderous one moment
as I decapitated daises with a stick,
then overcome with summer's opium,
numb-slumberous. I thought I'd always be a boy,
each day its own millennium, each
one-thousand years of daylight ending in
the night watch, summer's pervigilium,
which I could never keep because by sunset
I was an old man. I was Methuselah,
the oldest man in the holy book. I drowsed.
I nodded, slept—and without my watching, the world,
whose permanence I doubted, returned again,
bluebell and blue jay, speedwell and cardinal
still there when the light swept back,
and so was I, which I had also doubted.

I understood with horror then with joy,
dubious and luminous joy: it simply spins.
It doesn't need my feet to make it turn.
It doesn't even need my eyes to watch it,
and I, though a latecomer to its surface, I'd
be leaving early. It behooved me to stay awake
and sing if I could keep my mind on singing,
not extinction, as blurred green summer, lifted
to its apex, succumbed to gravity and fell
to autumn, Ilium, and ashes. In joy
we are our own uncomprehending mourners,
and more than joy I longed for understanding
and more than understanding I longed for joy.

Before the Fall

from *Salon*

It is the light, on summer evenings, drifting on till 9 P.M. or later, and slanting above the elms, the musky river; it is the scratchy smell of grass, the thunk of bat on cricket ball. It is the flow of a brackish stream, the twittery, gnattish nothingness that is a drowsy English town on a summer day going nowhere. It is the sound of bells tolling across the fields, and the morning walk to class when the dew is still on the grass.

It is, of course, nostalgia—geography's *deja vu*—that marks a large part of what we call the "sacred." Born in England on a winter's day, I grew up thinking of it only as the place I longed to flee. As soon as I could, upon the completion of my studies there, I got on a plane and never looked back. England is red-brick houses to me, and lowering grey afternoons, the inertia of a social system that has no room for growth, the soot and filth and dreariness of Industrial Revolution factories that blacken the already smudged sky on winter afternoons. Even on summer days, when I return, almost all that I can see is porridge-colored tower-blocks and circumscribed lives and hopes, the milk-bottles lined up outside the scruffy gardens as for a rain-storm that will never come.

Yet for all the unyielding griminess, England remains the place where I was a child, careless of the future and in a state of perpetual discovery. It is the place where I stepped outside the hours, and had no sense of yesterday or tomorrow. And so, even now, half a world and half a lifetime away, in the country where I've chosen to make my home (a romantic England, you could say, or an exotic one, so much like the place of my boyhood that on these rainy Japanese afternoons I half-expect to hear the cricket scores recited on TV), I find myself returning to some quality of light and languidness and suspension that belongs to an English summer evening, the insects twittering as the lights come on as in a garden production of *Midsummer Night's Dream.* *A sacred place*

A sacred place, I mean to suggest, is only a place where we get a taste of Eternity—and that taste comes strongest of all, or most repeatedly, when we are hardly conscious of it (children, the Romantics, among others, believed, still carry with them a memory of the Heaven they have just quit). The past is the site of our wounds, our fears, the habits that cripple us, the tangles we long to escape; yet it is—only it can be—the place from which we derive our most palpable sense of Heaven. Every visit to Eden has a quality of recollection.

Many of us travel, more and more, to the "sacred places" of the globe—to Angkor and Luxor and Cuzco—and partake there of the sacraments and rites of someone else's paradise; we are visitors, even trespassers, in a foreigner's alien church. Those powerful places have a sacredness that hits us as the glance from a magnetic stranger's eyes, but their magic is one that is not really ours to claim. The "sacred places" that lie in memory, individual as a thumbprint, or a scar above one's right eye, are the personal pieces of Heaven that are ours to carry round with us, our barely discernible memories of life before the fall. The place, the life, the weather may all be everyday and unremarkable, but when I hear the opening strains of a certain hymn, I am walking through the lanes of a neverending twilight, the sound of a choir coming from behind some stained-glass windows, in a place as magical to me as Tibet. A place whose tiny limits give out upon sheer boundlessness.

Closing my eyes, I see the sun declining over fields and fields. I hear a tennis ball being thwacked, and the return of a quiet unsmudged for a thousand years. I see the first outlines of a moon rising above the trees, the sluggish water, the silhouette of ancient spires. I think that sacredness means only having so strong a sense of trust that we hardly know the meaning of the word, and find a world without change even in the midst of "dark Satanic mills" and a land so familiar that we know it's home only because it's the place we always—always—long to flee.

You Could Believe

from *Ontario Review*

You could believe the city is more than you,
that when you lean into the chain-link fence
separating the axle plant from the world
you are satisfying a hunger to be God,
that when you climb the one hill in October
to count the stacks smoking in the dirty air
you see yourself divided into squares
of city blocks under an ungiving sky.
The hill's brow is your brow, the wild grass blowing
in the wind, the milkweed bowing and rising
as the trucks groan by, the air reddening
in the distance, the river, dark and still,
holding back its blood, they are who you are.
A child growing into a boy, a boy growing
into a man, you reach out for something
to take your breath. The elms and maples stay,
their leaves blackening as the rain comes down.
Can you imagine turning to the woman
on the bar stool next to you and soberly
recounting your name and all the details
of your secret self. Go ahead and try it.
She works afternoons at Briggs polishing
engine parts or parts of something vital.
She has a daughter in the seventh grade
sleeping alone at home, or so she hopes.

"Honey," she says, "have another one on me,"
and she unsnaps her purse and slaps a five
down flat on the bar. Don't be offended.
She's not laughing. It's Autumn of '96.
The black and white TV in the corner
has heard it all and it's not laughing either,
it too dreams of a world unlike this one,
everything in this place does what it can.

JACQUES LUSSEYRAN

What One Sees Without Eyes

Something has astonished me for a long time. It is that blind people never speak about the things they see. At least I never hear them talk about them to those who see with their physical eyes.

Rather often, however, when blind people are together, suddenly they tell each other what they perceive. Then why do they ordinarily keep quiet about this?

I think that basically the reason is rather simple. They keep quiet because of society. To live in society one must at any cost resemble everyone else. Society demands it. In order to adapt to the world of the seeing, blind people are obliged to declare themselves unable to see—and, believe me, I know what I'm talking about, for that has happened to me even when I knew very well that it didn't correspond to reality and was not true.

Therefore tonight, excuse me for not saying to you a single time that I am blind. I will not speak to you about blindness, but about its opposite.

To begin with, I have a very strong memory: something which stays alive for me as an experience every minute, but which presents itself to me, when I think about it, as a memory. It is what happened to me when I became blind at the age of eight.

I believed—oh, I believed, and with a great dizziness, as you may well imagine, despite my young age—that from the moment I lost my eyes, I would from then on never see again. And then that was not true. What a surprise! I still haven't forgotten it. I verified immediately and in a concrete way that I had not lost anything, or rather that what I had lost was of a practical order, and only of that order.

Oh, indeed, I could no longer walk around freely; I had to be accompanied. I was sometimes obliged to ask others for help—those who saw with their eyes, who were passing around me. But the others responded to me. Usually they responded very well. I learned very quickly that this was not very serious. No, truly, I had lost nothing at all.

What does this mean?

It does not mean that the situation must be explained in a moral manner or by poetic images—I will adamantly insist on that.

It means uniquely positive, concrete, and elementary things.

I had rediscovered inside myself everything which others described as being outside of us: on the exterior. And I verified for myself that they were wrong. They said, "But he can no longer see the light," or even, "If he says that he sees it, he is actually imagining it or remembering it." And people spoke to me of the marvelous memories I must have of the time when I could see. Or of the faculty that I possessed, as they put it, to an extraordinary degree: imagination. But, for my part, I was obstinately resolved not to believe them. I knew very well that I was not "imagining things." I knew that I was perceiving, that I was sensing.

Inside me was everything I had believed was outside. There was, in particular, the sun, light, and all colors. There were even the shapes of objects and the distances between objects. Everything was there, and movement as well.

I verified that sometimes the shapes I perceived inside myself were not exactly like those which others described to me. There were slight differences, little divergences. For example, a friend who had eyes told me that a wall at the side of the road was still quite a ways away from us, that it was about ten meters distant.

Rather strangely, I felt it much closer. And then, several years later, I understood where the difference came from: The wall was very large and very tall, much taller than the other walls in the neighborhood. So nothing had really changed for me. My blindness did not prevent the wall from being a wall. It didn't change its being strong, solid, and immobile along the side of the road.

This is how things went for me right from the beginning, and it was and still is amazing to me.

From the moment I became blind, I did not enter a world of privations supported by courage, to "see" heroically what others described to me. Not at all.

I entered a world of enchantment, but an enchantment which supported my life, which nourished me, because it was real. It was not an imaginary fairy-tale enchantment, and I sensed that clearly.

And now, at the interior of this positive enchantment, I found a small understanding which was immediately a very great prize for me which I treasure to this day: the nature of light.

I knew very well that most of those who see with their eyes—I hardly dare call them "the seeing," for there would be an unpleasant ambiguity to that—usually say that light comes to them from the outside, that they catch it like a ball which is thrown to them.

I know very well that is not true. I know the nature of light is not to be outside of us, but, on the contrary, within us.

Exactly what is this nature of light? I could not tell you. I don't know. I only know how it really manifests itself. It is an element that we carry inside us and which can grow there with as much abundance, variety, and intensity as it can outside of us. Maybe even more intensely, and in a more stable, better balanced way, inside rather than outside.

There was this phenomenon that surprised me: I could choose when the light came or went. Yes, I could make it appear or disappear. I had that astonishing power: I could light myself. You heard right: "light myself." That is to say, I could create a light inside me so alive, so large, and so near that my eyes—oh, it was very strange—my physical eyes, or what remained of them, vibrated, almost to the point of hurting, just as yours would hurt if you suddenly fixed them on the sun's ray too attentively. I could in the same way extinguish all, or almost all, light impressions, or at least reduce them, soften them into a monotonous gray, a sort of obscurity, whether pleasant or disturbing. In any case, for me the variations of light no longer depended on external phenomena— do I need to repeat that medically I was one hundred percent blind?—but on my own decisions.

All my childhood was sustained by these experiences and inclined—as you already must understand—toward joy. Not toward consolation—I have never needed to be consoled—but toward joy.

By all this, I learned at the same time that we should never give way to despair, that no matter what brutal and negative events occur in our lives, just as quickly the same sum of life is given back to us; that actually everything in the universe adds up to continuity. I no longer saw with the eyes of my body, as men of letters say, but with the eyes of my soul.

To tell the truth, I hardly need to involve my soul, because for me it was something much more direct, a great deal more physical, and quite simple.

Yes, there was continuity: I had lost nothing. I had been given as much as I had had taken from me, perhaps more.

When one realizes that, when one knows it from the age of nine or ten, I assure you it is not difficult to believe in God, because God is there. He is there under a form that has the good luck to be neither religious, nor intellectual, nor sentimental, but quite simply alive. And that is an extraordinary support for all the rest of life. I would sometimes forget that—I forget it even today—but that support remains alive. And when I do remember it, I have exactly the sensation of someone taking my hand, or that a ray of light—it is exactly this way—comes toward me and touches me. If I know what the ray of light is, I no longer have any problems.

Since becoming blind, I have paid more attention to a thousand things, and that this has allowed me to discover all sorts of aspects of the world that I probably would never have known otherwise. And these aspects are very comforting. They give life to everything. I'd like to give you some examples.

First of all, I perceived that sounds were not produced just by vibrating objects, but more generally, by all objects which make up our world, even those that we deem immobile or lifeless.

I observed, for example, that the wall which is here behind me also produces a sound. I say: "produces a sound."

Is it really a sound that I perceive in placing my attention on the wall? I'm not completely certain. But it is, if you wish, a shaking, something very light, but something repeated endlessly. I would say that it repeats as long as the wall stays behind me, exerting some force on my body.

Thus, the most apparently lifeless objects carry with them a potential for life as great as those which whirl and vibrate a lot—or are the most human.

What difference is there between a human voice and a tree's voice? Very slight, unless you have acquired the habit of understanding the human voice more rapidly than a tree's voice. But both are one voice.

I remember this experience. I've retold it often to my friends, it's so pleasant.

I discovered as a child that different species of trees don't have the same presence. In particular, I did not experience the same sensations when I passed along a street shaded by an oak tree that I did going down one shaded by a fir tree or an acadia.

During vacations in the country, when I had made friends with the landscape during the long weeks, I could distinguish the tree under which I passed by its volume, its configuration, the distinct sound of its shadow.

That's only one detail. But there are a number of details like that. And that's why, when I found myself in the presence of an unknown mountainous landscape, when I was still hundreds of feet or even a few miles away from the neighboring summits, I could give a general indication of their silhouettes! It was as if I saw them: I saw far beyond me the great outlines and shapes of the mountains. How did I know what they looked like? I knew absolutely nothing about them. Nonetheless they appeared to me—or, more precisely, I verified them within myself, exactly as I verified the presence of light.

Once again: I did not have to leave my armchair, I did not have to move, because things were inside me.

I began to verify that most of the particular sensations that I experienced and that I attributed just now to hearing, touch, or smell, always related essentially to the same sort of sensation.

I'm about to give it a name, which may not be a very good idea: a sensation of pressure.

The universe had weight and was always pressing against me. Which is to say that it presses equally against you.

All the objects in the universe seem to be masses of energy located somewhere, and it doesn't matter much where, except on the level of mechanics pure and simple: physical relationships.

Therefore, these masses of energy exist somewhere and draw near or far, making an impression on us, the whole affair being one of perception for us.

I mention again the example of the walls of this room.

The four walls of this room lean against me. Their life consists—to the extent that their life concerns me—of leaning on me from a certain distance.

Or preferably: I also lean on them. Yes, I lean on them by the simple fact, for example, that I think about them.

I think about the four walls of this room, simultaneously of these four walls. It is as if one of my hands were propped up against that wall on the right, and the other against the wall to the left, and two more against those in front of or behind me. It is as precise as that.

And it still seems that the walls exist as a point of encounter between these two pressures: that coming from them and that coming from me.

It seems almost that the walls are the conjunction, the union of these two forces, their equilibrium; I almost want to say their reconciliation.

I think that you feel to some extent that these remarks of mine are, if not surprising, at least difficult to express. Well, that's because we have the habit—and a very bad habit—of believing things are outside of our control, that they either come to us or don't, that they are stubborn as mules, that we will never be able to make them do what we want. Translation: that we are poor unfortunates, creatures forgotten by the universe, and that we—free, generous and heroic beings—cannot obtain the responses from things which we feel are our due.

That's true: we are in a battle against things. But it's not the things' fault. It would be so simple to catch them where they live and not somewhere else—and that place where they live is not outside.

What role does blindness play in this affair?

The answer is so simple that it's right under our nose. Blindness leads us to perceive more clearly, more immediately the connections between objects and the universe at large. Then we make some big discoveries.

So, as I was saying, objects exert pressure on us. We exert another pressure on them, or at least it seems that that's the way it is. And the world—of real spectacles, real images—is produced by the encounter of these two movements, at the same time.

When one knows this fact, when one thinks about it a little, the proportions of the universe change. One perceives a solidity, a new resonance.

There are echoes everywhere. There are presences everywhere. There is a rather marvelous exchange going on: between the concave and swollen, the full and the empty, between the explosive and the responsive. One doesn't have to touch a statue with one's fingers or the palm of the hand to know the statue.

That is what I want to say.

You know that your eyes are a very useful sense organ, for with them you can travel in an instant to numerous places, to numerous points on the surface of objects.

You can go very quickly, with your eyes. You can glide. Excuse me; I don't want to scold or insult you, but I am obliged to say to you: you glide too quickly.

This ends up becoming a frightening temptation for you.

Fingers don't glide.

With my fingers I can know this table. I am obliged to feel my way around it. That is to say, I make my fingers explore all its parts, one after another, until at last I know it all, completely. For indeed, if I have touched a smooth part on the left side of the table, I cannot yet know if I am going to find a big hole in the middle of the table. Why not? Maybe there is a hole. I will know it only when I come into tactile simultaneity with it. The touch gives the proof.

But it is possible, without eyes, to apprehend a part of an object and to know it immediately, instantaneously, in its entirety.

It is possible for a blind person to hear the voice of a man or woman speak just three words to recognize that man or woman as if they had been speaking for hours. How is that possible?

Is it really necessary that the blind person be a first-rate psychologist in order to have this facility, or have made long and detailed studies of human mechanics? Do you think so? It is sufficient, as always, to be attentive.

The part is equal to the whole. The hand conveys the arm. The arm conveys the whole body. The body conveys the past, present, and future actions of whoever inhabits it.

There is another thing to which the blind person becomes habituated very quickly, if you want to so much as give it a thought.

And what does it prove, this brief experiment, if not that things and people are not outside of us to discover and explore, but on the contrary that we already carry things inside of ourselves. They are there in advance. We require only a little shock, a very brief opportunity—just a flicker of movement or the sound of their voice, in order to perceive their presence.

All these things are naturally true for those who see, just as for those who don't see.

All that is a question of attention—and a question of the direction taken by us inside ourselves

Basically blindness gives a great force, that of discovery that the inner life is not at all what people imagine it to be.

When people speak of the inner life, they irresistibly—and one must add bizarrely—think of I don't know what construction, what imaginary fabrication: perhaps, a novel. That's the simplest word of all. Indeed, there are certainly some very good novels. There are those which give the illusion of reality and those which

don't do that at all. There are good craftsmen of the inner life—
and bad ones. That is what the majority of people believe—and
they take you for a great rogue if you seriously say to them that
you have a real inner life—"Ah, well, that fellow, he invents
things! He comforts himself as best he can! He is rather clever!" At
the very least they laugh at you, which happens very often, and
accuse you of not adapting to the modern world.

Well, it's not that way at all.

It is incontestable that certain inner lives are entirely fabricated, unfortunately. These are fictitious lives, and God knows
what there is to them.

The true inner life either is or is not.

If it is, it is not absolutely different from external life. It does
not oppose it. It is not in battle against the necessities of positive
existence: it contains exactly the same things as external life. Only
this time they are seen and perceived from within.

I have said here at least a good dozen times, "within us" or
"within me."

So what does that ultimately mean?

For as long as one merely uses the expression, one is still in the
world of language: with a meaning that is banal, loaded.

What is the "inside" that is inside us? And consequently, what
is this "inner" of inner life?

Is it necessary to represent things as if we were a husk, a large
shell which, like all shells, has at its center a space which is more
or less empty or full?

And is it true that a blind person very often sees things as if he
were lightly separated from them, as if only one part of them were
available to him, the other parts remaining on the surface, which
can only be scratched or grazed, not penetrated?

Sensations like this exist.

But to a very perceptible degree, this sensation of the husk or shell disappears.

And things are there, without space.

Yes, "without space."

You ask me: Is that possible? Have you found the recipe for inner life?

Alas! How could I explain to you? I hardly know what it is.

No. I know simply that things are there, are present, without having to attribute to them a particular position in the world.

When you look with your eyes, you say: "This ashtray is there, in front of me, just to my right." "That man or woman is over there; I see him or her in a precise position that is such and such in relationship to the neighboring position." You take into account the space and you imagine to yourself that the space you have imposed can not be destroyed, that in fact it exists, is substantial.

But, for experiential reasons once again, I think that is not true.

If, speaking from the depth of my blindness, I say to you: "Things are inside me," this "inside" is an inexact term since there is no actual inside. Things are presented in another way, that's all. I can then play with given space as much as I like. I can even imagine—and if you like, I can do it this very instant—the room in which you are in: I can see to the left the wall and the door. I then try, if I pay close attention, to imagine some people around you, there, sitting and looking. Well, naturally, these would be spatial facts.

But, be careful! Right now, I am playing, just amusing myself, creating a representation, if you like: a drawing.

If I think of a person, if we right now—go ahead, it's OK—were to think of Georges Saint-Bonnet, who is in Marseilles: Saint-Bonnet is not at all in this particular place. But he is. Not to the right or to the left or behind us. He is inside me, for I have, in thinking about him, the sensation of being located a little lower, even in my physical body, than I usually am. Closer to my heart than my head, I believe, and I'm not being sentimental.

Yes, but in reality, this is no longer a space.

Or instead, it is the only one which counts—that which we have made.

It is that space in which we support ourselves, in which we unite ourselves, in which we envelop ourselves, and, who knows, in which we create ourselves.

Being blind, I have made a certain number of practical observations about these things which I'd like to share with you.

Suppose I am sad. Or embarrassed. I have things which upset me. I am anxious. Armies of small pains race inside my head. I see black butterflies everywhere.

What happens then?

Suddenly I see almost nothing.

When I am sad, walking inside my house, I bump my forehead; I hurt my hand on a half-open door. And I no longer even have a sense of where I am.

This reminds me that I am blind, but blind in a way I don't like. That is to say, in a way which makes me different from others. Also I understand quickly that in order to no longer be blind in the way I detest, all I that I have to do is simply no longer be sad.

What a beautiful Godsend!

It is true that today I think in this clear and peremptory way. At the age of ten, I undoubtedly didn't tell myself things exactly this way.

I know in every case when I am in high spirits, when I am confident, when I observe within myself an air of joy, of life, of peaceful curiosity in regard to things, there are no longer any accidents. I no longer smash my face against objects. I have an impression of knowing them wonderfully well, sometimes of measuring them to the exact centimeter.

In fact, one could write whole books of the newest and most refined psychology on this theme or one like it. But all the books written would add nothing to the experience, which is the only thing that counts. I want to hold myself to that.

There is also what I have discovered when I was impatient. You see this is no longer exactly sadness, though impatience is in many regards a form of sadness. In a word, when I was impatient, I wanted everything to go faster. I wanted to eat quickly. And during this time when I was impatient, all the objects immediately started to turn against me like fretful children. They changed their positions. I could no longer trust them. There was a glass which was on the table, and which I had seen just a moment ago at the tip of my napkin. It disappeared a moment later. It was behind a bottle, and of course in trying to reach for it, I turned over the bottle.

Impatience moves objects in exactly the same way that sadness puts them in shadows, almost eclipses them, surrounds them by some sort of smoke or fog.

Joy clarifies everything.

How many times have I found myself quite simply walking along. And suddenly I receive one of these gusts of contentment, of, so to say, "joy" or "well-being," which is a marvelous feeling because one has no idea where it comes from. There is no known reason. It is as if life were tapping, like rain on a window-pane. One is content. I was content on the sidewalk. Paris became visible to me. I saw Paris. I knew how tall the houses were. I distinguished how wide the streets were. I perceived the automobiles coming and going. And people who approached me had a smell, a history, even before they spoke or I spoke to them. In short, for a brief second, I was all-knowing. I had eyes all around my head, and then, truly, I was no longer blind. It was actually even more than that, in a certain regard.

And it was all because I was content.

Let's look at these phenomena and verify especially their extraordinary positiveness, or rather their material character as opposed to their intellectual, moral, psychic, or social character.

The universe shrinks if I am afraid. It gets gloomy if I am sad. It goes crazy if I am impatient. It becomes clear if I am joyous.

But how does it happen that the universe can be so pliant as that? And then what is the hand which gives itself all these shapes, one after the other? Let's see: If the universe were one reality against which we were obliged to struggle because it was created long before we were, would it not be this way?

If the universe were mere necessity, if it were entirely mechanical, would it be so mobile? Would it allow transformations as concrete in perception as those we get from it?

Why does the universe—which could be a person, ultimately, someone fully adult before we were even born: out there, well-made, well-rounded, definite—why does it allow itself to grow and shrink, to shine forth or to darken its light? That seems almost absurd.

No. What happens, instead, is that we observe ourselves as the hand that manipulates this universe, which gives itself form— though that's an inadequate phrase—inside ourselves.

And we can verify that this hand is not in the objects of the universe that we perceive, but certainly elsewhere.

Thus, during the years following my accident, I lived in a kind of amazement, enchantment, a very beautiful dream.

That expressed itself for me in great lyric expansiveness and in poetry.

Don't worry, I have no wish to speak ill to you about poetry, but that marvel sometimes hid from me something which is more central to all marvels.

I'll try to be a little less obscure.

Having become blind, I had discovered enchanted worlds inside myself. I think you've felt them as well.

I had discovered enchanted worlds, and I was content with these enchanted worlds, and then, one day I was afraid.

I was afraid because it occurred to me, "Good heavens, what if, by chance or bad luck, I am the author of these enchanted worlds? What if I'm just making them up? If they're just hallucinations that I am entertaining according to some more or less suspicious process, some egocentric compensation for being blind? That would be frightful, because the world would no longer be as beautiful as I have made it, and one day I'll perceive the difference and that will hit me like a ton of bricks."

Then one beautiful day I recognized that it was not something I had fabricated, but that in fact it had all been given to me.

And given by someone. I say "someone" because that is the most suitable way to say it in words. By someone or something who, evidently, was very much inside of me, but who in another sense was not at all identified with myself.

In fact, I perceived in myself someone who saw all these wonders of the inner life, but who was not me. I profited from it, and then broke it down into parts, transformed it, arranged it, but in the end, it was not I who saw.

I recognized that there was indeed someone watching.

Someone watching deep within.

But this spectator himself did not have a history. And, for him, linear space had no meaning whatsoever.

Who was this someone watching deep within? Imagine for a second that he is identical to the manipulator—the hand—I have just spoken about: to whatever makes the universe expand larger, or shrink, or shine forth or darken. Imagine that he is the same as that. Everything suddenly explains itself.

And everything in fact is explained. There is inside each of us someone watching deep within. Someone who sees.

But whoever is watching is not whoever it is, in us, who sees with our physical eyes—a superficial person indeed—nor even whoever it is, in us, who sees with the eyes of the imagination: that is no longer enough.

He—the someone who's watching deep within—to tell the truth, he sees nothing.

He sees nothing because no spectacles of the inner or outer life interest him. He allows seeing. That's all.

Without him, indeed, we perceive nothing, neither with our physical eyes nor with our inner psychic look. He is more important; he counts for more than anything we perceive.

There is one other thing that I owe, I am almost certain, in large part to my blindness, or rather to which I owe the evidence of my blindness.

Blindness has allowed me to have contact—quite concrete and a good deal closer—with what is going on inside of us all. There are, if you like, whole dull areas of perception that have been elevated, and consequently salvaged.

I have had roughly the best seat in the house at this theater. I have become part of the scenery.

It's up to me to use blindness, to profit from it, to serve it. But in the end, that's how it is.

Yes, you see, when you learn that it is possible to pass beyond your physical eyes, when you discover all that the inner glance can observe, well, you perceive in the end the value of this intimate glance in and of itself. Is it not the essential part of us, something better than anything else? You are no longer content to just be blind once; you want to become blind a second time.

To become blind a second time, why?

And after the second time, a third!

To be blind by accident in the exterior world, in the physical world in one part of its manifestation, is one thing; but imagine also being blind, after that, to all the images of the inner world, to try to look beyond them—beyond the screen of images, in some way—into pure light.

Blind just once? What strange austerity!

There is actually no austerity, for then what we see of the world can never be suppressed, no matter what. Such spectacles indeed will always exist.

It is we, in relationship to them, who perhaps must change.

They will continue to be there, and they will defile us as much as ever, maybe more. And this can also truly be a great fountainhead, a great source for our growth.

Yes, what we see defiles us. One sees these spectacles in their succession, in their interminable progression. But one no longer has to be mixed up with them.

For there is inside of people a kind of glance.

This glance is not at all what one might imagine.

On the level of physical vision, it is carried by what we call eyes, those two organs well protected in the face. Well protected but nonetheless very fragile.

On the level of inner psychic vision, it is carried, if you wish, in a fashion a bit more subtle than on the physical level, but one that is still heavy, mixed up, complex: the power to represent images within ourselves.

But in the end, it's all the same power.

It is never completely exhausted, by either one of these visions.

It is a good deal more central than all that, and a good deal greater. It is up to us to reconcile it within ourselves.

To put it concisely and very simply, when I was eight years old, it was possible to see again, even though I had become blind, because vision is not an organ of the body, nor even an organ of the feeling imagination alone, but an essential power.

A power to help, to assist everything that is, or better yet, to convey in itself everything that is: the power that the spirit possesses to contain the whole universe—our link with the Principle, with God. For that's how it is.

That fountainhead at the bottom of us: I have called it someone watching deep within, also joy.

Perhaps it is exactly the same thing.

And one could almost ask if the only way we have of adapting our senses to the universe, of making better use of them—of seeing, hearing, touching, and sensing as best we can, of not "being blind"—is it not to pray, in the true sense of the term, which is to say to put ourselves in touch with God, as continually and as frequently as possible?

> For this joy is close to you,
> it is in you!
> None of you has a spirit so heavy,
> nor an intelligence so feeble,
> none of you is so far from God
> not to be able to find this joy in Him.
>
> —*Meister Eckhart*

I even dare believe that interior joy has a secret power to make luck more favorable. . . .

I have often noticed that the things I have done with a happy heart, and with no inner repugnance, have a habit of succeed-

*ing happily, even during games of chance, where it is only for-
tune which rules. . . .*

*It is useful to have a strong conviction that the things which
you undertake without repugnance, and with the freedom
which ordinarily accompanies joy, will not fail to succeed well.*

*Your Highness will allow me, if she pleases, to finish this let-
ter as I began it, and to wish her primarily the satisfaction of
the spirit and of joy, as not only as the fruits that one looks for
above all others, but also as a means to augment the grace one
has for acquiring them.*

   —René Descartes,
     Letter to Princess Elisabeth

ANITA MATHIAS

I Was a Teen-Age Atheist

from *Commonweal*

Flames leaped into the horizon. My parents, my sister, Shalini, and I abandoned our dinner to race up to the terrace and watch the blaze. It was Holi, the Hindu spring festival, an explosion of mischief celebrating the god Krishna's shenanigans with the cowgirls. Flung water balloons gushed vermilion; water pistols squirted indigo. Stranger smeared stranger with silver paint stolen from construction sites. Buckets—dishwater? urine?—were emptied from high apartment windows onto passersby. Riotousness and devilry burst forth, a ripe sore.

Durga, our tiny, curly-haired cook, cycled into town and returned, panting with news. A procession of Hindus, chanting *bhajans,* statues of Shiva, god of destruction, hoisted on their shoulders, had marched past the mosque and forced a pig into it. Rumors of Muslim vengeance for this desecration flew round the town. "I won't tell you in front of the *chhota memsahibs,*" Durga said. The Hindus retaliated. Jamshedpur, my North Indian home town, was 82 percent Hindu and 11 percent Muslim. The fire engines were silent as Muslim slums, homes, and businesses burned.

Mesmerized by the flames zigzagging into the horizon, I sat on the parapet, my legs dangling over the edge. In the boredom of boarding school, I had read of front-page disasters wistfully—hurricanes, earthquakes, landslides, floods, war. But nothing happened, except in the movies. I was seventeen and had just graduated from Saint Mary's Convent, Nainital, a century-old boarding school in the Himalayas run by German and Irish nuns—staid, staid.

I gazed down: fire devouring houses, crashing rafters, distant screaming. The effect was hypnotic, as in a cinema rustling with peanut-crunching, betel-nut chewing, enthralled throngs. But these were not sound effects—I snapped out of reverie—these were real people, just like me, burning to death. Suddenly sickened, I ran downstairs and locked myself in my room.

The police slapped a curfew on the town: A glare, a curse, a flung stone could spark a riot. Police stood at every street corner, their rifles cocked. The market shut down. Home deliveries of bread and milk stopped. The cook sifted out insects to make *parathas* from old whole wheat flour. It was romantic in a way, the *Indian Family Robinson.*

The Hindu-Muslim riots held little personal terror: I was Roman Catholic. My forebears from Mangalore on the west coast of India were converted in the mid-sixteenth century by Portuguese missionaries, backed by the Inquisition. It was the prospect of boredom that bothered me. At the first hint of violence, libraries closed their stacks as too-easy targets for arsonists. Though we lived in faculty housing on the campus of Xavier Labor Relations Institute, a business school run by American Jesuits at which my father taught, it was impossible to get books. How would I get through curfew without them? A compulsive reader, I went through our bookshelves: *Jane Eyre, Wuthering Heights,* I had read them several times. I shrank from rereading *The Return of the Native, Far from the Madding Crowd,* or *The Mill on the Floss,* though I loved those "classics."

I settled down with the books I had not already read: Christian books. My father bought them at parish jumble sales as though there were virtue in the purchase. He never read them. To my surprise, I was fascinated. *The Cross and the Switchblade,* David Wilkerson's tale of Christ's radiance transforming young gangsters and drug addicts in New York City, and Catherine Marshall's

Beyond Ourselves were vivid accounts of Christ bursting into everyday life, setting it to music, making it sweet. This felt very different from the fossilized Catholicism forced on us at boarding school.

My childhood had been totally immersed in Catholicism—saints, angels, rosaries, novenas, litanies. It was punctuated with those rituals—baptism, first confession, first Communion, confirmation—that can so entwine themselves with the fabric of your spirit that to slough off Catholicism is to shiver in uncertainty. It's like stripping off your skin. As a child, I unquestioningly accepted Catholicism, and believed what I was taught; that it was the only true faith. *Extra ecclesiam nulla salus:* Outside the church, there is no salvation.

When I was eleven, I read through a compendium of *General Knowledge* during the winter school holiday and discovered a new passion: Greek mythology. I abandoned my stamp and postcard collections to read everything I could find on the enchanted universe of Greek gods and goddesses. Then, I chanced upon an idea that shattered my religious complacency.

I read that primitive men and women, often devastated by nature, imagined it was God. They worshiped the sun as Apollo; corn, fickle in blight or plenty, was Ceres; the raging sea, they imagined, was the mighty god Poseidon; the north wind, Boreas. Flabbergasted mortals elevated the forces of erratic, uncontrollable nature into gods to adore and placate. I understood. And was Catholicism any different from this awe-struck, foolish approach to nature? I doubted it.

I became an atheist and fed off the secret knowledge of intellectual superiority. How benighted they were, these parents, grandparents, priests, and nuns who ran our boarding school—they and their rattling rosary beads and boring Masses, their sprinklings of holy water from Lourdes, their relics, holy pictures, apparitions of the Virgin, prayers both to and for any good soul that left this earth. Just eleven, I knew better. I whispered to cronies, "I am an atheist," as one might confide, "I am a murderess."

Sister Hermine, our stern-faced, square-jawed German principal, summoned her rebellious charges to her office and, from her lowest desk drawer, slowly drew forth her strap—a thick strip of leather. She rarely had to use it. At the mere sight, the victim whimpered in terror and repentance. I was the only girl she had ever strapped, Sister Hermine often said, shaking her head. When I was sent to the principal's office to apologize for calling Miss Fernandes—a teacher who had maliciously and unfairly punished me—a Gorgon and a bitch, I clarified "No, I didn't call her a bitch. I said a witch," which seemed worse. Since I refused to recant (I meant what I'd said) I was struck on the calves with the strap and let off apologizing. Sister Hermine was ambivalent about breaking her students' wills. "What's the merit in taming lambs?" my father's brother, Theo Mathias, a Jesuit, asked her when she was close to expelling me. "But if you get a lion cub, and tame it into a lamb, isn't that something to be proud of?" Sister Hermine agreed.

Still, she would be unimpressed by an eleven-year-old atheist, I thought. Outwardly, I went through enforced Catholicism—daily Mass; Benediction: a cascade of hymns every Sunday evening; adoration: silent prayer before the Blessed Sacrament every first Sunday; confession, rosary, stations of the cross, and choir practices. Inwardly, I scoffed, and as the habit of confidence grew, I rebelled. I got my friends to join me in crawling out of the choir room while Sister Cecilia, behind the organ, warbled in a holy dream. I embedded the altar candles at Mass with the sulfurous heads of match sticks, reducing the girls who strained to catch the hiss, the sputter, the odor, to convulsive giggles.

When I turned fourteen—no longer one of the "babies," or the "middle set," but a "big girl," especially in my own estimation—I knocked on Sister Hermine's door and announced that I did not believe in Catholicism, or in God for that matter, so please, please, could I not *have* to be a Catholic, and—especially—not *have* to go to church?

"I'd much rather join the non-Catholics at 'silent occupation,'" I protested. The Hindus, Muslims, and Sikhs were allowed to read, study, paint, or embroider, provided they sat at their desks in perfect silence—oh, oasis!—while we, we went to church.

"Can't I just obey the Ten Commandments and not go to church?" I asked.

She was amused. "What are the Ten Commandments?"

I rattled them off from years of catechism, but stumbled over "Thou shalt not covet thy neighbor's wife." "See, you can't even say the Ten Commandments. How can you obey the Ten Commandments?" Sister Hermine laughed. "You have to be a Catholic now. Wait until you are twenty-one. Then decide."

And that was that. I got no support from my parents for my desire to officially "lapse." They detested adverse attention. You are a Catholic, my mother said, whether you like it or not. Seven years to go.

I became openly defiant. As president of the debating club, I chose subjects like "God is dead," and "religion is the opiate of the people," speaking for the motion, annoying the nuns. My favorite writers were Matthew Arnold and Thomas Hardy. (I was not aware that doubt had a more modern face.) I embraced Hardy's bleak Learian vision—"As flies to wanton boys are we to the gods; they kill us for their sport"—his absent or malign god.

Still, the vanishing of God left a vacuum which was filled by restlessness, unhappiness, and puzzlement about the purpose of life. Like Ivan in *The Brothers Karamazov,* I concluded that if there was no God, there was also no immutable moral law, nothing intrinsically right or wrong. There was no one to reward goodness or punish wrongdoing in this world, and there was no world to come. So one could do whatever one wanted or, at least, whatever one could get away with.

I shared my new philosophy with my friends. We formed a gang, "the bandits," and our first exploit was our daily raids on Modern Store which catered to rich kids from the four expensive boarding schools in Nainital, and to the tourists and honeymooners who swamped the Himalayan resort. Kaye, Savneet, Bella, and I strolled into the store wearing the baggy sweaters of our convent uniform, designed to disguise nubile figures. We stuffed Cadbury's chocolate, Mills and Boon romances, stickers, cards, nail polish, and costume jewelry into our sleeves and up our sweaters. When our desks overflowed, the nuns noticed, made inquiries, then pounced on us. We were marched back to the shop with our booty and forced to apologize: "We are sorry, 'Mr. Modern.'"

Furious, I debated with my class teacher, the fiery, Irish Sister Josephine, through a long summer evening. Perched on a piano in the music room (a sacrilege), I argued that if "Mr. Modern" overcharged us all year, it was okay to even things occasionally by "swacking" from him. Her beautiful brown eyes kindled. "The Bible says . . ." she began. But I did not believe the Bible was "the Word of God," indisputable.

But at the same time—secretly—I began to crave a moral framework. How easy choice can be when there are absolutes, a road map through the maze of decisions. How wearying to thrash out the morality of every case, every time, all by yourself. I wished I could believe.

"You are experiencing an Augustinian restlessness," Sister Josephine said, quoting the saint: "Thou hast made us for Thyself, O Lord, and our hearts are restless until they rest in you." Pascal, she said, wrote of the "God-shaped vacuum" only God could fill. And I was God-bitten. Atheism is closer to faith than indifference is.

I was nicknamed "the naughtiest girl in school" after an Enid Blyton heroine. But being a rebel wasn't really fun despite its jaunty aura. If I could have been "good," I would have. When the nuns predicted a conversion experience for me, I feared it. I wanted it. Their naughtiest girls often become the "holiest," they claimed. For was not Saint Augustine a rake, and Saint Francis a playboy, and, as for Saint Mary Magdalen . . . ?

When we were to be confirmed, I was eleven. Sister Magdalene, an enormous, squint-eyed British nun, persuaded me to take her name. "Mary Magdalen was a notorious sinner who became very holy. Take her name, and she will ask God to give you the grace of a great conversion," she said. The old story—flamboyant rebellion later swinging to passionate devotion. I did not ask "Maggie" why she compared me to a supposed prostitute, harbor to seven demons. I composed scandalous poems about the nuns: "Sister Secunda eloped with a *gunda,*" a bandit. I ran away from school with Micky, the school sheepdog. In revenge for being sent out of class, I locked my teacher and classmates into the classroom throughout an afternoon. Such things were surely wicked. But too awkward, alas, too "nice," to refuse Sister Magdalene, I became Anita Mary Magdalene Mathias, adopting that stodgy, dated name I hated. The classic coming-to-faith trajectory had its appeal. I wondered if the "Mary Magdalen" might prove prophetic. Would I suddenly turn "good," perhaps even, in a blaze of glory, become "a great saint"?

I might convert like Paul. A bullet of hatred, galloping to Damascus to kill and destroy, he is struck off his horse and glimpses divinity. "Saul, Saul, it is hard for you to kick against the goad." "Who are you, Lord?" "I am Jesus whom you persecute." His life acquires a purpose: "the surpassing greatness of knowing Jesus Christ, my Lord." "For me to live is Christ, to die is gain," he writes. How wonderful, I thought, to convert just like that, your life transformed—but I lacked both belief and an object of devotion.

Father Clement Campos and Father Ivo Fernandes, handsome Redemptorist priests with twangy-voiced charm, preached our annual retreats: an aesthetic delight, days of hymns and silences, resounding oratory, and prayer by candlelight led by a luscious male voice. And every year we, who from March to December rarely saw a man except the chaplain, developed monstrous, predictable crushes.

"And is anyone here an atheist?" the priest asked provocatively on the first retreat evening as he polled our group of Catholics, Hindus, Muslims, Sikhs, Jains, Buddhists—and atheists. And every year, I raised my hand.

For the next week, they worked on me—private conferences and counseling, private prayers for healing from whatever trauma brought me, a Catholic girl of good family, to this strange pass. A foot away from the man's animated brown eyes, how easy conversion seemed; how it would please this appealing priest.

"Get up at 5 A.M. tomorrow," the priest said, "and sit alone. Watch the sun rise on those snow-tipped mountains and ask yourself, 'Could this grandeur come to be by accident?'" So I raised my eyes to the Himalayas, waiting to be surprised by faith. Gazing up at the mountains, I thought, as I was expected to— "Maybe, maybe. . . ." But back down in the valley, any belief born of eloquence and hormones left with the good-looking priest.

Still, I was fertile soil at seventeen as I read the Bible while confined to the house during those Hindu-Muslim riots. On the patio where I sat reading, the sun, a ball of vermilion fire, sank beneath the emerald fortress of trees, lit by the orange-crimson flowers of the Flame of the Forest and the red and yellow Royal Poinciana. I continued reading after dusk by the glow of a kerosene lamp. Was Jesus Christ who the New Testament claimed he was: the God who made and loves us, the creator of the universe, cornerstone and crux of human history, the zigzag of the jigsaw that makes sense of everything else?

Paul says, "He is the image of the invisible God. All things were created by him and for him . . . and in him all things hold together."

And Jesus asked them, "Who do you say that I am?" And Peter answered, "You are the Christ, the son of the Living God."

Who do you say that I am? Who do you say that I am? Driven by an inchoate hunger, I read and reread the New Testament, my thirst growing even as it was quenched. Gradually, my cherished objections—the lack of scientific proof; the myth-like aspects of virgin birth and a Christ resurrected from the dead; that Christianity was the credulity of fishermen given form and credibility by Paul's sophisticated intellect—crumbled like clay gods. No, this was not mythology. It differed from the tales of Mount Kailash, Mount Olympus, and Asgard that I had devoured. It differed in the sense of, well, holiness. It had the taste of truth. Jesus' words sang in me like music, like poetry. I found myself praying, "Lord, I believe. Help thou my unbelief."

I gradually surrendered the intellectual high ground of cold reason: What I do not see with my eyes, or feel with my hands, I will not believe. I could not spar against the Christ I apprehended dimly—I who did not understand cars, or logarithms, or tides, or love. It's possible the Gospels are true, I conceded. It's plausible. Intellect can bring you to the brink of belief. Faith is the missing link. I believed: in a leap of the heart as rationally inexplicable as the leap from affection to love. For like love, faith is the heart's knowledge. "Lord," I prayed. "I believe. You are the living God. I will follow you, wherever you lead. I will do your will insofar as you make it clear to me what it is." I did not quail at this largesse, this scattering of blank checks. I did not add, "but be merciful,

Lord. Be sensible." With an air of adventure, of rusty doors wrenched from their sockets, revealing fresh vistas, I prayed: "Show me, Lord. What should I do?"

I would dedicate my life to Christ, I decided. How then should I live? "A life of love!" How exactly, I did not know, but, being seventeen, I wanted to do something dramatic and do it swiftly. "I want to be a pen in God's hands," I wrote in my journal, "picked up and used, leaving light where I have written."

My first impulse, to fly off from Jamshedpur to help David Wilkerson of *The Cross and the Switchblade* in his work with teen drug addicts and gangsters in Harlem, wasn't exactly practical. While casting about for a vocation, I volunteered in the Cheshire Home for physically handicapped and mentally retarded children, on the outskirts of Jamshedpur. Here, in the postage stamp of my world, I tried to practice the kindness at the heart of Christianity, without which words are noisy gongs, ardor and alms worth little. I lived with the Vincent de Paul nuns and was captivated by their life of prayer, quiet work, and silences. "How beautiful this serene life is, governed by the pealing of bells," I wrote in my journal. "Scaling inward mountains—lovelier by far than a life of distraction, worries, gossip, and moneymaking, a life inimical to the spirit."

Catholic children brought up by nuns or priests brace themselves against a vocation: a tap on the shoulder, inward marching orders, an imperative you can ignore, but at the cost of your soul. At some time, we all think we've caught it: That's it, we are the chosen of God, chosen for a lonely, lovely way, another bride of Christ.

Now, I began, obsessively, to wonder if I had a religious vocation. God was the only thing that was real, I kept reminding myself, and all else—college, marriage, career, social life, money—was vanity. I wanted to find a way to live, always, close to Christ, tasting his joy and peace. Surely leaving "the world," becoming a nun, was the only way to do that.

While at the Cheshire Home, I read Edward Le Joly's *Servant of Love* about Mother Teresa's congregation, the Missionaries of Charity. How utterly radical they were in their following of Christ, I thought, as I read of their austere life, stripped down to essentials. They owned but two saris, a Bible, and no more than could fit into a bucket—their "suitcase" when they traveled. How seductive to slough off everything, to live deep in the embrace of Christ, the creator of the universe, friend sufficient for every need. Wow! Without training, with impetuosity, they plunged into all manner of human misery, their reach widening year by year, their mandate simply to serve "the poorest of the poor," defined broadly: lepers in Yemen, shut-ins in Melbourne, crazed drug addicts in New York, freezing homeless people in London, orphans in Peru, tramps near the Vatican, the dying destitute in Calcutta. The energy of it all and, unconsciously, I guess, the prospect of adventure dazzled me. They did just what Christ commanded, I thought, impressed: I was hungry and you gave me something to eat, I was sick and you looked after me. Whatsoever you do to the least of my brethren, that you do unto me. I felt an inner push, a shove toward this congregation, so literal in its imitation of Christ.

In a burst of headstrong lucidity, I sloughed off the destiny my parents had mapped for me: college, followed by (an arranged) marriage. No, I would become a Missionary of Charity. I would help those unable to help themselves. I would feed constantly off the light and joy of Jesus. The notion glowed.

Minutes after I'd returned from the Cheshire Home, full of bright decision, I announced it to my parents. I left the room swiftly as I saw my father's face freeze. My mother followed me. "Go and see your father." The muscles of his face worked. There were tears on his cheeks. "Why must you bounce from one extreme to another?" he asked. "You've always found it impossible to conform. In the convent, 'It's yours not to reason why.' It will be a life of exhausting manual work. Mother Teresa recruits simple women from the villages and you're an intellectual snob. You'll have nothing in common with them. Your mind will atrophy. You will be bored!

"However, if you are sure that God is calling you to this . . ." he acquiesced eventually. "But go slow. Be sure. Wait." Wait! "I will not wait," I said. "I will call them today. I have heard my vocation."

I left for the convent that August, feeling, with the naiveté of late adolescence, holier already, as if the Christian's life task of "being conformed to the image of Christ" could be accomplished in a dramatic grab for holiness, and showy, though worthy, doing would speed the slow, almost imperceptible process of transformation called sanctification. I grew. I grew through the next two years, through the aspirancy, postulancy, and novitiate. I grew through work in the orphanage, with the mentally retarded and the dying destitute; through prayer and Scripture study; through friendships and conflicts and the "testing of vocations," and through the tears and humiliation. And I grew through sickness and exhaustion that never let up, and eventually made the whole enterprise untenable, and which, after I left, was diagnosed as tuberculosis.

I left the convent sadly, with a sense of falling off, to study English as an undergraduate at Oxford University, to go to graduate school in creative writing in America, and later to forge myself into a writer as a faculty wife in suburban America—the less poetic path. I still see Christ as the wisdom that created the universe. I still see following him as the sanest way to live, a way I am committed to. The Christian imperatives which Jesus with his

Gordian-knot-slashing directness reduced to two—to love God mightily and to love your neighbor as yourself—remain the same. There is just more distraction. The traditional monastic disciplines—prayer, meditation, adoration, the beautiful liturgy of the hours, and "spiritual reading"—served to draw one's thoughts back to Christ, the breadth and depth of his love, and his enabling grace. It now takes ingenuity to carve for myself a circle of silence to feed on Scripture and the transforming presence of Christ it houses, and to live contemplatively, mindful of Jesus not only amid the beauty and tranquillity of my garden, my writing, and my books, but amid a child's cries and crankiness, the crucible of marriage, and the haste and busyness which haunts America as poverty haunts India. Nurturing two young children, creating a loving family life, running a peaceful household—the demands to give of oneself are constant, without the convent's periodic sanctioned escape into the sacred ivory spaces of psalmody and song. In fact, I now consider domesticity, marriage, and motherhood a smithy in which the soul can be forged as painfully, as beautifully, as amid the splendid virginal solitudes of the convent.

haste + busyness [handwritten margin note]

WILLIAM MAXWELL

The Education of Her Majesty the Queen

from *DoubleTake*

Once upon a time, when airplanes couldn't be counted on always to rise into the air and the motorcar was still a novelty, there was a princess who married a commoner. Reluctantly her father put aside his expectations for her—she was intelligent and capable and would have made a wise and popular queen—and named his nephew, whom he did not like, as his heir apparent. The Princess was obliged to live on her husband's salary, though if she had married the ruler of no matter how small a state or principality, Parliament would have voted an annual stipend sufficient for her every comfort. Fortunately her husband had a salary, but this had its unfortunate side, for it meant that he was in trade, a thing which it would take several generations for the family to live down, and meanwhile she and her husband were not invited to houses where they would have been most welcome if they had been living at the expense of the Nation.

The house they lived in was hardly bigger than a cottage, and no one who was at all knowledgeable would have considered that one ill-tempered old woman in the kitchen and a lame man to clean the stable and fill the woodbox twice a day was keeping an establishment. But the Princess never tired of the view from her bedroom window, which was of a pond with geese on it, and willow trees. And if she found herself doing things that formerly were done for her, she did not mind. To gain her father's consent to her marrying, and the consent of Parliament as well, had required a great deal of obstinacy on her part, from time to time the shedding of tears, and even a certain amount of what in other circumstances would have been described as blackmail, and she did not care to give anyone an excuse for saying I told you so. To tell the truth, she did not by ordinary standards have much to complain of, and when she did allow herself to complain it was always to her husband and always about her mother.

She was an only child, and because the Queen did not have any other sons and daughters to visit or offer advice to, she came rather oftener than was tactful and sometimes she came rather earlier in the morning than it was convenient to receive her. The Princess, having kissed her husband good-bye and lingered over her second cup of coffee, would start to make the bed and empty the slop jar, and before she had done either one there would be a noise outside of carriage wheels and horses' hooves and she would peer out of the bedroom window just in time to see a footman in the palace livery jump down from the box and open the door of the royal coach, and Her Majesty would emerge from the cavernous gilt interior dressed as for a levee and with a little black boy to hold up her train, at a quarter of nine in the morning. Though the Queen was never alone from the moment she woke up or even at night, when she had to ignore the majestic snores beside her in order to fall asleep herself, she was lonely and missed her daughter. So she came and sat on a rickety chair in the tiny bedroom, and when the Princess put clean sheets on the bed the Queen would say, not in criticism, really, "You shouldn't have to do that"—for she had never lived anywhere but in a palace, with a staff of hundreds to dust and sweep, to light the fires and make the beds and polish the silver and wash the crystal chandeliers in soapy water and keep up appearances, and she judged everything from this rather special point of view.

Whether the Princess was hanging out the clothes or making an Easter cake or sewing a button on her husband's shirt, it was the same, so far as the Queen was concerned—for having always had someone to do these things for her, she could not help feeling that there was something improper about doing them for oneself. And when the babies started coming and the Princess nursed them, the Queen would shake her head commiseratingly and say, "You shouldn't have to do that. I had a wet nurse for you, and I am told that many women give their babies a bottle," and afterward she would complain to His Majesty that the Princess had been short with her.

Though the Princess had cut herself off from the line of succession by marrying a commoner, she continued to be universally admired. Her children grew up healthy and handsome, with, for the most part, A's on their report cards, and they never hesitated to bring their friends home—a thing that would not have been permitted if they had lived in a palace—and before the family sat down to a meal somebody always had to count noses. The Princess's husband had the look of a contented man and everything he put his hand to turned out well. Before long, instead of complaining to her ladies-in-waiting about the cramped quarters her daughter was living in, the Queen now complained about the stairs, and the way her grandchildren left their boots and cricket bats and clothing all over three floors of a rather large town house. Though she was not a stupid woman, she nevertheless had the feeling that in a properly run household toys did not stay in the middle of the living-room floor for people to trip over but reverted to the toy chest when children were tired of playing with them, and petticoats and dresses, of their own accord, either ended up hanging from a hook or a rod in the closet or found their way to the laundress.

When she first noticed a gray hair among the Princess's dark brown tresses, the Queen not only was disturbed by this not uncommon misfortune but attributed it to the fact that her daughter *would* do things that she should have allowed other people

to do for her, though there were no other people but the ill-
tempered cook and the lame man—the one now quite old indeed
and deaf and half blind, so that she had to cook mostly by feel,
and the other too feeble to keep the woodbox filled and clean out
the stable and so he would bring his grandson to do it for him.
On days when neither the lame old man nor the boy showed up,
the Princess cleaned out the stable and filled the woodbox herself.
Her hands were reddened from housework and she lost the soft
look that people have who are continually waited on, but she was
a fine-looking woman, with a proud carriage and a light in her eye
that only those have who have managed to live exactly the life
they wanted to live. Still, her mother went on saying, "You
shouldn't have to do that," in a voice more than faintly tinged
with sympathy, and the Princess eased her feelings by saying afterward to her husband, "I would love to know what she thinks I
ought to be doing."

But naturally she knew the answer, which was: being a
princess, being waited on. In the royal palace everything, or so it
appeared, was taken care of by some chamberlain or lord-of-the-
bedchamber or lady-in-waiting or flunky in livery—with one exception, and that exception was perhaps an oversight: there was
no one to attend to the ill or the dying. The court doctor came
and prescribed emetics and repeated bleeding, after which the
personage grew much weaker and deathly pale from the loss of
blood. And rumor of what was happening spread through the
palace, and both the courtiers and the servants, fearing that they
would lose their place at court, were so busy currying favor with
probable successors that the invalid's slop jar went unemptied and
his sheets unchanged.

When the Queen took sick, the King was out of the country
on affairs of state. He sent ambassadors daily to inquire about her
condition, when it would have been much better if he had come

himself. The Princess left her house in the charge of her oldest daughter and went every day to the palace to look after her mother. The Queen was indeed grateful to have her. And when her daughter brought her a tray with a nourishing soup she had made the night before or fluffed up her pillows or drew the curtains to shut out the glare, she said in a weak voice, "You shouldn't have to do this." She said it largely out of habit, for by this time it was reasonably clear that if the Princess did not do these things for her mother, nobody else would. On the last morning of her life, the Queen opened her mouth to say something and the Princess, who was sitting at her bedside, holding her hand, bent down closer, expecting to hear the tiresome words once more. Instead, with an effort, her mother said, "It seems that nobody can die for me. I have to do it all by myself." She stopped, seeing that her daughter's eyes had filled with tears. When two tears ran down the Princess's cheeks, the Queen reached out and wiped the tears away, lovingly, with her hand. It was the first time in her life she had been moved to do something for somebody else, and she died quite happy.

The End of Growth

from *Mother Jones*

I am, perhaps like most Americans, Guruphobic. Bhagwans, swamis, saffron-robed saints of every sort leave me cold. I can find out the truth for myself, dammit—isn't that the point of having a library card? And so it was a novel experience for me to sit in an ashram in a fog-swept corner of Marin County, California, talking with a man named Eknath Easwaran, whose followers sat by the dozens watching our interview, nodding at each of his statements, beaming at him. I felt a long way from the little Methodist church that serves as home page for my ill-defined faith.

And yet it was a thrill. Partly because I'd read most of Easwaran's calm and wise books over the years, and even tried to follow his commonsense advice on how to meditate. But even more because, as a young man, Easwaran had visited Gandhi at his ashram in central India, had walked with him in the late-afternoon heat, and in certain ways had his life changed. I would come no closer to Gandhi than this.

"I have gone for walks with him, and none of us could keep his pace," Easwaran told me. "He walks like the sandpiper on the beach. The wave can never catch him." That lightness marks every picture of Gandhi. He is skin and bones, wearing almost nothing, usually smiling with amusement. He looks, literally, as if he might blow away. Certainly he was the frailest-looking leader of recent times, and certainly he was among the toughest. "The first time I went to see Gandhiji, I joined a small group waiting outside his cottage, where a meeting had been taking place the whole day," said Easwaran. "I expected someone very irascible, and then the door opened and there came out a teenager in his 60s, looking as though he had been spending the whole time playing bingo. That really struck a deep chord in me."

That lightness, of course, did not come from playing; it came from the hard work of renunciation. Gandhi gave up the passion for sex, for money and possessions, for distraction, for comfort. He renounced, at root, the right to put himself first, choosing instead to live for others.

An American journalist once asked him, "Can you tell me the secret of your life in three words?"

"Yes," chuckled Gandhi. "Renounce and enjoy."

Very few large questions survive the gory politics of the 20th century. Fascism has no intellectual defenders (though of course, in its many forms, it has innumerable ammunition-toting practitioners); the various Marxist creeds have dried up and blown away. Some form of liberal capitalism, pushed by a global marketing machine, holds sway in most places, though tattered by the regular collapse of emerging economies. The giant figures of the dwindling century are still giants, but they are stable and fixed in our minds: Hitler, the archetype of pure evil; Lenin, that of ideological fixation; and FDR, an icon of triumphant pragmatism.

Of the century's household names, only Gandhi's, I think, remains in flux. What is his legacy? Nonviolence? In a sense, though even his native India seems to have utterly repudiated his example by firing off nuclear weapons last year. I think he must be measured more by his idea that a deep moral sense might provide an alternative to politics as usually practiced. His call for moral perfectibility—for a radical, renouncing humility—seems to have been even more completely rebuffed by history. Since his time, we have grown to embrace consumption as the one true creed.

Yet his example remains intriguingly full of possibility—there is the sense that perhaps we haven't followed his ideas far enough to see if they really do run into some dead end, or whether they might open whole new passages. He is the one great figure that has not yet been balanced in the checkbook of our century, the one big loose end. And that idea of renunciation—un-American as it sounds—lies near the center of it all.

Since Gandhi seems increasingly a romantic figure, we need to remember that for many years this sandpiper was near the heart of the world's affairs. He not only drove the British from India, he also began the attack on the logic of apartheid in South Africa and on the legitimacy of colonialism the world around. Within India he launched the (still-unfinished) battle for the full civil rights of the most oppressed, the Hindu untouchables.

Even after his death, though Nehru and his dynasty paid only lip service to the Mahatma's ideas as they strove to Westernize the subcontinent, others kept the faith. Vinoba Bhave led the Gram-dan movement, walking the length and breadth of the country trying to persuade whole villages to own their land in common. He met with real successes, as did another Gandhi lieutenant, Jayaprakash Narayan, who led the opposition to Indira Gandhi (no relation) and her autocratic rule. The Chipko, or tree-hugging, movement of northern India, the farmworker protests of California's Central Valley, the civil rights movement launched by Martin Luther King Jr.—all owed explicit debts to Gandhi's ideas, strategies, and examples. Sit-ins, "going limp," boycotts: These were tactics inspired by the Indian satyagrahis. In South Africa, where Gandhi had begun his work, his influence lingered through the antiapartheid fights; in the Middle East, teams of Mennonite Christians intercede between Jews and Arabs in tense towns like Hebron; Witness for Peace volunteers have traveled to

Central America to try to shine some outside light on dark places. "One tends to find the events and people who make up the as-yet-untold narrative of nonviolence tucked away in apparently unrelated corners," writes Gandhian scholar Michael Nagler. "You must somehow run across these events and people and hold their story together with the glue of your own insight."

But if one is being honest, one must say this: A Gandhian style of politics does not remotely come close to controlling any corner of the earth. It is principally a method of the fringes, of the pro-testers, and even there it competes with the various time-honored techniques of violence and scapegoating. What dominates the planet's politics, of course, is money, especially the pursuit of a global consumer culture. And that consumer culture comes with an ideology all its own. Instead of the debate that raged through most of modernity—between the idea that you need to change people in order to create a benign system (Gandhi's view) or change systems to allow the good in people to flourish (the Marx-ist idea)—we've come of age under a new idea so powerful it has blown those other two away.

The appeal of laissez-faire capitalism, as it spread around the world until it vanquished even the Soviets, was simple: You needed neither a change in structures nor a change in human nature. In-stead, the bad side of human nature—the greed, competitiveness, and materialism that so bothered Gandhi—could be counted on to magically produce wealth, wealth enough that many people could actually enjoy the easy life that the utopians and commis-sars could only promise. That is the revolutionary idea of our time, and it has cast into a sepia shadow the two earlier ideas; both Gandhi and Lenin seem distant now. We distrust moralizing as thoroughly as we distrust government; in a cynical age, our ul-timate trust is in the notion that trust is unnecessary, that we should each simply advance our own cause.

And it should be said that this approach has yielded more fruit than the others—certainly more than the horror show that was communism, probably more than all the good works inspired by Gandhi. With all the more-necessary-than-ever caveats about the gross inequality the market has created, it is nonetheless true that global capitalism has lifted living standards in many places, lengthened lives, improved nutrition, broadened education. It may have ended forever the argument between the moralist and the revolutionary, replacing them both with the logic of the cash register and the trading floor.

Or maybe not. The "problem" that unrestrained global capitalism seems to solve with such power is the problem of how to make things grow. Making economies larger, making harvests bigger, producing more stuff. By and large, demand really has created supply, and it may well have done it much better than the Gandhian method, which would be: "Share. And don't want so much anyway."

But what if the problem of the 21st century presents itself in a different form? Newspapers are full of crises: the worst drought in 30 years across the mid-Atlantic, the highest summer temperatures on record across Russia, and the second straight year of wild floods along the Yangtze. All these problems—and a thousand more—can plausibly be laid to growth, and to global warming in particular. Our fossil fuels raise the atmospheric temperature, and since warm air holds more water than cold, we see increases in evaporation and precipitation, drought and deluge. Scientists report that 1998 was the warmest year in recorded history; that spring now comes a week earlier across the Northern Hemisphere; that even the salinity of the oceans is changing as melting glaciers gush forth freshwater into the sea. Our growth now alters every physical system on the planet's surface, and those above it as well.

In December 1997, the world's nations met in Kyoto, Japan, to talk about this climatic change. They began with a few hard facts, physical and political, on the table. First, there is only so much atmosphere in which to dump the byproducts of our growth. Second, the planet's population is expected to grow by 50 percent in the next 50 years, to 9 or 10 billion. And most of those people will be poor, and will want to live better.

So the debate, for all its technicalities, is pretty clear. Rich countries, and therefore rich people, need to use far less fossil fuels, thereby costing themselves some money. And they will have to transfer money and technology to poor countries, to help them build alternative energy systems. If we don't—well, China and India have enough cheap coal in their mines to boost the atmosphere's carbon content by half in the next century.

Many other environmental problems—from deforestation to the depletion of fisheries—come down to the same basic point. If you have to take care of more people, and if endless growth is becoming less desirable—well, then, the problem might become how to share.

Here's an image I've had in my head for a long time: A long line of white-robed saints and gurus and cranks stretches back down through the ages, at least to the Buddha. Jesus is there, and St. Francis, and Thoreau, and Gandhi—all the people we've theoretically revered and mostly ignored. They are asking us to change, and to do it for spiritual or moral reasons. To make our lives more perfect. We ignore them because change is too hard and because we like being human, especially those of us on top.

Their line is joined by another of men and women in white lab coats. Scientists, physicists, ecologists. This rank is much shorter;

it stretches back just a decade or two. They, too, are asking us to change, but for quite practical reasons having to do with higher temperatures, ultraviolet levels, and the rate of species extinction. Forget aesthetics—they'd like us to live more simply because the amount of carbon in each cubic liter of atmosphere is growing much too fast.

I have tried, sporadically, to meditate following the advice in Easwaran's simple and lovely book, *Meditation*. In it he urges novices not to go beyond half an hour, for fear they may "plunge deeply inward" to a world of emotion and psychology they are not yet prepared to handle. For me this has never been a problem. I may be the planet's worst meditator, unable to calm my mind for more than a few seconds before some thought, commentary, plan, slogan, or accolade pops up on my screen. My mind chatters on with its stuff even as I'm trying slowly to repeat the inspirational passages that Easwaran recommends in his writings, fragments from all the world's scriptures and many of its gurus. One of the most encouraging of those passages—included in Easwaran's book *God Makes the Rivers to Flow*—is from Gandhi himself:

> I know the path: it is straight and narrow
> It is like the edge of a sword.
> I rejoice to walk on it.
> I weep when I slip.
> God's word is: "He who strives never perishes."
> I have implicit faith in that promise.
> Though, therefore, from my weakness I fail a thousand times,
> I shall not lose faith.

What does it mean to walk that straight and narrow edge? If it means to follow the set of ascetic disciplines that marked Gandhi's life, then the kind of politics I have been calling Gandhian is not a politics at all, but an almost athletic endeavor that will be confined to the monasteries and ashrams. As George Orwell pointed out in his ambivalent elegy for Gandhi, "Many people do not wish to be saints," especially if sainthood involves giving up sex with your spouse or, after St. Francis, grinding ashes into your food so it will taste worse. But are there disciplines—real *disciplines*—that might be adopted by enough people in this time and this place to make some kind of actual difference in the affairs of the world? In the temperature of the planet?

Easwaran's ashram has produced one book that really reached a mass audience: *Laurel's Kitchen,* a vegetarian volume that sits next to *The Moosewood Cookbook* on a million kitchen shelves. Eating lower on the food chain is a discipline of sorts—it means rearranging the logic you grew up with. And if large numbers of people practiced it, some of the pressure on the world's farms and fields would ease; we'd be growing more grain for our bodies and less for our cows. For many people—as indeed for Gandhi—changing the ways they eat is the first step in changing other patterns, the first step toward some deeper politics. Gandhi would have agreed with the '60s credo that the personal is the political, but he would have giggled at the notion that "liberation," that "doing your own thing," was the way out. Renunciation! It sounds so nasty, like some purgative to force down your throat, some syrup of ipecac for a consumer world. But it's an idea that may slowly be starting to acquire a new valence.

It's easy enough to sneer at the "voluntary simplicity" movement, the quietly spreading notion that we might want to reduce the quantity of getting and spending in our lives. In many of its manifestations, it's not much more than the latest affectation from Northern California or Vermont, an excuse to acquire a whole new set of stuff (quilts!) or to feel holier-than-thou. Still, the spread of the simplicity idea is enormously interesting, precisely because it comes from the richest parts of the rich world.

The problem with protest politics has always been that it's easier to organize the oppressed than the oppressors. The former have only to throw off their fear; the latter have to discard their habits. And yet it is not unheard of. I've spent time in the southern Indian province of Kerala, a state of 30 million people. There, in the 1930s, under the deep influence of Gandhi, many Brahmans began renouncing their privileges and giving up their lands. Not all, by any means, but not just a few either. The result has been a state with some of the most equal wealth distribution on earth, and a place where—despite an annual income per capita of $222—both the average life expectancy and the literacy rate approach our own.

So it is possible to imagine, at any rate, that what begins in Marin might have some wider effect, that renunciation might spread. But only if it actually makes people happier than the alternative, the consumer culture we all grew up in. Renunciation seems like such a joyless word. But remember that Gandhi's secret for living was "Renounce and enjoy!" Here is the secret reason that some people in the rich world have begun to get rid of some of their stuff, move to smaller homes, eat lower on the food chain, ride bikes, reduce their expenses, and scale back their careers: If you can simplify your life, and it requires a certain minimal affluence to do so, then you can have more fun than your neighbors.

This was not always so. For a long time in our lives, materialism was more fun. Why? Because we didn't have much stuff. We lived on the farm or in the slum, we lived through the Depression, our material lives were pretty bleak. Each new thing added some comfort, some convenience. And in most of the world it still does—in those Keralite villages, a chair is still a luxury in most huts. But here, among the middle and upper classes, we've reached a saturation point where new things no longer provide an added increment of pleasure. You can sit in only one chair at a time. The hours of work required to pay for a slightly better chair aren't worth it. Our food is rich, our wines pungent, our clothes luxe.

In fact, more of the same threatens to overwhelm our lives. In a 1998 poll, only 28 percent of respondents said they usually felt "joyful" at the end of the holiday season. Why? Because the holidays we celebrate developed in a different age, when a pile of shiny stuff really turned us on, when holiday shopping was an adventure. But we have, by now, so much stuff that our main worry is where on earth to put it all. More packages don't do it for us.

What does come increasingly as a thrill, I think, are those things that money can't buy. Time, chief of all. In their hugely popular book, *Your Money or Your Life,* Vicki Robin and Joe Dominguez asserted that "money is simply something you trade life energy for." Their suggestion: Trade as little time as necessary to make your living, mostly by cutting back on expenses. Their followers, saving their pennies and buying bonds, retire years before the rest of us, to spend an extra hour at the breakfast table sipping some, yes, herbal tea, and then volunteering with a youth group or hiking or gardening or whatever it is that makes their lives whole. They "renounced"—the boat, the big vacation home, the cruise, whatever it was. They enjoyed.

Say this notion kept spreading. Might it lead, even theoretically, to a new kind of polities? We are in a period of almost unbelievable affluence in the rich world. Not evenly shared, obviously, but unbelievable nonetheless. As the parents of the boomers pass away, something like $10 trillion will pour into the hands of their children. That money can be spent pursuing more of the same. The average home, which has doubled in size since World War II even as the number of its occupants has shrunk, can double again.

Or it can be used to make the transition to a less hectic life, one in which we don't work too many hours, don't fit the rest of life in around the edges, don't try (and increasingly fail) to meet our emotional needs with more buying.

Sooner or later we will face the problem of stasis. Having grown as large as we can both in numbers and in appetites, we will need a different idea to balance our economies, our politics, our individual lives. *The thing that comes after growth is elusive.* It's as elusive for the left as for the right and the center, all of whom believed for most of this century that "more" was the answer and differed mainly on the means.

The rest of the advice of the 20th century is used up, like bubble gum that's lost its flavor. Some of that advice—Lenin's, say—was pretty bad to begin with. Some was pretty good, though it seems now to be leading us into box canyons. But we've barely begun to chew over Gandhi's advice. It may be too strong for us in the end. Yet if we're going to keep our species' impact on the planet in check, I'm not sure I can think of a politics other than Gandhi's that offers much promise.

ROBERT MORGAN

Family Bible

from *Image*

The leather of the book is soft
and black as that of Grandma's purse,
brought west by horse and wagon, kept
on mantel shelf and closet plank.
The red dye on the edge has faded.
The marriages recorded, births
and deaths set down in pencil and
in many inks and hands, with names
and middle names and different dates
and spellings scrawled in berry juice
that looks like ancient blood. And blood
is what the book's about, the blood
of sacrifice and blood of lamb,
two testaments of blood, and blood
of families set in names to show
the course and merging branches, roots
of fluid in your veins this moment.
You open crackly pages thin
as film of river birch and read
the law of blood and soar of blood
in print of word and print of thumb.

RICHARD JOHN NEUHAUS

Born Toward Dying

from *First Things*

We are born to die. Not that death is the purpose of our being born, but we are born toward death, and in each of our lives the work of dying is already underway. The work of dying well is, in largest part, the work of living well. Most of us are at ease in discussing what makes for a good life, but we typically become tongue-tied and nervous when the discussion turns to a good death. As children of a culture radically, even religiously, devoted to youth and health, many find it incomprehensible, indeed offensive, that the word "good" should in any way be associated with death. Death, it is thought, is an unmitigated evil, the very antithesis of all that is good.

Death is to be warded off by exercise, by healthy habits, by medical advances. What cannot be halted can be delayed, and what cannot forever be delayed can be denied. But all our progress and all our protest notwithstanding, the mortality rate holds steady at 100 percent.

Death is the most everyday of everyday things. It is not simply that thousands of people die every day, that thousands will die this day, although that too is true. Death is the warp and woof of existence in the ordinary, the quotidian, the way things are. It is the horizon against which we get up in the morning and go to bed at night, and the next morning we awake to find the horizon has drawn closer. From the twelfth-century *Enchiridion Leonis* comes the nighttime prayer of children of all ages: "Now I lay me down to sleep, I pray thee Lord my soul to keep; if I should die before I wake, I pray thee Lord my soul to take." Every going to sleep is a little death, a rehearsal for the real thing.

Such is the generality, the warp and woof of everyday existence with which the wise have learned to live. But then our wisdom is shattered, not by a sudden awareness of the generality but by the singularity of *a* death—by the death of someone we love with a love inseparable from life. Or it is shattered by the imminent prospect of our own dying. With the cultivated complacency of the mass murderer that he was, Josef Stalin observed, "One death is a tragedy; a million deaths is a statistic." The generality is a buffer against both guilt and sorrow. It is death in the singular that shatters all we thought we knew about death. It is death in the singular that turns the problem of death into the catastrophe of death. Thus the lamentation of Dietrich von Hildebrand: "I am filled with disgust and emptiness over the rhythm of everyday life that goes relentlessly on—as though nothing had changed, as though I had not lost my precious beloved!"

It used to be said that the Victorians of the nineteenth century talked incessantly about death but were silent about sex, whereas today we talk incessantly about sex and are silent about death. In 1973, Ernest Becker's *The Denial of Death* contended that Freud had gotten it exactly backwards. It is not true, said Becker, that our fear of death is rooted in our denial of sex, but, rather, that our fear of sex is rooted in our denial of death. Throughout history, and in many cultures, sex and death have been engaged in a *danse macabre,* and not simply at the shadowed margins of erotic fantasy where dwell the likes of the Marquis de Sade.

In sex and death are joined beginning and ending, the generative and the destructive. In today's culture we chatter incessantly about both sex and death. They are subjected to the specialization of experts, of therapists, ethicists, and the like. Sex and death have been "problematized," and problems are to be "solved" by sexual technique and the technology of dying. Victorian reticence about sex and our former reticence about death may have mystified both, although the probable intent was simply to put them out of mind. In any event, we have now embarked with a vengeance upon a course of demystification. Now there is nothing we cannot talk about in polite company. It is a great liberation. And a great loss, if in fact both sex and death partake of mystery. Mystery is attended by a fitting reticence.

Death and dying has become a strangely popular topic. "Support groups" for the bereaved crop up all over. How to "cope" with dying is a regular on television talk shows. It no doubt has something to do with the growing number of old people in the population. "So many more people seem to die these days," remarked my elderly aunt as she looked over the obituary columns in the local daily. Obituaries routinely include medical details once thought to be the private business of the family. Every evening without fail, at least in our cities, the television news carries a "sob shot" of relatives who have lost someone in an accident or crime. "And how did you feel when you saw she was dead?" The intrusiveness is shameless, and taboos once broken are hard to put back together again.

Evelyn Waugh's *The Loved One* brilliantly satirized and Jessica Mitford's *The American Way of Death* brutally savaged the death industry of commercial exploitation. Years later it may be time for a similarly critical look at the psychological death industry that got underway in 1969 when Elizabeth Kübler-Ross set forth her five stages of grieving—denial, anger, bargaining, depression, and acceptance. No doubt many people feel they have been helped by formal and informal therapies for bereavement and, if they feel they have been helped, they probably have been helped in some way that is not unimportant. Just being able to get through the day without cracking up is no little thing. But neither, one may suggest, is it the most important thing. I have listened to people who speak with studied, almost clinical, detail about where they are in their trek through the five stages. Death and bereavement are "processed." There are hundreds of self-help books on how to cope with death in order to get on with life. This essay is not of that genre.

A measure of reticence and silence is in order. There is a time simply to be present to death—whether one's own or that of others—without any felt urgencies about doing something about it or getting over it. The Preacher had it right: "For everything there is a season, and a time for every matter under heaven: a time to be born, and a time to die . . . a time to mourn, and a time to dance." The time of mourning should be given its due. One may be permitted to wonder about the wisdom of contemporary funeral rites that hurry to the dancing, displacing sorrow with the determined affirmation of resurrection hope, supplying a ready answer to a question that has not been given time to understand itself. One may even long for the *Dies Irae,* the sequence at the old Requiem Mass. *Dies irae, dies illa / Solvet saeclum in favilla / Teste David cum Sibylla:* "Day of wrath and terror looming / Heaven and earth to ash consuming / Seer's and Psalmist's true foredooming."

The worst thing is not the sorrow or the loss or the heartbreak. Worse is to be encountered by death and not to be changed by the encounter. There are pills we can take to get through the experience, but the danger is that we then do not go through the experience but around it. Traditions of wisdom encourage us to stay with death a while. Among observant Jews, for instance, those closest to the deceased observe shiva for seven days following the death. During shiva one does not work, bathe, put on shoes, engage in intercourse, read Torah, or have his hair cut. The mourners are to behave as though they themselves had died. The first response to death is to give inconsolable grief its due. Such grief is assimilated during the seven days of shiva, and then tempered by a month of more moderate mourning. After a year all mourning is set aside, except for the praying of kaddish, the prayer for the dead, on the anniversary of the death.

In *The Blood of the Lamb,* Peter de Vries calls us to "the recognition of how long, how very long, is the mourners' bench upon which we sit, arms linked in undeluded friendship—all of us, brief links ourselves, in the eternal pity." From the pity we may hope that wisdom has been distilled, a wisdom from which we can benefit when we take our place on the mourners' bench. Philosophy means the love of wisdom, and so some may look to philosophers in their time of loss and aloneness. George Santayana wrote, "A good way of testing the caliber of a philosophy is to ask what it thinks of death." What does it tell us that modern philosophy has had relatively little to say about death? Ludwig Wittgenstein wrote, "What can be said at all can be said clearly; and whereof one cannot speak thereof one must be silent." There is undoubtedly wisdom in such reticence that stands in refreshing contrast to a popular culture sated by therapeutic chatter. But those who sit, arms linked in undeluded friendship, cannot help but ask and wonder.

All philosophy begins in wonder, said the ancients. With exceptions, contemporary philosophy stops at wonder. We are told: don't ask, don't wonder, about what you cannot know for sure. But the most important things of everyday life we cannot know for sure. We cannot *know* them beyond all possibility of their turning out to be false. We order our loves and loyalties, we invest our years with meaning and our death with hope, not knowing for sure, beyond all reasonable doubt, whether we might not have gotten it wrong. What we need is a philosophy that enables us to speak truly, if not clearly, a wisdom that does not eliminate but comprehends our doubt.

A long time ago, when I was a young pastor in a very black and very poor inner-city parish that could not pay a salary, I worked part-time as chaplain at Kings County Hospital in Brooklyn. With more than three thousand beds, Kings County boasted then of being the largest medical center in the world. It seems primitive now, but thirty-five years ago not much of a fuss was made about those who were beyond reasonable hope of recovery. They were almost all poor people, and this was before Medicare or Medicaid, so it was, as we used to say, a charity hospital. They were sedated, and food was brought for those who could eat. The dying, male and female, had their beds lined up side by side in a huge ward, fifty to a hundred of them at any given time. On hot summer days and without air-conditioning, they would fitfully toss off sheets and undergarments. The scene of naked and half-naked bodies groaning and writhing was reminiscent of Dante's *Purgatorio.*

Hardly a twenty-four-hour stint would go by without my accompanying two or three or more people to their death. One such death is indelibly printed upon my memory. His name was Albert, a man of about seventy and (I don't know why it sticks in my mind) completely bald. That hot summer morning I had prayed with him and read the Twenty-third Psalm. Toward evening, I went up again to the death ward—for so everybody called it—to see him again. Clearly the end was near. Although he had been given a sedative, he was entirely lucid. I put my left arm around his shoulder and together, face almost touching face, we prayed the Our Father. Then Albert's eyes opened wider, as though he had seen something in my expression. "Oh," he said, "Oh, don't be afraid." His body sagged back and he was dead. Stunned,

I realized that, while I thought I was ministering to him, his last moment of life was expended in ministering to me.

There is another death that will not leave me. Charlie Williams was a deacon of St. John the Evangelist in Brooklyn. (We sometimes called the parish St. John the Mundane in order to distinguish it from St. John the Divine, the Episcopal cathedral up on Morningside Heights.) Charlie was an ever ebullient and sustaining presence through rough times. In the face of every difficulty, he had no doubt but that "Jesus going to see us through." Then something went bad in his chest, and the doctors made medically erudite noises to cover their ignorance. I held his hand as he died a painful death at age forty-three. Through the blood that bubbled up from his hemorrhaging lungs he formed his last word—very quietly, not complaining but deeply puzzled, he looked up at me and said, "Why?"

Between Albert's calm assurance and Charlie's puzzlement, who is to say which is the Christian way to die? I have been with others who screamed defiance, and some who screamed with pain, and many who just went to sleep. Typically today the patient is heavily sedated and plugged into sundry machines. One only knows that death has come when the beeping lines on the monitors go flat or the attending physician nods his head in acknowledgment of medicine's defeat. It used to be that we accompanied sisters and brothers to their final encounter. Now we mostly sit by and wait. The last moment that we are really with them, and they with us, is often hours or even many days before they die. But medical technology notwithstanding, for each one of them, for each one of us, at some point "it" happens.

It has often been said that each death is unique, that each of us must die our own death. Enthusiasts such as Walt Whitman gild the inevitable. "Nothing can happen more beautiful than death," he wrote in *Leaves of Grass.* In "Song of Myself" he trumpets: "Has anyone supposed it lucky to be born? / I hasten to inform him or her, it is just as lucky to die, and I know it." Good for him. "Why fear death?" asked Charles Frohman as he went down with the sinking *Lusitania.* "Death is only a beautiful adventure." Fare thee well, Mr. Frohman. If each life is unique, and it is, then it would seem to follow that each death is unique. I will not dispute the logic of that. And there is no doubt an element of adventure in moving into the unknown. But in my own experience of dying, it struck me as so very commonplace, even trite, that this life should end this way. Perhaps I should explain.

Several lawyers have told me that it would make a terrific malpractice suit. All I would have to do is make a deposition and then answer a few questions in court, if it ever came to trial, which it probably wouldn't since the insurance companies would be eager to settle. It would be, I was assured, a very big settlement. The statute of limitations has not run out as of this writing. But I will not sue, mainly because it would somehow sully my gratitude for being returned from the jaws of death. Gratitude is too precious and too fragile to keep company with what looks suspiciously like revenge.

The stomach pains and intestinal cramps had been coming on for almost a year. My regular physician, a Park Avenue doctor of excellent reputation, had told me long ago how pleased he was with the new techniques for colonoscopy. It meant, he said, that none of his patients need die of colon cancer. His partner, the specialist in these matters, did one colonoscopy and, some weeks later, another. After each mildly painful probing up through the intestines, he was glad to tell me that there was nothing there. Then, on Sunday afternoon, January 10, 1993, about five o'clock, after four days of intense discomfort in which there was yet another probe and yet another x-ray, I was at home suddenly doubled over on the floor with nausea and pain. The sensation was of my stomach exploding.

My friend George Weigel was visiting and he phoned the doctor's office, but the doctor was on vacation. The doctor covering for him listened to the symptoms and prescribed a powerful laxative. (I said that this story would smack of the commonplace.) Much later, other doctors said that the prescription might, more than possibly, have been fatal. They said they never heard of several colonoscopies not detecting a tumor, and shook their heads over a physician who would prescribe a laxative after being apprised of symptoms indicating something much more seriously wrong.

Weigel had the presence of mind to bundle me off—pushing, pulling, half-carrying me—to the nearest emergency room, which, fortunately, was only a block from the house. The place was crowded. I strongly recommend always having with you an aggressive friend or two when you go to a hospital and are really sick. A large and imperiously indifferent woman at the desk was not about to let anyone jump the line of waiting cases, relenting only when Weigel gave signs that he was not averse to the use of physical violence. She then sat me down to answer a long list of questions about symptoms and medical insurance, which I tried to answer until I fell off the chair in a faint, at which point she surmised she had an emergency on her hands. The experience so far did not instill confidence in the care I was likely to receive.

Very soon, however, I was flat on my back on a gurney, surrounded by tubes, machines, and technicians exhibiting their practiced display of frenetic precision, just like on television. The hospital's chief surgeon, who happened to be on duty that night, ordered an x-ray that showed a large tumor in the colon and declared there was no time to lose. I was wheeled at great speed down the halls for an elevator to the operating room, only to discover the elevators were out of order. By then I had been sedated and was feeling no pain. In fact, I was somewhat giddy and recall trying to make a joke about the contrast between the high-tech medicine and the broken-down elevators. A guard showed up who said he knew how to get the number six elevator working, and then I was looking up at the white water-stained ceiling of the operating room, and then there was someone putting a mask over my face and telling me to breathe deeply, and then there was "Now I lay me down to sleep . . . ," and then there was the next morning.

The operation took several hours and was an unspeakable mess. The tumor had expanded to rupture the intestine; blood, fecal matter, and guts all over the place. My stomach was sliced open from the rib cage down to the pubic area, then another slice five inches to the left from the navel for a temporary colostomy. I've noticed that in such cases the doctors always seem to say that the tumor was "as big as a grapefruit," but my surgeon insists the blackish gray glob was the size of "a big apple." After they had sewed me up, the hemorrhaging began, they knew not from where. Blood pressure collapsed and other vital signs began to fade. What to do? The surgeon advised my friend to call the immediate family and let them know I would likely not make it through the night. The doctors debated. To open me up all over again might kill me. On the other hand, if they didn't find and stop the hemorrhaging I was surely dead.

Of course they went in again. The source of the effusion of blood was the spleen, "nicked," as the surgeon said, in the ghastliness of the first surgery. Given the circumstances, I'm surprised that parts more vital were not nicked. The spleen removed and the blood flow stanched, they sewed me up again and waited to see if I would live. The particulars of that night, of course, I was told after the event. "It was an interesting case," one doctor opined in a friendly manner. "It was as though you had been hit twice by a Mack truck going sixty miles an hour. I didn't think you'd survive."

My first clear memory is of the next morning, I don't know what time. I am surrounded by doctors and technicians talking in a worried tone about why I am not coming to. I heard everything that was said and desperately wanted to respond, but I was locked into absolute immobility, incapable of moving an eyelash or twitching a toe. The sensation was that of being encased in marble; pink marble, I thought, such as is used for gravestones. The surgeon repeatedly urged me to move my thumb, but it was impossible. Then I heard, "The Cardinal is here." It was my bishop, John Cardinal O'Connor. He spoke directly into my right ear, repeatedly calling my name. Then, "Richard, wriggle your nose." It was a plea and a command, and I wanted to do it more urgently than anything I have ever wanted to do in my life. The trying, the sheer exercise of will to wriggle my nose, seemed to go on and on, and then I felt a twinge, no more than a fraction of a millimeter, and the Cardinal said, "He did it! He did it!" "I didn't see anything," said the surgeon. So I tried again, and I did it again, and everybody saw it, and the Cardinal and the doctors and the technicians all began to exclaim what a wonderful thing it was, as though one had risen from the dead.

The days in the intensive care unit was an experience familiar to anyone who has ever been there. I had never been there before, except to visit others, and that is nothing like being there. I was struck by my disposition of utter passivity. There was absolutely nothing I could do or wanted to do, except to lie there and let them do whatever they do in such a place. Indifferent to time, I neither knew nor cared whether it was night or day. I recall counting sixteen different tubes and other things plugged into my body before I stopped counting. From time to time, it seemed several times an hour but surely could not have been, a strange young woman with a brown wool hat and heavy gold necklace would come by and whisper, "I want blood." She stuck in a needle and took blood, smiling mysteriously all the time. She could have said she wanted to cut off my right leg and I would probably have raised no objection. So busy was I with just being there, with one thought that was my one and every thought: "I almost died."

Astonishment and passivity were strangely mixed. I confess to having thought of myself as a person very much in charge. Friends, meaning, I trust, no unkindness, had sometimes described me as a control freak. Now there was nothing to be done, nothing that I could do, except be there. Here comes a most curious part of the story, and readers may make of it what they will. Much has been written on "near death" experiences. I had always been skeptical of such tales. I am much less so now. I am inclined to think of it as a "near life" experience, and it happened this way.

It was a couple of days after leaving intensive care, and it was night. I could hear patients in adjoining rooms moaning and mumbling and occasionally calling out; the surrounding medical machines were pumping and sucking and bleeping as usual. Then, all of a sudden, I was jerked into an utterly lucid state of awareness. I was sitting up in the bed staring intently into the darkness, although in fact I knew my body was lying flat. What I was staring at was a color like blue and purple, and vaguely in the form of hanging drapery. By the drapery were two "presences." I saw them and yet did not see them, and I cannot explain that. But they were there, and I knew that I was not tied to the bed. I was able and prepared to get up and go somewhere. And then the presences—one or both of them, I do not know—spoke. This I heard clearly. Not in an ordinary way, for I cannot remember anything about the voice. But the message was beyond mistaking: "Everything is ready now."

That was it. They waited for a while, maybe for a minute. Whether they were waiting for a response or just waiting to see whether I had received the message, I don't know. "Everything is ready now." It was not in the form of a command, nor was it an invitation to do anything. They were just letting me know. Then they were gone, and I was again flat on my back with my mind racing wildly. I had an iron resolve to determine right then and there what had happened. Had I been dreaming? In no way. I was then and was now as lucid and wide awake as I had ever been in my life.

Tell me that I was dreaming and you might as well tell me that I was dreaming that I wrote the sentence before this one. Testing my awareness, I pinched myself hard, and ran through the multiplication tables, and recalled the birth dates of my seven brothers and sisters, and my wits were vibrantly about me. The whole thing had lasted three or four minutes, maybe less. I resolved at that moment that I would never, never let anything dissuade me from the reality of what had happened. Knowing myself, I expected I would later be inclined to doubt it. It was an experience as real, as powerfully confirmed by the senses, as anything I have ever known. That was some seven years ago. Since then I have not had a moment in which I was seriously tempted to think it did not happen. It happened—as surely, as simply, as undeniably as it happened that I tied my shoelaces this morning. I could as well deny the one as deny the other, and were I to deny either I would surely be mad.

"Everything is ready now." I would be thinking about that incessantly during the months of convalescence. My theological mind would immediately go to work on it. They were angels, of course. *Angelos* simply means "messenger." There were no white robes or wings or anything of that sort. As I said, I did not see them in any ordinary sense. But there was a message; therefore there were messengers. Clearly, the message was that I could go somewhere with them. Not that I must go or should go, but simply that they were ready if I was. Go where? To God, or so it seemed. I understood that they were ready to get me ready to see God. It was obvious enough to me that I was not prepared, in my present physical and spiritual condition, for the beatific vision, for seeing God face to face. They were ready to get me ready. This comports with the doctrine of purgatory, that there is a process of purging and preparation to get us ready to meet God. I should say that their presence was entirely friendly. There was nothing sweet or cloying, and there was no urgency about it. It was as though they just wanted to let me know. The decision was mine as to when or whether I would take them up on the offer.

There is this about being really sick, you get an enormous amount of attention. I cannot say that I did not enjoy it. In the pain and the nausea and the boredom without end, there were times when I was content to lie back and enjoy the attention. It was a kind of compensation. Over these days there were hundreds of cards and letters and phone calls and, later, brief visits—the last by people who sometimes betrayed the hope of having a final word with what they took to be their dying friend. Some of those who checked in I had not seen in years. Nor have I seen them since, so busy are we with our several busynesses. Sickness is an enforced pause for the counting up of our friends, and being grateful.

In all the cards and letters assuring me of prayer, and almost all did offer such assurance, there were notable differences. Catholics say they are "storming the gates of heaven" on your behalf, and have arranged to have Masses said. Evangelical Protestants are "lifting you up before the throne." Mainline Protestants, Jews, and the unaffiliated let it go with a simple "I am praying for you," or "You are in my prayers." One gets the impression that Catholics and evangelicals are more aggressive on the prayer front.

Then there were longer letters laying out the case for my getting better. A friend who is a constitutional scholar at an Ivy League university wrote a virtual lawyer's brief summing up the reasons for dying and the reasons for living, and came down strongly on the side of my living. It was very odd, because after that there were a number of similar letters, all arguing that I should stay around for a while and assuming that I was undecided about that. I was undecided. This struck me as strange: at the time of crisis and in the months of recovery following, I was never once afraid. I don't claim it as a virtue; it was simply the fact. It had less to do with courage than with indifference. Maybe this is "holy indifference," what the spiritual manuals describe as "a quality in a person's love for God above all that excludes preferences for any person, object, or condition of life." Aquinas, St. John of the Cross, and Ignatius Loyola all write at length about such holy indifference. All I know is that I was surprisingly indifferent to whether I would live or die. It probably had less to do with holiness than with my knowing that there was nothing I could do about it one way or the other.

On the other hand, there was the message: "Everything is ready now." As though the decision were mine, to stay or to go. A friend who had written with his son the story of his son's several years of waging a heroic battle against a horrific series of cancers sent me their book, inscribed with the admonition "to fight relentlessly for life." It was very kind, but I was not at all disposed to fight. More to the point were those letters calmly laying out the reasons why it would be better for others, if not for me, were I to live rather than to die. Over the slow weeks and slower months of recovery, I gradually came to agree. But still very tentatively.

When I was recuperating at home and could take phone calls, those calls became a staple of everyday existence. There were dozens of calls daily; closer friends called every day. Somebody was always on call-waiting. I enjoyed it shamelessly. Although I was often too tired to talk, when I had the energy I related in detail, over and over again, every minuscule change in my condition. With a credible display of intense interest, people listened to the problems with colostomy bags and the latest wrinkle in controlling the nausea that came with chemotherapy. And always in my talking, I was on the edge of tears. I, who had seldom cried in my adult life, was regularly, and without embarrassment, blubbering. Not in sadness. Not at all. But in a kind of amazement that this had happened to me, and maybe I was going to die and maybe I was going to live, and it was all quite out of my control. That was it, I think: I was not in charge, and it was both strange and very good not to be in charge.

Tentatively, I say, I began to think that I might live. It was not a particularly joyful prospect. Everything was shrouded by the thought of death, that I had almost died, that I may still die, that everyone and everything is dying. As much as I was grateful for all the calls and letters, I harbored a secret resentment. These friends who said they were thinking about me and praying for me all the time, I knew they also went shopping and visited their children and tended to their businesses, and there were long times when they were not thinking about me at all. More important, they were forgetting the primordial, overwhelming, indomitable fact: we are dying! Why weren't they as crushingly impressed by that fact as I was?

After a month or so, I could, with assistance, walk around the block. Shuffle is the more accurate term, irrationally fearing with every step that my stomach would rip open again. I have lived in New York almost forty years and have always been a fierce chauvinist about the place. When you're tired of London, you're tired of life, said Dr. Johnson. I had always thought that about New York, where there is more terror and tenderness per square foot than any place in the world. I embraced all the clichés about the place, the palpable vitality of its streets, the electricity in the air, and so forth and so on. Shuffling around the block and then, later, around several blocks, I was tired of it. Death was everywhere. The children at the playground at 19th Street and Second Avenue I saw as corpses covered with putrefying skin. The bright young model prancing up Park Avenue with her portfolio under her arm and dreaming of the success she is to be, doesn't she know she's going to die, that she's already dying? I wanted to cry out to everybody and everything, "Don't you know what's happening?" But I didn't. Let them be in their innocence and ignorance. It didn't matter. Nothing mattered.

Surprising to me, and to others, I did what had to be done with my work. I read manuscripts, wrote my columns, made editorial decisions, but all listlessly. It didn't really matter. After some time, I could shuffle the few blocks to the church and say Mass. At the altar, I cried a lot, and hoped the people didn't notice. To think that I'm really here after all, I thought, at the altar, at the *axis mundi,* the center of life. And of death. I would be helped back to the house, and days beyond numbering I would simply lie on the sofa looking out at the back yard. That birch tree, which every winter looked as dead as dead could be, was budding again. Would I be here to see it in full leaf, to see its leaves fall in the autumn? Never mind. It doesn't matter.

When I was a young man a parishioner told me, "Do all your praying before you get really sick. When you're sick you can't really pray." She was right, at least in largest part. Being really sick—vomiting, and worrying about what will show up on the next blood test, and trying to ignore the pain at three o'clock in the morning—is a full-time job. At best, you want to recede into relatively painless passivity, and listen to your older sister reading Willa Cather, as my sister read to me, during those long nights, *My Antonia, Death Comes for the Archbishop, Shadows on the Rock,* and at those times I could have wished it to go on and on. Not that it mattered, but it was ever so pleasant being ever so pampered.

People are different around the very sick, especially when they think they may be dying. In the hospital, bishops came to visit and knelt by my bedside, asking for a blessing. A Jewish doctor, professing himself an atheist, asked for my prayers with embarrassed urgency. His wife had cancer, he explained, "And you know about that now." Call it primitive instinct or spiritual insight, but there is an aura about the sick and dying. They have crossed a line into a precinct others do not know. It is the aura of redemptive suffering, of suffering "offered up" on behalf of others, because there is nothing else to be done with it and you have to do something with it. The point is obvious but it impressed me nonetheless: when you are really sick it is impossible to imagine what it is like to be really well; and when you are well it is almost impossible to remember what it was like to be really sick. They are different precincts.

I had lost nearly fifty pounds and was greatly weakened. There was still another major surgery to come, to reverse the colostomy. You don't want to know the details. It was not the most dangerous surgery, but it was the third Mack truck, and for a long time afterward I barely had strength to lift my hand. Then, step by almost imperceptible step, I was recovering and dared to hope that I would be well again, that I would stride down the street again, that I would take on new projects again. Very little things stand out like luminous signposts. The first time I was able to take a shower by myself. It was dying and rising again in baptismal flood. When one day I was sent home from the hospital after another round of tests, I was told that, if I did not urinate by five o'clock, I should come back to the emergency room and someone would put the catheter back in. My heart sank. It was quite irrational, but going back to the emergency room would have been like recapitulating the entire ordeal of these last several months. I could not endure the thought. When at four o'clock I peed a strong triumphant pee, my heart was lifted on high, and with tears of gratitude I began to sing with feeble voice a Te Deum. I thought, "I am going to get better." And I allowed myself, ever so tentatively, to be glad.

That was seven years ago. I feel very well now. They tell me I might be around for another twenty years or so. Medical science, perhaps arbitrarily, says five years is the point of complete recovery when you are reassigned to your age slot on the actuarial chart. But just to be safe, the tests continue on a regular basis. Next Monday we get the latest report on the CEA (Carcinoembryonic Antigen), the blood indicator of cancerous activity, although the doctor says the test is really not necessary. But I think I am well now. It took a long time after the surgeries, almost two years, before the day came when I suddenly realized that the controlling thought that day had not been the thought of death. And now, in writing this little essay, it all comes back. I remember where I have been, and where I will be again, and where we will all be.

There is nothing that remarkable in my story, except that we are all unique in our living and dying. Early on in my illness a friend gave me John Donne's wondrous *Devotions Upon Emergent Occasions*. The *Devotions* were written a year after Donne had almost died, and then lingered for months by death's door. He writes, "Though I may have seniors, others may be elder than I, yet I have proceeded apace in a good university, and gone a great way in a little time, by the furtherance of a vehement fever." So I too have been to a good university, and what I have learned, what I have learned most importantly, is that, in living and in dying, everything is ready now.

JOHN PRICE

Man Killed by Pheasant

from *Orion*

So I'm driving east on highway 30 toward Cedar Rapids, Iowa. It's a four-lane and because I'm an eldest child I'm driving the speed limit, around fifty-five, sixty miles per hour. I'm listening to Hendrix cry "Mary"—imagining, as usual, that I am Hendrix—when in the far distance I see some brown blobs hovering across the highway: one, then two. By the way they move, low and slow, I guess they're young pheasants. But two is a pretty small brood, I think, so as I near the place of their crossing I look to the right, across the empty passenger seat and into the grassy ditch to see if I can spot the whole clan. Suddenly there is a peripheral darkness, like the fast shadow of an eclipse, and something explodes against the side of my head, erupting into a fury of flapping and scratching and squawking. Somehow, in an act of almost miraculous timing, one of the straggling pheasants has flown in my driver's side window. And being the steel-jawed action hero I am, I scream, scream like a rabbit, and strike at it frantically with my left arm, the car swerving, wings snapping, Hendrix wailing, feathers beating at my face until, at last, I knock the thing back out the window and onto the road. I regain control of the car, if not myself, and pull over, to cry.

That's the time I should have been killed by a pheasant. For a couple of reasons peculiar to that summer, I recall it often. It occurred, for one, while I was on my way to teach a technical writing course at a nearby community college. This "distance learning experience" took place exclusively by radio wave, with me in an empty room on campus and my fifteen students scattered at sites within a 100-mile radius. The technology was such that my students could see me, but I couldn't see them. To converse we had to push buttons at the base of our microphones, so that each class felt like an episode of Larry King Live: *Judy from Monticello, hello, you're on the air.* "The future of higher education," my supervisor called it. And I never did get the hang of the camera. I'd turn it on at the beginning of the class and there, on the big screen monitor in front of me, would be a super close-up of my lips. I'd spend the next few minutes jostling the joy-stick, zooming in and out like one of those early music videos until I found the suitable frame. Sometimes my students would laugh at this, and I'd hear them laughing, but only if they pushed their buttons. If there was an electrical storm nearby, I wouldn't hear them laugh at all.

On the way to such a displaced, bodiless job, a near-death experience had some additional currency. As did the larger natural disaster unfolding around me. It was the summer of the great Iowa floods, 1993, and the reason I was on Highway 30 to begin with was that my usual route to campus had been washed out by the swollen Iowa River. This was a serious situation—people had been killed and Des Moines, our distant capital, had been without water for over a week. "Nature Gone Mad!" the national news media called it.

Although aware of the widespread suffering, I was privileged to watch the whole thing unfold more gently from the roadways of my rural commutes. And what I saw was a wilderness of birds. Bean fields suddenly became sheer, inaccessible places where egrets stood piercing frogs in the shallows, where pelicans flew in great cyclonic towers, where bald eagles swung low to pick off stranded fish. Perched on soggy, neglected fence posts were birds I hadn't seen since early childhood, bobolinks and bluebirds and tanagers. Their color and song drew my eye closer to the earth, to the ragged ditches full of forgotten wildflowers and grasses—primrose and horsemint, big blue and switch—safe, at least for a while, from the mower's blade. The domesticated landscape of my home had gone wild and I was mesmerized by it.

Toward the end of the summer flooding, when the dramatic presence of wild birds dwindled, I thought a lot about Noah, about those end days on the Ark between the release of the raven and the return of the dove, between a knowledge of a decimated landscape and a faith in one that, through decimation, had become reborn. I wondered if Noah, like me, was of mixed emotions, suspended between hope and despair, witnessing the flood waters swell then recede, the wetlands become cropfields again, the wilderness become tame, the unknown become known, the miraculous become mundane.

When it was all over, I thought I understood Noah's first impulse, once on dry land, to get drunk and forget. I had lived my entire life in Iowa, the most ecologically devastated state in the Union, with less than one-tenth of one percent of its native habitats remaining. "Tragic" is what the ecologist Wes Jackson has called the plowing up of this prairie region; "one of the two or three worst atrocities committed by Americans." Not that I'd ever cared—it's hard to care about a wild place you've never seen or known. Yet in those short, flooded months of 1993, I witnessed a blurry reflection of what Iowa had once been: a rich ecology of wetlands and savannas and prairies, alive with movement and migration. Alive with power. Under its influence, I felt closer to my home landscape than ever before. So when that power slipped from view, I was surprised to find myself in grief, longing to chase after it. But where would I look? Having spent most of my life wanting to leave the Midwest, in what place or experience might I find the reasons to stay, to commit?

Death by pheasant didn't immediately come to mind. Although, in the wake of the floods, death was part of what I longed for. Or rather the possibility of a certain kind of death, one that, appropriately enough, is associated with birds. You know the kind of death I'm talking about, to become lost in a vast landscape, to die, as Edward Abbey has described it, "alone, on rock under sun at the brink of the unknown, like a wolf, like a great bird. . . ." It is the kind of potential death that in my mind helps define wilderness as a place worthy of respect, a place of consequence and power and a kind of fearful freedom. My German friend calls this freedom *vogelfrei,* which loosely translates into "free as a bird." Far from the positive gist we associate with this phrase, *vogelfrei* refers to the state of being cast out from the tribe, so free you will die in the open, unburied, to be picked apart by birds. It is a state of fear and vulnerability and movement, one that might have the ability, especially here in the agricultural Midwest—a place seemingly without fang, without claw, without talon—to make us more observant of the natural world, more humbled by its power to transform us.

At first flush, my collision with the pheasant didn't seem to hold that kind of possibility. But it could have. If, for example, this had happened to me as a child or adolescent or as a member of a New Age men's group, I might have made something more of it. After all, as a boy some of my favorite comic book heroes were mutations of man and animal—Spiderman, for example, and Dr. Lizard, and Captain America's sidekick, the Falcon. Imagine, in my case, the comic-book story that could have developed: a mild-mannered English professor is struck in the head by a wayward pheasant, his blood mingling with the bird's while, coincidentally, a cosmic tsunami from a distant stellar explosion soaks the whole scene in gamma radiation. Emerging from the smoldering rubble:

Pheasant Man. No, *Super* Pheasant Man! As Super Pheasant Man, our mild-mannered professor finds he has acquired some of the bird's more powerful features—its pride and daring, its resilience, its colorful head feathers—learning to use them for the good of humanity while at the same time fighting the darker side of his condition, namely, a propensity for polygamy and loose stools.

But I was not a boy when I met that unlucky pheasant on Highway 30, which is too bad, because for a long time afterward I found nothing particularly hopeful or uplifting or powerful about the experience. Instead, I saw my life, and death, made a joke, just like the place where I grew up. Imagine the regional headlines: *Iowa Man Killed by Pheasant. Mother Files for Hunting License.* Imagine the funeral where, in the middle of singing "I'll Fly Away," one of my more successful cousins whispers to his wife: *And it wasn't even a big cock pheasant that killed him. It was just a little baby pheasant.* And imagine that hypothetical men's group who, in their wailful mourning of my death, botch up the spirit animal ritual and condemn my soul to be borne not on the wings of an eagle or a falcon, but on those of a pheasant, stubby and in-sufficient, struggling to get us both off the ground, never getting more than maybe fifteen feet toward heaven before dropping back down to earth with a thud and a cluck.

No thank you. I do not wish to become one with the pheasant, either in this life or in the next. Yet I wonder if there isn't some-thing to our togetherness. Seen through the history of the land, this bird and I have been colliding for centuries. Having evolved together on the grasslands of distant continents, we were both brought to this country by the accidents of nature and technology and voyage. As Americans, the pheasant and I have come to share cultural ties to certain important historical figures, like Benjamin Franklin, whose son-in-law was one of the first to attempt to in-troduce the ring-necked pheasant, a native of China, to this country. (His release was unsuccessful, partly, I'd like to think, because it occurred in New Jersey.) Its introduction to Iowa over a century later was also by accident, taking place during a 1901 windstorm near Cedar Falls that blew down confinement fences and released two thousand of the birds into the prairie night. They've remained here ever since, sharing with my people an affinity for the Northern Plains to which we've both become anchored by the peculiarities of the soil. This soil, loess, and glacial till, is migrant and invasive, like us, having been carried here from ancient Canada by wind and by ice. Its rich organic loam, black as oil, brought my farmer ancestors to the region and has, at the same time, held close the range of the ring-necked pheasant, lacing the bird's grit with calcium carbonate. Because the ring-neck requires an abundance of this mineral, it doesn't stray far, not even a few hundred miles south into the gray prairies of, say, lower Illinois. Although the soil there is slightly older, shaved from native limestone, it is, for the pheasant, less nutritious.

So, the pheasant and I remain settlers in this region, watching as others of our kind move on or migrate. As such, we have come to share some of the same enemies, like the fencerow-to-fencerow, get-big-or-get-out agricultural policies of the 1970s and '80s. These policies, enacting yet another vision of migration, dramatically expanded agricultural exports and, at the same time, led the region to the farm crisis of the 1980s, to the flight and impoverishment and, sometimes, death of thousands of industrial and farm families. For the pheasant as well, despite set-aside programs, this fencerow-to-fencerow world has held its own kind of impoverishment, a destruction of habitat so thorough that two hundred pheasants have been known to crowd a shelter-belt only a hundred yards long. In such a bare-naked world a good blizzard, like the one in 1975, has the power to wipe out seventy to eighty percent of a local pheasant population in a single evening.

Yet in sharing enemies, we have also been, together, the common enemy. To the prairie chicken, for instance—one of the many native citizens that had the unfortunate luck to precede us here in the "heartland." For almost a century European settlers hunted and plowed down prairie chicken populations in Iowa. But some argue it was the ring-necked pheasant that finished it off, destroying its eggs, occupying its nests, and interrupting, seemingly out of spite, its dancing-ground rituals. Since then, efforts to restore prairie chickens have usually had to correspond with significant reductions in pheasant populations. Most of those efforts have failed, largely because reducing pheasant numbers around here is about as easy and popular as reducing our own. The difficulties are partly economic: in Iowa, we hunt and eat this bird to the tune of about one and a quarter million a year. It's one of our biggest tourist attractions. But I wonder, too, if we don't see in this bird, at some unconscious level, a dark reflection of our own troubling history in the American grasslands, our role as ecological party crashers, as culture wreckers. Our role, ultimately, as killers and thieves. To question the pheasant's claim on the land is, in some way, to question our own.

It's unfair, of course, and dangerous to project our sins onto another species. When tossing around ethical responsibility the difference between us, between instinct and intent, is significant. But the pheasant needn't worry about taking the blame. Hardly anyone around here gives them a second thought. That indifference was part of my problem when searching for reasons to care about my home landscape. In relation to that bird, as to most of the familiar, transplanted wildlife around me, I felt nothing. The pheasant was common, and the last thing I wanted to feel as a Midwesterner was common. Since early adolescence I'd been fleeing a sense of inadequacy shared by many in this region, a sense of self marked—as Minnesotan Patricia Hampl has said—by "an indelible brand of innocence, which is to be marked by an absence, a vacancy. By nothing at all." For Midwesterners like me, the complex, the worthy seemed always to be found elsewhere. Not here in this ordinary place, this ordinary life.

So not surprisingly, during the years following the floods, I sought a new relationship to the Midwest not in the ragged and familiar land immediately around me, but in the distant and, in my imagination, more exotic landscapes of the Black Hills and Badlands in western South Dakota. What I discovered in those places did indeed transform me. I saw for the first time elk bugling and mating, at home on their native prairies. While sitting in a fly-plagued prairie dog town, I saw for the first time a bison bull wallowing in the brown dust. On the grasslands near Bear Butte, where Crazy Horse once sought vision, I saw for the first time a falcon stoop to kill a mallard, the native cycles of predator and prey, of wild death, still lingering. Even *vogelfrei,* that fearful freedom—I felt it for the first time in this region while walking lost in the deep earth of the Badlands. My journey through these distant *journey* places toward commitment has been awkward, fragmented, and at times pathetic, even comic. Yet the significance of these experiences cannot be underestimated, how they have worked to cure a lifetime of ignorance and indifference. How, to use spiritual terms, they have filled what once was empty.

But if the spiritual journey to a place begins, as Kathleen Norris claims, with fear, then it was not the bison or the falcon or the Badlands that first drew me closer to the region in which I had been raised. It was the pheasant. That particular baby pheasant—there on a highway in eastern Iowa—which almost, as my sister would say, rocked my world. In a sense, that's exactly what it did. It made me wake up, become more observant of what's lurking in the margins. What's lurking there, despite the rumors, is the possibility of surprise, of accident, of death. And if it's possible in this overdetermined landscape for a pheasant to kill a man, then why not, too, the possibility of restoration, renewal, and, at last, hope?

But that's a romantic stretch, and at the time of the incident itself I didn't feel particularly worshipful of its surprise. As I sat in the car wiping hot tears from my face, I just felt lucky—*thank God it wasn't a two-lane!*—and then ridiculous. The whole thing was so absurd it might have been a dream. I carefully leaned my head out the window to see if the pheasant was still on the road. It wasn't. I thought about going back to find it, to see if it was injured, but decided against it—after all, it was only a pheasant. Besides, I was late for work where in a few minutes I would be taking my own precarious flight through the airwaves, across the flooded land, to students I would never see, never truly know.

I started the car and eased back onto the highway. As I approached cruising speed I saw something move out of the corner of my eye. I jerked, swerving the car a little. A feather. An ordinary brown feather. Then another and another—there must have been a dozen of them—floating in the breeze of the open window. They tickled and annoyed me. Yet for reasons I still can't explain, I kept the window open—just a crack—enough to keep the feathers dancing about the cabin. And that's how I, the man almost killed by a pheasant, drove the rest of those miles, touched by its feathers in flight, touched by an intimacy as rare and welcome, in my tragic country, as laughter in a storm.

A pheasant flying into his car + face through an open window, awakens the author to a new sense of place + life.

Rivers and Mountains

from *Parabola*

Fall was coming to California. You could feel it in the hot, sere winds that occasionally blew down the canyons to rattle the sycamores across from our house. Just below our kitchen window the Carmel River flashes under a stand of trees. In July and August the river is little more than a brook racing down stone terraces shrouded by willows. In the morning the ravine is sun-shot and changes color with every hour's shift of light. By late afternoon the river canyon is hot and settled; stacked clouds the color of pale slate tower above the mountains to the south.

Over this short section of river we witnessed extraordinary changes in the passage of a season. The river chiseled two new channels and deposited tons of smooth granite stones forty feet from our door. Canadian geese came and went and came again. The water changed from the mud-saturated brown of winter to the empyrean blue of spring. We were, however, still outsiders in this riparian drama and never really learned the vernacular of the water. Although we heard the water's eloquent speech, there were only glimmerings of its teachings.

In *Shobogenzo, Keisei-Sanshoku, (Valley Sounds, Mountain Sights,)* Dogen Kigen wrote:

> *At the moment of this true training, valley sounds and valley sights, mountain sights and mountain sounds all bounteously deliver eighty-four thousand gathas. If you are generous in surrendering fame and wealth, body and mind, then the valley*

and mountains will also be generous (in delivering the dharma discourse).

Dogen's nature writings evoke a reconciliation with something we cannot name—some larger aspect of life only alluded to like a vague memory in the body. Another part of that reconciliation is discerning the mystery, seeking to decipher the teachings of mountains and waters. What are the lessons of landscape?

My daughter Pilar, three years old and fearless, loves nothing more than wading along the shallow shoreline outside our house. On the Fourth of July it was eighty-three degrees and we were knee-deep in the slow current, threading our way upstream, moving over submerged rocks as if great weights were tied to our feet. Pilar randomly stalked minute fish swimming against the current. Pairs and threesomes of mallards lifted from the water and pounded the late summer air furiously to put distance between us.

Holding hands, we walked barefoot upstream quietly in the water, stepping delicately over stones. Besides the water sounds, there was just immense silence. We stopped and listened to the water. She asked me for a story: I did not have one. Listening, she turned in delight and announced. "Daddy, this water is talking."

Sometimes we *do* hear water talking. In listening to the river a kind of silence prevails, broken only by the rush of water over rocks. Such a silence is more like faint echoes, each a series of dim reverberations. They continue deep inside you, distant yet familiar. The language of the river is not any known language, but a language nonetheless. It is familiar to the body and communicates a watery eloquence. It tells of the nature of water, of how it lives and functions there.

In *Keisei-Sanshoku,* Dogen tells the story of Su Tung-p'o (1036–1101), a Sung poet from China who was enlightened by the sound of water:

> Sounds of brooks are nothing but a gigantic tongue.
> Figures of mountains are none other than Buddha's body of
>   purity.
> Eighty-four thousand gathas since last night—
> How shall I explain them to others at another time?

Sometimes the sermons are in the sound of the thrush by the brook, the beat of a hummingbird's wings, or the wind in dogwood trees; sometimes they are in the screech of a car alarm or the murmur of a refrigerator.

Walking upstream, we paid attention to the single prevalent feature of the landscape—flux and change. Moving slowly, we noticed small occurrences in the constantly changing riverbed: the random order of stones against the current, each sequence of rocks the result of unceasing movement. Though seemingly insignificant, these small events are clearly imparting a collective language of rivers.

Walking in water returns a sharpness of attention. The point of view from the river is singular; it points to our relationship with the watershed and to ourselves. Nothing is so unfamiliar as the well-known when viewed from the perspective of walking in a river. We think we understand our life, who we are, and our place in the sweep of things. We think we live in a world that makes sense. Then—sometimes vividly—the rug is pulled out from under our long-held assumptions. We temporarily misplace our map. The narrative we've made up about our life no longer has meaning beyond the transitory arrangement of images. Perspective starts listing this way and that—and the truth about the world is disclosed: Things are constantly in flux, and nothing is essentially anything apart from the rest of the world. Spending time by a river, or at a funeral, or in a zendo can sometimes demonstrate this point.

Further upstream we found a number of extraordinary pale gray rocks. Pilar became interested in the relationship between rocks and the tiny fish and their seemingly random darting movements. She was not so interested in knowing names of things but in the relationship between them—how they were connected to one another.

Mountains are not mountains, yet they are nothing but mountains.

The logic of Dogen Zenji can be an incisive shock to our understanding of the world. He makes us question not only the outside world and its objective validity, but also our pact with the world, our way of relating to what we encounter, and our self. At the same time, Dogen's nature writing is also singularly gratifying. We are invited to explore absolute water and are made aware of our complicity in it, and that is why we are drawn again and again to this thirteenth-century monk's writing: to remember that the eastern mountains travel on water, and that the blue mountains' walking is our own walking. To remember that our meeting with birds, convenience stores, cars, trees, and water is meeting ourselves. For Dogen, this convergence is a rare occasion to meet, grow, and create.

As we waded along the shaded bank, fat steelhead trout rolled along the bottom of a deep pool. We both turned as the sycamores shimmered in the wind. Only the beginnings of branches were visible under the foliage, as though a few thin arms supported the mass of trembling leaves. Black birds shot from the trees, tilting into the afternoon sky. Then it was still. That was when I looked at Pilar, her arms spread for balance in the aspect of a cross. I spoke silently to myself, in my mind, but not with sentences—just images. Then I did not think anything at all, but simply stood there in a state resembling curiosity and wonder. The quiet of the riverbed had ceased to be something that we observe; now it was something we were part of. Or our quiet had joined the stream's quiet. Just below my knees the Carmel River pulled with enormous purpose toward the Pacific Ocean. My daughter showed me that I'd been fortunate in being given the chance to discover mountains and rivers, sky and trees in a context that restored to me the religion of my childhood—which was primarily gratitude and awe.

You must know this: Mountains are neither the human world nor the heavenly world. Do not judge mountains by human standards. If you do not apply human standards to them, who can entertain a doubt about the flowing or nonflowing of mountains?

In the *Mountains and Waters Sutra*, Dogen Zenji says, "You should clearly examine the green mountains walking and your own walking." Since I first read these lines some years ago, the image of green mountains constantly walking has never been entirely absent from my mind's eye. I might be talking with someone and the sawtooth image of mountains would appear momentarily between us, like great green sails hovering across the horizon. Mountains endlessly walking.

Mountains are not fixed over time. Some geologists have suggested that the exposed rock in the Santa Lucia range may have had seafloor origins of a depth of fourteen miles below the surface, and that much of the rock originated 1800 miles away in the latitude of Acapulco, Mexico. The mountains of Big Sur form perhaps the most geologically complex continuous mountain chain in the United States. The range is composed of differing elements of rock, pieces of ancient volcanoes and primordial mountain chains, layers of sea floor and stream sediment. A complex network of faults runs northwest by southeast and roughly follows the coast's directional orientation. Small tremors are common, and the entire range moves whenever the massive San Andreas Fault is active. In fact, the geological narrative of these mountains is one of continuous wrenching by opposing plates. Many geologists think that the most recent uplift began 1.8 million years ago and continues today at roughly the rate fingernails grow.

The walking of these mountains and rivers extends ceaselessly beyond this narrow canyon up into the Carmel River watershed where unseen rivulets, arroyos, and streams create an elegant and complex system. But the overpowering presence, beyond the waters and mountains themselves, is one of transformation and elemental intelligence. The waters we walk in are the teaching themselves and serve as a kind of rescuing operation for us. Reminders of wildness and process, serenity and chaos. Reminders of ourselves.

After a time, we entered a deeper pool—the water startlingly clear. With no leaves on the surface, it was difficult to discern the water's plane, and the fish appeared to float on a current of air. As we walked, small fish darted out of sight, and when we stopped they would appear again, curious.

I spoke with a dim knowledge of the names of plants and fish and insects and birds. Gradually I began to say less. The longer we spent in the river, the more effortlessly and quietly we moved. The effect was intoxicating, providing a sense of attention and affinity with the water. I did not want to feel again the sequence of daily events, of analysis and deliberation—just the affirmative hues of physical activity. Pilar, fish, rock, wind, and water were all joined by movement and light, creating a sort of participatory haiku. Some type of exchange seemed to transpire, but the nature of the transaction seemed unknowable in everyday terms.

One of Dogen's spiritual ancestors asked his teacher, "Why don't I hear the sound of inanimate things teaching?"

The teacher replied, "You don't hear it yourself, but you shouldn't hinder that which does hear it."

DAVID RENSBERGER

Thoughts from My Roof

from *Weavings*

I should begin by telling you why I am on my roof in the first place. Not that it's all that much to tell. We recently added a fireplace to our house, and the chimney needed a cap, a kind of metal hood to go over the opening and keep out the rain and leaves. So we went to the hardware store and bought one, and then it was simply a matter of climbing up onto the roof and installing it.

That's why I went up on the roof. A simple matter. But why am I still sitting here, looking around and thinking? That's simple, too: because I'm afraid to come down. The fact is, I'm afraid of heights. I was scared coming up. I'm absolutely terrified to start back down.

Getting up on our roof shouldn't have been all that hard. It's a modest house, and the edge of the roof is only eight feet or so from the ground. I didn't even need to extend the extension on the ladder. The roof isn't particularly steep, either. The ground there is soft, fairly moist, with a few wood chips, a little ivy. I probably wouldn't get hurt if somebody *threw* me off the roof.

But this is not about rational considerations. It's about fear. With the top end of the ladder propped against the roof, I started climbing resolutely upward. There was no one else home, which meant no one to hold the ladder, but also no one to witness my ridiculous terror. Even the neighbors (thank goodness) were not around. I got to the edge of the roof, and then faced my first real challenge. I had to get off the ladder and onto the roof. This meant climbing nearly to the top of the ladder, and then taking a little step up and to my left. I couldn't do it.

I'd used this ladder once or twice to climb up to really high places, where I had to pull the extension out all the way. Near the top of the extension, on the third rung down, there is a warning label, the kind of helpful admonition that the government and the lawyers make everybody put everywhere these days. "CAU-TION!" it says, in big red letters, "This is not a step! Do not stand on it. YOU MIGHT FALL!" This is a profoundly unnecessary piece of advice for anyone with my kind of anxiety. I already knew I might fall; the thought never left my mind for a second, and this little reminder only increased my paranoia.

Even climbing to the roof today, with no need for the extension, that warning stuck in my mind. I was paralyzed there on the ladder, unable to take the short step that would have me up on the roof. I stood there for five minutes, maybe longer, seeing the simple thing that I had to do, and completely incapable of doing it, for fear that that little step would be my last, that it would send me flying, or rather falling, into oblivion.

It's more than a little embarrassing to admit that I had to appeal to divine intervention to lift my foot and move less than a yard. I finally took refuge in the thought, *God is my helper.* I repeated these words over and over, and finally got my left foot onto the roof without incident. From there the rest of me followed pretty easily. I was on the roof; and I quickly moved behind the chimney, which is a wide one, so that I could sit against it in such security that even I stopped worrying about falling.

It took only a few minutes to put the cap in place, naturally. And that brings me to where I am now, sitting on the roof, still behind the chimney, unable to get down. There's no rush about getting down, of course. I don't have anything urgent to do. In fact, it occurs to me that maybe I don't really need to come down at all. The view is interesting from up here. I can see my neighborhood from a different vantage point. The weather is fine. Why not just stay where I am?

Coming down would involve getting out from behind the chimney, taking a completely unprotected step toward the edge, and then pivoting on my left foot in order to turn around and place my right foot on the ladder, which might or might not stay in place as I do so. This seems like a huge risk to take for a very small benefit (namely, going into the house and getting on with my life). Taking out my own appendix sounds less dangerous right now. So I will sit here and just think a little while longer.

I am thinking about what a nice day it is up here, about how lovely the neighborhood is. I am thinking about God, and how silly it was for me to have to repeat "God is my helper" to get up on the roof in the first place. It strikes me as extremely generous of God to tolerate these little absurdities, a real mark of divine love to smile over our childish behavior and forgive.

I am also thinking about fear. Why am I so afraid, and what am I afraid of? I am afraid that gravity, something built into the universe, will overcome my ability to hold on to where I am and draw me against my will through the air and into the ground. I am absolutely certain that I would not be badly hurt if that happened. I can see the ground, see how close it is and how soft it is. A little bruising, a little shaking up, is the worst that could happen. I envision breaking a bone and having to drag myself into the house and get to a phone to call for help; but even then I wouldn't die. None of this matters, though: I am afraid of falling, maybe not so much of the landing itself as simply of the falling.

But why am I so afraid of this, since it probably won't happen, and even if it did happen nothing very bad would likely result? Something inside me seems convinced that with my first step I will go sliding inexorably down off the roof. If I stand up, it's almost as if the ground is sucking me down onto it, and nothing I do can stop it. The edge of the roof seems to be drawing me toward it, as if I have no power to put my foot down in a safe place. No movement seems safe; only staying put can guarantee that I won't fall down. Perhaps a therapist could help me with this. It might be a good idea to see one, and finally get over this nonsense, so I can enjoy mountains and canyons and perform simple household tasks. Of course, I'll have to get down off the roof in order to find a therapist; and how can I do that?

FEAR AND HOPE

So I keep sitting here and thinking about fear. What *is* fear? Fear, it strikes me, is closely related to hope. Both are responses to an unknown future. As long as I stay where I am, I am guaranteed not to fall. I'm behind the chimney, and it's not going anywhere. (Even this I have to repeat to myself for reassurance.) Movement of any kind gets me into unknown territory, though. I can have no certainty of where I will go, where I will end up. I may not like where I am; it may not seem like a permanently suitable place to stay; but at least I know what is happening to me here.

Fear—this kind of fear, anyway—is a reaction to the unknown, based on uncertainty. "YOU MIGHT FALL!" Yes, I might! There's nothing to prevent it, really, nothing that I can be sure of. I don't *know* what will happen. I know several things that might happen, and I can't trust that the ones I don't want won't happen. So I am afraid, responding to this uncertainty about an unknown future with flight from it, with retreat into a motionless paralysis that keeps me right where I am, useless as that place may be.

Hope is the other side of the same coin. Hope also reacts to the unknown, but does so on the basis of some kind of certainty. I am talking about biblical hope now, not the kind of hope that we associate with helpless wishing and longing. "I hope that call comes today" is not the same thing as "Rejoice in hope" (Rom. 12:12).*

---

*Scripture quotations are from the New Revised Standard Version.

The hope I'm talking about is grounded in something certain; it is the hope whose assurance is faith (Heb. 11:1). Hope, in this sense, involves trust, a trust in God that is itself rooted in the certainty of divine love. God loves us, and we trust that love; and because of this trust we respond to the unknown future with hope.

Having hope that is based on confidence in divine love, we face the unknown knowing one thing: whatever may happen to us, we will not be destroyed, for nothing can separate us from the love of God (Rom. 8:39). The unknown remains unknown. Hope does not remove that uncertainty, but matches it with the certainty that all unknowns rest in the power of the God who loves us. We might fall; we might hit the ground hard; but it will not be the end of us, because God does love us and will stay with us, even if we ourselves will not always be aware of the divine Presence. In that hope, we can move forward, even into a future that may well hold things we rightly dread. We can move because we are confident that, even if we do not know the consequences of each footstep, God does, and God cares.

Fear, as the opposite of hope, results from not trusting God and God's love. The way to overcome fear, then, is a renewal of trust, of faith, of confidence in the love of God. My little chant, "God is my helper," is not quite so silly after all. At least it points me in the right direction. It reminds me that God *is* available to me in love. The piety of Psalms 91:11–12—that God will command the angels "so that you will not dash your foot against a stone"—may be more a poet's hyperbole than a pledge to be taken with absolute literalness. But, even from my roof, I can pray, "When I thought, 'My foot is slipping,' your steadfast love, O LORD, held me up" (Ps. 94:18).

I am still repeating, "God is my helper," and still a little ashamed of it, but I am climbing down from the roof. A fear this overwhelming, even if it is baseless, can only be faced with a source of hope, and for me that hope is in God, however cravenly I may express it. It is hard, hard, hard to face that first step, and then to launch myself over onto the ladder. But how good it feels coming down! I'm off my roof! I'm on the ground! Thank God! "For you have delivered my soul from death, my eyes from tears, my feet from stumbling" (Ps. 116:8).

FEAR AND RESURRECTION

There are much worse things to be feared in the world than falling off a roof. People who have confronted death or some genuine evil may be a bit impatient with my little roof phobia, and not unreasonably so. But even the big fears, I think, have hope as their opposite. Paul writes that an experience that brought him face to face with death taught him to rely "not on ourselves but on God who raises the dead," and that as a result he had set his hope on this God (2 Cor. 1:9–10). The women at the tomb of Jesus in Mark's gospel are in need of just this hope.

Mark, probably the first gospel to be written, ends abruptly, to say the least.* "So they went out and fled from the tomb, for terror and amazement had seized them; and they said nothing to anyone, for they were afraid" (Mark 16:8). Yes, the tomb is empty; yes, the stone is rolled away; yes, there is an angel (or at least a young man in white) who tells the women, "He has been raised; he is not here" (v. 6). But is this any way to end an Easter story?

Mark does not portray these women as weak or cowardly. They alone had watched the crucifixion of Jesus; there is no mention of

---

*Mark's ending is so abrupt and problematic that copyists reproducing the gospel in later centuries felt compelled to improve it by making shorter or longer additions, in which the women do tell Peter and the others, and Jesus appears to them and gives them mission instructions.

male disciples being present (Mark 15:40–41). They were there on Sunday morning, by themselves again, to do what had to be done. Was anybody looking forward to handling a day-and-a-half-old corpse? There was plenty of bravery in their actions; yet the last word we have about them from Mark is *afraid*.

People in Mark's gospel show fear for several kinds of reasons. The disciples and others are afraid when Jesus' divine power is revealed: when he heals (5:15, 33) or walks on water (6:50) or is transfigured (9:6). At other times, fear is the result of a lack of faith (4:40; 5:36). The women's fear at the empty tomb may be the first kind, terror at finding oneself in the presence of an unmistakable act of God. But their unwillingness to speak suggests the sort of fear that results from too little sense of divine activity, rather than too much. They have hardly begun to know the God who raises the dead, and their fear of what now lies ahead overwhelms them. Staring into this tremendous unknown, the only movement they feel safe in is flight away from it, back to where they know they're safe. To talk about what they've been told would likewise mean moving forward into the unknown. Better to stay paralyzed, silent and unmoving.

We should not think too harshly of them. Would we have done any better? And eventually they must have spoken, or their story could not have been told at all. Still, Mark's ending comes as a challenge to the reader, a conclusion that is left inconclusive, left open for the reader to finish. Will we join the witnesses in their fear, or in their later testimony? What will we make of these events, and what will they make of us? Will we let fear keep us from moving into the unknown future? Or will we find hope in the God of resurrection?

Down from my roof, I can have no pretension to a courageous faith. I will have to think some more about fear, and faith, and hope. I do know that the divine gift of life experienced in the

risen Jesus gives me a ground for hope when only fear seems possible. I may never get over my fear of heights, at least not without
a long struggle. But there is something that can be set against
every sort of fear. It is the knowledge that God—God who raised
Jesus from the dead—does love me, and the confidence that that
love will never fail, and the hope that comes from realizing that all
unknown futures lie in the hands of this loving God.

PATTIANN ROGERS

The Background Beyond the Background

from *The Georgia Review*

On an autumn afternoon, perhaps selecting
apples from a crate or examining pickled beets
and onions in a jar, or watching two honeybees
at one red clover, we stand unaware
before a background of behest and sanctity.

Or floating down a river through elm
and cottonwood shadows, past sandbar
willows and lines of turtles on sunning logs,
over underwater thickets, bottom beds
of leaf roughage and mud, we are, all the while,
made finely distinct upon a more distant
background of singularity.

Anywhere we turn, this background
stays, a domain for mortal and immortal,
for crystal grids, for shifting furls of smoke,
for structure and fallibility, for each nexus
of sword and cross.

Atop a barn roof, a glossy green-tailed
rooster with auburn feathers lifts his wings
against a backdrop of dawn. Is it the passing
moment of occupied event or the passing fact

of barnyard morning that creates the impression
of presence before this silk of elusive
light behind light?

Like a clear horizon at the edge of a wide
field, the background beyond the background
of sky reveals most explicitly the figures
of those that come before it—elephant
or ostrich or seed-heavy grasses, saint,
sow, runt or sire, summer lightning,
blowing ice. It achieves us all.

Far, far beyond those far mountains of stone
and cavern against which I am outlined now
there is another background—translucent,
stolid, eloquent, still.

MARJORIE SANDOR

Waiting for a Miracle: A Jew Goes Fishing

from *The Georgia Review*

One Saturday morning, waist deep in the Colorado River, I glanced up to see a dozen Hasids in long black coats and fedoras standing on the bridge above me. I closed my eyes to dismantle this hallucination, but when I opened them the Hasids were still there, gazing down at me, mournfully stroking their beards. I made a cast—into the trees. I made another and missed a strike. The men frowned and moved on, but it was too late: I knew myself judged. What kind of chutzpah was this, a Jew trying to walk in harmony with nature? And in the water, no less, that famous Christian element. Is there a posture in the world that smacks more of the desire for premature transcendence than this business of standing midstream, trying to raise fishes from the deep?

All day I felt my klutziness—my absolute fishlessness—like a curse; I wondered idly if there was a prohibition against fishing on the Sabbath. Before this, I'd figured myself the usual beginner with a long way to go, but that day, watched by smart trout below and wise Jews above, I began to think I wasn't fated to improve. What if I wasn't so much a bad fisherman as a person struggling hopelessly against an ancient tribal destiny?

On the other hand, what were a bunch of pious Jews doing on a western riverbank on a Sabbath morning, gazing down at an angler and the water too, their pallid faces bearing the expression of fishermen everywhere: that absorbed, childlike alertness, everything in the world forgotten but the river and what might lie beneath its surface? Surely they'd come further than any fisherman to stand on the bank of this river, which now, under a passing cloud, turned that promising greeny-gray that says *trout* to some people, and in so doing, says something about the mysteries we all wait for: Divine before you see it, mortal when you do.

The smallest, most idle speculation kept tugging at me, right through summer and into fall, a thousand miles from a brief humiliation on the trout stream. Maybe it's the academic life. At any rate, it was winter in the middle of north central Florida; I was teaching my classes at the university and not fishing. Otherwise I cannot account for my behavior. As if in a dream, I stopped at our library's Judaica collection and introduced myself to the man in charge. "Just offhand," I said, "do you have anything on Jews and fishing? Rivers, water, fish—whatever you can dig up. I don't care what."

The librarian raised his eyebrows as high as they would go, then sighed. "I can see you've never been in here before. Listen, sweetheart, a Jewish fisherman is going to be as hard to dig up as a Jewish athlete. I mean, sure, we all want to be Sandy Koufax." He gave a mysterious little laugh. "I'll see what I can do."

Overnight, I considered the librarian's sad eyebrows and felt again that eerie chastisement, as if I'd transgressed and he'd been divinely sent to return me to the fold. Of course I knew the old stereotype. How many Jewish sportsmen can you name, let alone fishermen and hunters of wild beasts? Ask anybody: we've been stuck indoors for centuries, huddled over closely printed texts, difficult theorums, and violins, developing myopia as well as serious allergies to grass and trees. The trouble is built right into our linguistic heritage: our scholars tell us that in Yiddish, so famous for its juicy expressions and lively rhythms, there are only two words for flowers—rose and violet—and no names at all for wild birds. To this information, a friend of mine once added, "True, maybe, but we've got thirteen ways to call somebody a shmuck."

It's been said that this linguistic leaning came out of necessity. Our forefathers lived in cramped ghettos inside hostile cities, so who had time to go naming birds when any minute the peasants coming down Market Street might turn out to be real evildoers?

But a scholar writing about the Jewish painter Marc Chagall exclaims, not without a certain proud petulance, "The Jewish Genius has no respect for nature." He says our struggle didn't start in the ghetto, but goes way back. The ancient Jewish poets themselves are responsible; they showed a deep, even intimate knowledge of the natural world, which they saw ultimately as a "house that has a lord and master." When Jehovah "turns his face away, the shining beauty of the world vanishes. He takes his breath away, and all is dead and withered." So, from the beginning, nature is a pale business next to the luminous personality of God.

This particular scholar was trying to explain how rough it is to be a Jewish painter. "The Jew gave out his expression in song," he says. "He did not create a plastic art." But our writers haven't fared any better with nature. Isaac Babel, a Russian Jew who grew up around the turn of the century in Odessa's Moldavanka Quarter, claimed this ignorance of nature "a Jewish handicap to be overcome." In his short story "Awakening" a young boy is forced by his father into violin lessons even though he hasn't the slightest speck of talent. In this family's worried world, the hopes of the whole community rest upon the shoulders of musical prodigies, "those wizened creatures with their swollen blue hands." The boy does the unthinkable: he plays hooky from his lessons and goes daily to the harbor, desperate to learn to swim. But, he says, "the hydrophobia of my ancestors, Spanish rabbis and Frankfurt money-changers, dragged me to the bottom."

He is rescued from this "struggle of rabbis versus Neptune" by a kindly old Gentile naturalist who says, "What do you mean the water won't hold you; why shouldn't it?" This wonderful man becomes a kind of writing mentor too. He encourages the boy to learn the names of flowers, trees, and animals: "And you dare to write?" he says. "A man who doesn't live in nature, as a stone does, or an animal, will never in his life write two worthwhile lines."

Babel doesn't give us a happy ending—or any kind of ending at all. He's a Jewish writer after all, still waiting for the Messiah with the rest of us. In the final paragraph, the boy remains trapped in the book of Genesis, crying out to us his desire to learn the names of things:

> *Moonlight congealed on bushes unknown to me, on trees that had no name. Some anonymous bird emitted a whistle and was extinguished, perhaps by sleep. What bird was it? What was it called? Does dew fall in the evening? Where is the constellation of the Great Bear? On what side does the sun rise?*

Even as he tells us this, he is being dragged deeper into the ghetto, to his grandmother's house, to wait out his father's anger. He is taken there by a frightened aunt who holds him tightly by the arm, lest he try to run away again from "the smell of leeks and Jewish destiny."

Moonlight congealed on bushes unknown to me too, I wanted to cry, from the other end of the century and another continent. I'm afraid I've got the ancestral handicap, the predisposition for the study of shmucks over trout. My fishing friends are patient: they spiel off information about feeding habits, about the names of crucial insects and their stages of development, but I just stand there, amazed by the mere sounds of the words, by the knowledge that there is such knowledge, letting the facts themselves run through my brain as through a sieve. Is this why, in college wild-life biology, I went blank during multiple choice? I married a Gentile who valiantly struggled to teach me the names of a few of Adam's creatures. I'd get starling, goldfinch, sparrow, and he'd be proud, the dazzled parent of a limited kid.

So what's my excuse? God knows I can't claim Yiddish as a language in my life—apart from a few phrases, it went out of our family when my Ashkenazi grandmother Jenny Horwitz died. Nor was I sent to the violin master by my father, who was, in fact, more like the young Babel himself, a deep-city Jew with a trembling confused crush on the wilderness. Under my father's tutelage, we car-camped tentatively on the margins of California's mountains and deserts; we cooked on a Coleman stove and ate Van Camp's pork and beans straight from the can. He couldn't teach us the constellations or tell one cactus from another, but he was forever sighing happily, his eyes moist with pleasure at the spectacle before him. In our family's most celebrated photograph, he is walking into the vast reaches of the Mojave with the *Wall Street Journal* tucked under one arm and a portable toilet seat under the other.

This was only the beginning: my father's life dream was to live in a house overlooking the Pacific. Never mind that the cliff he selected had a fault running beneath it—in itself this was a distinction, the ultimate proof that he'd gotten out of the Chicago ghetto. I can see him standing on the deck of that house with his hands on his hips, Moses and Balboa at once: "Paradise can wait," he'd cry. "This is close enough for me."

Until his mother-in-law, our grandma Jenny Horwitz, left the safety of Indiana and came west herself to keep an eye on us, the

Pacific was my father's domain, all messianic pleasure and no threat at all—a fantastic playground, the great reward. He would drag us out on the deck to watch the sunset. Once or twice a summer, the newspaper announced that the grunion were running, and he'd wake my brothers and me in the pitch black of two A.M. to stand on the beach with flashlights, waiting for the miracle of the little fish that came in on the tide and stood straight up in the sand to deposit their eggs.

The house itself—did my father buy it because it looked like a boat? It was long and skinny with rust stains dripping down the windows, and he went so far as to call the lower floor "below decks." Even the telephone number pleased him, for it was only one number off from that of a deep-sea charter operation in Newport Harbor, with the deliciously dark name of Davy Jones's Locker. It was for him a matter of special pride that fishermen sometimes called our house in the hour before dawn, wanting to know what time the boat left. My mother felt differently. When the phone rang at that hour, he once told me, she turned pale and held her hand to her breast as if the great trumpet had at last been blown.

For years my father's passion reigned supreme among us, reaching its highest expression in the library below decks where, over the shelves of old medical texts and volumes of art history, and in defiance of my mother's good taste, there hung a huge, stuffed marlin he'd caught on his once-in-a-lifetime fishing trip off Mexico. I used to lie in that room with my eyes closed, taking in the musty and fantastic odor of learnedness all around me. When I opened them, there was the marlin, with its long sharp whatchamacallit pointing north toward the harbor, its glass eyes prophetically glazed and indifferent to the jumble of history beneath. Is this, then, the source of my own hopeless passion—the smell of old books forever wedded to the image of a great fish?

· · ·

I didn't expect to hear from the librarian, but there he was the next morning, whispering his news into the telephone. "You wouldn't believe, Miss," he said. "I've got a whole cart for you! When are you coming in?"

A two-tiered library cart was loaded down with books, and in the books were heaps of warnings, blessings, fish fables, advice, recipes, amulets, and gravestone symbology—the whole megillah. "Look at this," he said, leaning over *The Encyclopedia of Jewish Symbols,* his voice trembling with emotion. "Long ago, our people fished for their livelihood!" He seemed suddenly bruisable, on the verge of research hysteria, and before I knew it my midwinter curiosity about Jews on a riverbank had transformed into a subject for obsessive study: Fish as Jewish Symbol. That's what librarians do to you, isn't it, or maybe it's just Jewish librarians?

Under his watchful eye, I read everything he gave me. What a mess I'd gotten myself into: a crazy stew of Jewish advice and admonition, centuries of wisdom, leaning toward ecstasy but always holding off the outcome—from the beginning a serious double bind of desire and prohibition, be it the catching of a fish or the arrival of the Messiah. First, the good news. From one encyclopedia I learned that "Fish were created on the fifth day, and God blessed them. . . . Fish, man and the Sabbath are thus connected in a threefold blessing. Moreover the Sabbath is said to be an anticipation of the messianic era which will be inaugurated by the eating of the legendary fish Leviathan." From another, I discovered that fish were believed to bring good luck, and in Eastern Europe some boys were called Fishl as a good omen against the evil eye. From commentaries on the fables of Rabbi Nachman, I learned that in Judaism, water is connected with charity and is, by extension, a metaphor for the environment of the Torah itself:

"Your charity is like the waves of the sea" (Isaiah). In the beautiful logic of this commentary, it follows that the tzaddik or holy man who dwells in it is—metaphorically speaking—a fish.

I was rising like a fish myself with all this hope when, in *The Encyclopedia of Jewish Symbols,* I got hooked in the mouth. It turns out that not one name of a species of fish has come down to us in Hebrew, just as the flowers go unspecified in Yiddish. The Old Testament, I read, does not mention any particular fish by name. *Dag* and *nun* are the generic terms covering all species, and by the dietary laws fish are divided simply into clean and unclean. "Fishing from a river or pond is forbidden on Sabbath and on holidays," I read, and blushed to recall my transgression on the Colorado. A dour entry on fish and fishing noted with mysterious brevity that "the fish cult" probably originated in Babylonia, then spread to Syria and other lands, receiving a high symbolic rank in Christianity. In Deuteronomy, the Hebrews are expressly forbidden to worship the fish. By the time we get to Numbers, our ancestors in the desert are deep in the singsong of wistful complaint: "We remember the fish, which we were wont to eat in Egypt."

You can see how we lost the knack for the lusty, intimate pleasure of the strike. Add a few more dietary restrictions, go inland for a few centuries, and you've got a cultural tendency. I was wading into a swamp of divine and folksy terror, with a smidgen of joy dangled on a line to tease me upward, to give me, as it is said, "a foretaste of Paradise." In parable after parable, smart little fish rise up and advise the fisherman to catch them not now but later, when they're nice and fat. "For then there will be a festival in your house," and so on. Jewish philosophy in a nutshell: Worry now; later, much later, we'll party.

Then it happened. Sitting there surrounded by books, oppressed by the faint but tenacious smell of leeks and Jewish destiny, I came upon a little fish fable that concluded with one of my Ashkenazi grandmother's sayings: "Eat," she used to say. "Eat, or be eaten."

With a grandmother like this, who needs the law? Jenny Horwitz's ghost was rising in a sea of texts, laying her dry little fingers on my arm, making sure she got the last word. She was our family terror: a tiny woman who bristled with business sense and insect phobias, who'd grown up in cramped communities first on one side of the Atlantic, then on the other. She died at ninety-four, when I was nearly ten, but not before pouring into my mother's ears a cupful of worry leveled at nature and the condition of dreamy distractedness it was known to inspire in children. She must have sensed from afar our father's gift for temptation. From Indiana came thick, blue envelopes complete with enclosures on earthquake prediction, the fatal sting of the scorpion, the violin spiders and starved coyotes straying down from the coastal hills, the great white sharks that roamed the Pacific. The state of California was reduced in her private geography to a vortex of catastrophe in which our house stood dead center.

In the library, I was feeling some thinned-out version of Babel's Odessa fever, looking for redemption in a Jewish fish story since I was beginning to think I'd never get it on the river—but did I say redemption, that gift that traditionally belongs, along with fishing and river immersions, in the province of Christianity? No chance. I had a sudden vision of Jenny standing over me in the kitchen of our beach house, as grave and prophetic as one of Babel's hydrophobic ancestors, those inescapable Spanish rabbis and Frankfurt money-changers.

She had come at last to California to see for herself what trouble we were in. This was diabolical timing, because my father had just pronounced me old enough to go out on the half-day boat.

"She'll catch her death," she cried. This was hard on my mother, who'd grown up under Jenny's worried eye in the Midwest and had, from the beginning, uneasy feelings about the house on the fault line, the marlin in the library, and the big blue chaos beyond. My mother was no match for either her husband or Jenny, and for the time being, it appeared that my grandmother—and the rabbis—had triumphed. That summer I was detained in the living room or taken across the street, away from the ocean and "into town" on obscure errands. It worked. By summer's end, I felt the presence of sharks whenever I swam in the surf—surely the great Leviathan himself waited just beyond my toes, his warm bubbles nearer and nearer. Ten minutes and I would gulp my way shoreward. When I came up for air, I knew Grandma Jenny was watching me from the window, pale and shrewd. The dangers of drowning or being eaten alive were only half of it: why was I wasting my time when I could be studying or at least getting smart about real life, on land?

My grandmother has been dead thirty years now, and my father for twenty. But my mother still lives in the house on the cliff. She loves it, she says; she can't bring herself to move inland, though she is plagued from morning till night by salt corrosion, the cliffside eroding under her, the trouble in the water pipes my father laid at right angles to save expense, the moaning of the great Pacific itself as the tide comes in.

Not to mention the phone calls. They come, as always, at four in the morning, when she is in her deepest sleep. She sits up in bed and puts her hand to her pale, pale breast. What else could it be but bad news? Beyond her window the waves are banging against the foot of the cliff, and the deep voice on the phone says, "This is Davy Jones's Locker, right? How's the fishing?"

"God only knows," she says, and hangs up.

She takes a long time to get back to sleep, her heart is pounding so, but she never turns off the ringer. "What if it's one of you children calling," she says, "and something is terribly wrong? What if they're calling about you, that you've finally fallen into one of your big, fast rivers?"

My rivers? A little miracle: she has gone so far as to link me with rivers. A crazy spark of hope, mixed with ancestral fear, rises in me as it must have in my father when, far out in the Sea of Cortez and out of sight of any land, he got that first tug on his line, the sign of the big fish coming at last to meet him, all beautiful iridescence and darkest warning.

"Don't worry, Mom," I say. "I'm incredibly careful." But this is only partly true. The truth is that a beginner is bound to wade deeper every time, to cast farther out into the next mysterious depth. I think of Isaac Babel and my father, of the passionate yearning to break into a new world, to discover a new language. Of course it's always dangerous, a new vocabulary. It's the language of the mortal wilderness, not the immortal garden. Maybe those two are the ones who keep me fishing, waiting for a local miracle, a foretaste of paradise. I'll think of them the next time I step off a riverbank and into that swift and irresistible current, out of my native element or on my way back into it—who can say?

JIM SCHLEY

Devotional

from *Orion*

Now we live our life
    upon the marriage breadth—
stripped of outer bark,
sawed and planed lengthwise
    then jointed in dovetails, and
    hand-polished,
        confiding as never before
with body-sundering confidence;
        the sealed secrecy of youth
    opened wide
to leave any light glean
on its grain.

One, another. And we
        multiplied: how can this
    irreducible child
    with her speed and gaiety
be? Flesh and blood
        exponential in its blue-eyed force,
    a genetic bouquet.
A blur as she grows.

Overhearing overhead
    the ripple of steps upon floorboards

as we rest arm in arm,
     sharing a chair.
Upstairs in the room where we made her,
        she plays "This Old Man" with sticks
on lids from emptied jars.

   Hear one plea
when I pray, that each of us three
       will live to be old.
Willingly at last would I
   place a faith in vacant air,
obediently strung to the buoyant invisible
      we stride beneath,
         glad-footed trio of marionettes.

Because simply
   arranging our daughter's bedclothes, with a tug
     on the linen releasing
perfume of perspiration and chamomile soap
       will set off such trembling
     in dissolved morning light;
   then folding your clothes
just laundered, dried by the wood stove—
       the sense of smell is ravenous
   as you know, for these
      blessed scents of kin:
   the cotton jersey you work in,
     or stockings for nights of singing
       translucent as fragrance,
jade dress and cream-colored blouse,
   mine to hold as I fold them.

. . .

    If I might be
so bold,
       if I may—
Give us these days.

When Evil Is "Cool"

from *The Atlantic Monthly*

I begin with three stories, three moral tales.

In late-medieval Avignon a certain man gained the confidence and the warm friendship of a good-hearted and wealthy Jew. The man lived in the Jew's home and became his closest confidant. One evening the man came home in despair. He told the Jew that someone had denounced both of them to the Inquisition—the one as a despicable Jew, the other as a renegade from the only true religion. They would soon be imprisoned, tortured, tried, and burned at the stake. But the man had a solution. The Jew should sell everything he had and charter a fully equipped ship, onto which he could load his fortune. The two of them would quietly sail away to safer shores. All these plans were rapidly carried out. Then, during the night before the planned departure, the man rose stealthily, robbed the sleeping Jew of his last possessions, and slipped away aboard the ship with all its treasure.

But this is only half the tale, and does not reveal the full dimensions of the man's evil. Before escaping, this "friend" denounced his benefactor to the Inquisition and arranged that its agents would seize the Jew early on the morning of his own flight. A few days later the Jew died horribly by fire. His treacherous friend has come to be known as the Renegade of Avignon.

At nightfall outside a remote New England village early in the nineteenth century, a lime-burner named Bartram was tending his kiln. Its flame-framed metal door looked like a private en-trance to the infernal regions. Announced by a frightening roar of laughter, the previous owner of the kiln returned after many years' absence. He declared to Bartram that he had found what he set out to seek: the Unpardonable Sin. Where had he found it? The wanderer laid his finger on his own heart and scornfully laughed again. Some local residents assembled to acknowledge, though hardly to celebrate, their fellow's return, and to hear about his ob-sessive quest for the Unpardonable Sin. Strange omens during the evening, among them a dog's suddenly chasing its tail, suggested that the devil was lurking in the neighborhood. The guests had uncertain knowledge that the former lime-burner had carried out fiendish psychological experiments on young and old. Left alone, finally, to tend the kiln for the night, the wanderer recalled that he had not, properly speaking, *found* the object of his quest. Rather, he had *produced* the Unpardonable Sin. For in seeking that knowl-edge, his fierce intelligence had separated from and outrun his heart.

In the morning Bartram did not find the returned wanderer. But in the hottest part of the kiln he discovered a snow-white lump of lime in the shape of a heart.

Living alone in a Paris garret, an idle young bohemian medi-tated on the sudden, perverse spurts of energy that can interrupt a life of laziness and boredom. Such urges lead one to unthinkable acts—such as starting a forest fire or lighting a cigar next to a powder keg—just to see what will happen, to tempt fate.

One morning the young man awoke in a mood to perform such an outrageous act. Seeing below in the street a window-glass vendor, *un vitrier,* with his stock of panes in a pack on his back, he summoned the vendor to climb up the six stories to his garret. He asked for tinted glass, which the vendor did not have. In a rage the young man kicked the vendor back out into the staircase, where the tradesman almost stumbled under his heavy load. Then, watching from the balcony, the young man dropped a flower pot just as the vendor reappeared in the street, and thus broke his stock of glass to smithereens. This vicious prank might damn him, the young bohemian said to himself, but it also brought a moment of infinite bliss.

These three narratives cannot aspire to tragic or epic proportions. Their intimacy, combined with a certain mystery of the inexplicable, gives them the status of moral enigmas.

The Renegade of Avignon was not content to abscond with the good Jew's entire fortune; this traitor, who would be assigned to the lowest circle in Dante's Inferno, also contrived to have his victim burned at the stake. The story appears about two thirds of the way through Diderot's widely influential underground dialogue, *Rameau's Nephew* (1761). The parasitic, clowning nephew half jocularly and half seriously cites the tale to show how one can become a "great personage"—the Renegade displayed "unity of character" in his sustained viciousness. The nephew calls it "sublimity in evil," and enthuses over the deeds. His interlocutor, *Myself*, presumably speaking for Diderot, observes, "I don't know what horrifies me more, the villainy of your Renegade or the tone of voice you use to tell his story."

In the second tale many readers will have recognized Nathaniel Hawthorne's story "Ethan Brand" (1850). This dark tale implies that Brand has done unspeakable things to a local girl and to others, and has come to some understanding with the devil. But the essence of the Unpardonable Sin is neither of these. It lies in the sin of intellectual pride, in undertaking in the first place the search for the Unpardonable Sin. That overweening ambition turned Brand's heart to stone. "Ethan Brand" offers a strong parable of Forbidden Knowledge, in which the desired and prohibited goal is to discover ultimate evil.

The young Parisian who gratuitously and fiendishly victimized a poor glass vendor inhabited the imagination of Baudelaire in one of his prose poems, "The Unfortunate Glazier." Consisting of a few pages written around 1862, it may well have been read by Dostoevski, whose *Notes From Underground* (1864) sounds like a sustained recasting and elaboration of Baudelaire's vignette. In each of these works the author created a principal character who approaches cruelty and crime as psychological and intellectual experiments. Cultivating their most selfish impulses, both characters reach a point of practicing sheer wickedness without purpose or cause. Neither commits a capital crime, but their logic could easily lead them in that direction.

One thing these three tales establish is that evil comes in several forms. The Renegade of Avignon premeditated his theft and his treachery over time. He plotted how to obtain the Jew's cooperation in his scheme and then how to eliminate his benefactor with hideous cruelty. The latter crime was largely unnecessary, a kind of maestro's flourish or fiend's laughter. That is the part of the story that Rameau's nephew finds sublimely evil.

Ethan Brand spent even longer than the Renegade in meditating on and finally carrying out his project—discovering the Unpardonable Sin, the ultimate evil, which not even the love of God can wash away. Presumably, Brand believed that his quest would serve mankind and would bring him some form of reward and satisfaction for his devotion to a lofty goal. The story has a strong Faustian ring. But there is more evidence to consider. When Bartram saw Ethan Brand lay his finger on his heart to designate where he had found the Unpardonable Sin, the simple limeburner came to a conclusion never denied elsewhere in the story: he must be dealing with "a man who, on his own confession, had committed the one crime for which Heaven could afford no mercy." Only after an offstage, undescribed point of no return did Ethan Brand comprehend that the terrible knowledge he sought in the world and in other people resided in himself. Curiosity and pride blinded him until the time for redemption had passed. The Unpardonable Sinner could now only return to his starting place and destroy himself by leaping into the inferno that had originally inspired his nocturnal meditations on evil.

Baudelaire's bored bohemian neither plotted a crime nor sustained any purposeful mental activity. Through the absence of meaningful occupation he became the victim of sudden willful actions that seemed to serve no personal interest. The reward he claimed was *"dans une seconde l'infini de la jouissance."* This instant of mental voluptuousness stands for a reverse epiphany, a negative transcendence toward baseness and inhumanity. All of us can feel and have felt this tug toward what is vile, and have yielded to it in varying degrees. The fragile compact we live by declares that we should not follow these impulses too often or too far. Baudelaire reported in formal verse and in prose poetry on his recurrent encounters with these reverse epiphanies, these glimpses into the abyss. His power as a poet arises from the way his lines create tensely divided feelings about evil, composed of both fascination and revulsion. Rameau's nephew would have found nothing sublime about such an attitude—no unity of character.

Each of these tales concentrates on a particular form of evil. And in each case evil has a strong presence, a perverse stature not reduced or redeemed by any other force in the story. Moreover, each story obliges us to ponder an implied greatness *of* evil—its claim on our admiration as a dynamic element of reality—and an implied greatness *in* evil of certain dark personages.

In order to deal with this vast subject on a small scale, I must leave aside major figures like Milton's Satan and Goethe's clownish Mephistopheles. Instead I shall comment on three short quotations that may concentrate the matter for us.

The complete text of one of Blaise Pascal's most troubling *Pensées* runs to four sentences.

> *Evil is easy. Its forms are infinite; good is almost unique. But there is a kind of evil as difficult to identify as what is called good, and often this particular evil passes for good because of this trait. Indeed, one needs an extraordinary greatness of soul to attain it as much as to attain good.*

Elsewhere Pascal wrote insistently that man's greatness resides in his capacity to think: we are frail reeds, but reeds capable of thought. What, then, is this unexpected and even inappropriate "greatness of soul," summoned from nowhere to explain a particularly rare form of evil? Did Pascal envision a moral and metaphysical mission like Ethan Brand's to search out a special form of evil that could pass for good? Possibly. But he provided too little evidence to guide our conjectures, offering a riddle without a solution.

Pascal's contemporary, François, Duc de La Rochefoucauld, wrote even more succinctly on the same moral question: *"Il n'appartient qu'aux grands hommes d'avoir de grands défauts"* ("Only great men can have great faults"). La Rochefoucauld did not write, "The greater the personage, the more destructive the faults." Perhaps that is presumed evident. Instead he introduced a pun on the word *grand,* or "great." *Grand,* like "great," can mean "worthy of admiration and respect," and also, more neutrally, "large in extent, big." "Great men" employs the first meaning, "great faults" the second. When the two are said together, we hear a certain moral greatness and worthiness being attributed to the faults of the great—that is, to evil. Has La Rochefoucauld given us something more profound than a flippant pun? I think he has. Through the ironies that sparkle in the word "great," he offers us a warning against the influence of such powerful figures. So crisp a maxim does not fade away.

The eighteenth-century English scholar and critic Samuel Johnson was, unlike Pascal and La Rochefoucauld, disinclined to reduce a complex moral quandary to a cryptic maxim and move on. In his *Rambler* essay on the modern novel (1750) Johnson stated the quandary clearly and then inserted a severe "but" that cuts in the opposite direction from Pascal's "but."

> *There have been men indeed splendidly wicked, whose endowments threw a brightness on their crimes, and whom scarce any villainy made perfectly detestable, because they never could be wholly divested of their excellencies; but such have been in all ages the great corrupters of the world, and their resemblance ought no more to be preserved, than the art of murdering without pain. . . . Vice, for vice is necessary to be shown, should always disgust; nor should the graces of gaiety, or the dignity of courage, be so united with it, as to reconcile it to the mind.*

Johnson believed so strongly in the persuasiveness of literature that he disapproved of assigning sympathetic traits to immoral characters. This principle became the basis for his first criticism of Shakespeare: that the dramatist was more concerned to please us than to instruct us. I find Johnson's aversion to villains of mixed temperament naive and obtuse, if only for reasons of verisimilitude; we continue to expect fiction to be true to life in some essential way. But Johnson was dead right in insisting—as did Plato and Rousseau—that what we encounter as literature and as entertainment has a strong effect on us, not just on our feelings and imagination but also on our behavior. Nearly a century passed before a fully articulated doctrine of art for art's sake came on the scene to separate art from life. More than two centuries later a free-market publisher and pornographer, Larry Flynt, has been heroized in a movie as a champion of free speech, has been invited to law-school debates, and has stated without challenge, "Adults can read anything they want without being corrupted." Dr. Johnson's understanding of human nature reached deeper than Larry Flynt's.

I see four categories of evil.

Natural evil occurs in the form of elemental disasters and scourges, which may affect any of us and over which we have limited control. In the years immediately following the Lisbon earthquake of 1755 the intellectual and theological debate over the meaning of that event helped to shake the foundations of the Christian faith.

Moral evil refers to actions undertaken knowingly to harm or exploit others in contravention of accepted moral principles or statutes within a society. These actions are subject to judgment and punishment, mitigation and aggravation, repentance and remission. In societies that have been shaped by Western traditions, Greco-Roman law and Judeo-Christian ideals merge in a gradually changing heritage that defines morality.

Radical evil applies to immoral behavior so pervasive in a person or a society that scruples and constraints have been utterly abandoned. The Marquis de Sade, the Soviet gulag, and the Nazi Holocaust belong to this form of evil, so extreme that it can no longer recognize its own atrocity. Lenin stated it forcefully: "The dictatorship means—learn this once and for all—unrestrained power based on force, not on law."

Metaphysical evil designates an attitude of assent and approval toward moral and radical evil, as evidence of superior human will and power. Thus forms of evil arising from human agency are given a status as inevitable—effectively a reversion to natural evil. And thus the cruelest of monsters and tyrants are normalized in the perspective of history and in their evolutionary survival of the fittest. Metaphysical evil nullifies all attempts to establish constraints through law and social compact. The twentieth century has conferred astonishingly widespread respect for metaphysical evil by honoring the thought of Nietzsche.

Though such definitions and distinctions may supply us with ideas and nuances to argue about, I continue to find greater revelation about evil in narratives. Stories supply details of character, of setting, and of the passage of time, which are the essentials of our moral existence. When a number of cultures concur in identifying an author as profoundly illuminating about a particular aspect of life, we have good reason to read that author with attention. On the subject of evil Dostoevski has few close rivals. He frequently presented different versions of a single situation: the failed attempt by an individual or a group to extend the moral evil of his or their actions into the purer and more intense domain of radical evil. Even *Notes From Underground,* behind its compulsive comedy and satire, sketches in a weak version of this situation. *The Possessed* and *Crime and Punishment,* in contrast, develop a strong version that overrides elements of comedy and satire. Dostoevski's major works deal primarily with forms of evil and fanaticism released by "new ideas." In this respect Dostoevski remains astonishingly timely. His work occupies an essential place in literature curricula. Raskolnikov anticipates the essence and the allure of

Nietzsche's thought; his friend Razumihin and the police inspector Porfiry provide a mature rejoinder, both spoken and lived, to these destructive new ideas.

Anton Chekhov grew up in much the same society as Dostoevski, and through his medical practice and his professional familiarity with prison culture knew as much about the underside of life as Dostoevski did. Why don't we turn to Chekhov, as we do to Dostoevski, to inform ourselves about the compulsions and the evasions of evil? Chekhov's plays and stories contain despair to the point of suicide, pointless and fatal duels, perfidy and deception in endless variations. Chekhov was essentially more of a realist than Dostoevski, whose force often lay in a strong proclivity to melodrama, caricature, and hallucinatory scenes. In an 1887 letter to M. V. Kiselev, Chekhov defended a story called "Mire," about a grasping provincial courtesan who half corrupts two intelligent and respectable cousins. Literature must be able to portray all of life, Chekhov insisted, including "the dunghill," even though the depiction of evil affects readers in very different ways. Echoing the French critic Hippolyte Taine, he said, "A writer should be as objective as a chemist." Yet Chekhov wrote this stout defense of literary freedom with reference to a singularly innocent story. In "Mire" the two cousins misbehave a bit, but their embarrassed laughter at their own behavior is an appropriate response to their social situation. "Mire" is almost too strong a title for a story in which evil emerges briefly from the milieu and is absorbed back into it. Even the stunningly self-reliant woman who impresses both men with her poise and talents seems more a challenge to stuffiness than a sinister and corrupting influence.

Like most of Chekhov's stories and plays, "Mire" is a work without a villain. Chekhov depicted everything, dung-hills and all. Yet the self-deprecating, tentative actions of his characters leave the impression that in their weakness they exist as the victims of natural evil. Awful things happen, but no one must assume full moral responsibility for them. Not even Natasha, the most self-absorbed and unfeeling character in *Three Sisters,* fills the role of a moral agent driving the action, like Stavrogin in *The Possessed.* Chekhov dealt with evil, but he pushed it constantly in the opposite direction from that of Dostoevski, moving it through prolonged silences and inappropriate laughter toward natural evil, about which we can do very little. Dostoevski, with prolonged intellectual discussions and growing horror, moved evil toward radical evil and its self-justification. As a result, Chekhov is consoling to read, Dostoevski disturbing.

A year ago a group of high school students in Pearl, Mississippi, conspired to murder some fellow students and their parents. (At least five incidents of school homicide have followed.) The dynamics of the group and the motives for the killings may never become entirely clear. But such an event is not unprecedented. Seventy-five years ago a similar homicide and a celebrated trial shocked the nation. Nathan Leopold, age nineteen, and Richard Loeb, age eighteen, two precocious college graduates in Chicago, both from wealthy families, kidnapped and murdered Bobby Franks, a fourteen-year-old boy who lived in their neighborhood, and then tried to extort a ransom from the boy's family. As the result of their bumbling and some remarkable police work, they were caught, and they confessed.

The two youths were neither deprived nor mistreated. They could look forward to a brilliant future. Why this senseless crime? They sought a thrill, the kind of elation in a momentary experience that Baudelaire imagined. But they planned for it over a long time. They hoped it would demonstrate that they could conceive and carry out a perfect crime. And such a crime would demonstrate their superiority to, and exemption from, the ordinary laws of mankind.

The young men's defense was conducted by Clarence Darrow, the most famous trial lawyer of the era. He had them plead guilty without plea bargaining; that way they would appear before a judge alone. The hearing, with many witnesses for both sides, lasted more than a month. Having avoided an unwanted jury trial through guilty pleas that acknowledged the sanity of his clients, Darrow deployed witnesses and arguments to prove that the defendants were mentally impaired. In his magisterial summation, published in newspapers nationwide, Darrow cited the influence on Leopold of Nietzsche and his superman philosophy. He turned it into a mitigating circumstance. "Your Honor, it is hardly fair to hang a nineteen-year-old boy for the philosophy that was taught him at the university." Darrow said that the fact that Leopold lived and practiced the superman myth was evidence of a "diseased mind."

The most persuasive, finally successful part of Darrow's argument was against the inhumanity of capital punishment as no improvement over an eye for an eye. The judge sentenced Leopold and Loeb to life plus ninety-nine years. But along the way Darrow had stretched and even exceeded legal limits in his effort to transform guilt or conscious evil into insanity. The prosecutor, Robert E. Crowe, in his summation, quoted Theodore Roosevelt's response to a plea of insanity by a prisoner on death row: "I have scant sympathy with a plea of insanity advanced to save a man from the consequences of crime when, unless that crime had been committed, it would have been impossible to persuade any reasonable authority to commit him to an asylum as insane." No friend or familiar had ever considered Leopold or Loeb mentally incompetent before their crime. And Crowe felt compelled to reveal Darrow's deepest convictions about the nature of crime. He read to the packed court and into the historical record a statement Darrow had made twenty years earlier to prisoners in the Cook County jail in Chicago: "The reason I talk to you on the question of crime, its cause and cure, is because I really do not believe the least in crime."

It sounded for a time as if Darrow were being put on trial. First, he partially excused the boys' evil actions by attributing them to the influence of Nietzsche's ideas, the ideas of a man who went mad. Second, he had publicly advocated ideas about social determinism and the nonexistence of crime and moral responsibility. These ideas, if accepted, would not merely mitigate the crime; they would undermine the entire judicial system in which Darrow was participating, and would eliminate from social relations any guiding principles of good and evil, sanity and madness, innocence and guilt. This disturbing revelation close to the end of the trial did not halt Darrow's juggernaut against capital punishment. But it demonstrated that highly articulate and influential people close to the criminal-justice system may entertain notions about the nature of evil and free will that are utterly at odds with the basic principles of that system.

The last story I want to examine is neither a literary work nor a court case. The movie *Pulp Fiction* (1994) represents several murderous episodes in gory detail, sets all the action in a criminal milieu where such episodes are considered normal and justified (with the exception of one awkward accident), and surrounds the incidents with small talk and compulsive wisecracking. After one has adjusted to the thick layer of obscenities, a frequently used four-letter word emerges as descriptive of the character trait being held up by the film for admiration: "cool." Mr. Wolf, the chief mobster's troubleshooter, efficiently and unflappably directs the cleanup of everyone's bloody mess and restores the normal order of crime. Mr. Wolf provides the nearest approach to a moral center in the story. He is supremely cool.

One brief scene, in which a character chooses the cruelest available weapon with which to escalate the already extreme violence of the scene, unmistakably satirizes the conventions of splatter films. He picks up and then rejects, one after another, a hammer, a baseball bat, and a chain saw, settling finally and triumphantly on a samurai sword. This is vaudeville. Is it possible that the director, Quentin Tarantino, intended to mock the film industry's crass exploitation of criminal violence? Some viewers and critics believe that he did. But the movie as shot and edited displays itself as complicit with the criminal violence it depicts. Except for the scene just mentioned, nothing suggests that this film sees around or beyond the horrible actions it portrays with the utmost cool. By depicting evil in this fashion the film neutralizes it—absorbs it into ordinary life, broken by a few thrills and laughs, and desensitizes us to evil.

After I had presented a similar analysis of *Pulp Fiction* in a lecture on Swift and satire, a few of my students defended the movie vehemently as satire. They maintained that it sensitizes the audience to violence and crime. We did not persuade one another. I continue to find, after further viewings, that *Pulp Fiction* mitigates the behavior it represents, as Darrow tried to mitigate the evil deeds of Leopold and Loeb even after legally conceding their guilt. But in one respect *Pulp Fiction* carries us further away from responsibility and guilt than Darrow did. In the ideal of cool complicity in criminal violence lurks the suggestion, spotted by Pascal and La Rochefoucauld, of greatness *in* evil and *of* evil. Plausibly, a form of that greatness can be found in a few tragic roles. Aeschylus' Orestes kills his own mother to avenge her murder of his father. Orestes then undergoes the sufferings of exile, and of the Furies' wrathful pursuit, followed by ritual cleansing of his crime. In Aeschylus, however, greatness is less in and of evil than in *overcoming* evil and attaining wisdom. The cool of *Pulp Fiction,* in contrast, transports us first into the pervasiveness of radical evil and then back to Rameau's nephew's metaphysical evil—his approbation of the Renegade of Avignon. Evil is not overcome. Evil is accepted and admired.

I close with a troubling quotation from Emerson. Toward the end of "Experience," one of his most skeptical and disillusioned essays, Emerson made a remarkable statement about evil: "We believe in ourselves as we do not believe in others. We permit all things to ourselves, and that which we call sin in others is experiment for us."

The term "experiment," cousin to "experience," links Emerson's thoughts to Ethan Brand's search for the Unpardonable Sin and to Baudelaire's bohemian who indulges his perverse cruelty. And Emerson's transformation of objective sin into subjective "experiment" suggests a method of discovering greatness in evil, as imagined by Pascal and La Rochefoucauld. In this strongly observant passage Emerson appears to take no stand, to observe from afar. Then, a dozen or so lines later, comes a sentence that casts light on every case and every story I have cited: "For there is no crime to the intellect." I read that sentence as strongly cautionary to our era. Our culture, in particular the institution of the university, has contrived over the past few decades to transform sin and evil into a positive term: "transgression." As used by post-modern critics, "transgression" refers to conduct that aspires to Emerson's moral experiment and to an implied form of greatness in evil. On an intellectual level, which Leopold and Loeb feverishly extended into deliberate actions, evil can become supremely cool.

Let us beware of applying our intellects to condoning evil or to making ourselves into "splendidly wicked" people. Twice this century has spawned overwhelming state terrorism—in communism and in fascism. We cannot afford such blindness to history and such naiveté as to embrace the morality of the cool.

Rearranging the Clouds

from *Tricycle*

It's been two weeks since I took a vow of silence and as far as I can tell, no one has noticed. When people come into the kitchen, I simply nod as they talk, mastering the art of "um," that neutral little sound that expresses so much, reveals so little. I sense that my reputation as a good conversationalist increases daily.

When I first went silent, I brought a small pad and pen with me into the kitchen at the retreat center. I kept fingering the pad and pen in my pocket, planning to write, "Silence." Or maybe, "Silent Vow," but I've never had to use either.

Instead of basking in a round of applause, I stand by the big Hobart mixer, dumping in flour and salt, listening to its steady drone, hearing it for the first time as a sculpture of sound rather than an irritating noise that you have to talk over. The slosh-slosh of the dishwasher, the hiss of the burners, the controlled clamor of the fan in the hood of the stove—all have become my friends, allies in a world without speech.

I remember the long Sunday afternoons in South Carolina when I would hide under the giant ferns and listen to the streams of talk from aunts and grandparents, all mingling in a living river of familiar voices. It seemed normal to me that the same stories, with the same digressions about who was kin to whom, would be told over and over. I took it for granted that when a gap opened, someone had to rush in to fill it up with words, sounds, stories.

But when talk is happening, other things can't, don't. It is these other things that I am seeking. Something new is coming; this need for silent disengagement is just a sign. I have a decision to make and don't want to contemplate it with a cluttered mind.

This caution is something new. Usually, I just leap without thinking. Move across the country on a whim, marry someone I barely know, walk out of an ideal situation into chaos, let myself be sucked into an unknown future by who could say what force. It seems to happen about every four years.

It's been exactly that length of time since I became a chef, since I left behind the cool, dry order of the academy for the hot, wet chaos of the kitchen.

Before I landed on the pizza line, I had combed the want ads for a week. I hated the sound of most of the jobs "suitable" to a well-brought-up, over-educated thirty-six-year-old woman who suddenly finds herself out of a relationship, out of a job, and out of money all in the same week.

Assistant Museum Curator; Manager Trainee; Executive Secretary: All required subservience, respectability, panty hose. When I saw the ad for Assistant Chef, I felt my inner landscape shift.

Why not? I loved food, loved to cook, loved to eat. In the past few years, only food had seemed real, tangible. Everything else had become words; words about words. And I was good in the kitchen—our dinner parties were famous throughout the English Department, if not Arts and Letters. To be able to create an intricate meal and then not to have to sit down and eat with the guests was a pleasure I'd never even imagined.

When I answered that ad, life as I had always known it stopped dead in its tracks at the restaurant door. In its place, I entered a world of heat and pressure that seemed always to be on the verge of explosion—a threat to those within.

The pizza parlor eventually led to a job as executive chef at the Bluegrass Horse Center, getting out meals, driving that train. By the time I first came to the retreat, at a place I'll call Dorje Ling, I was tired of having to manage an unruly crew, sick to death of food and more food. All I wanted was a vacation from cooking. I looked forward to the promise of peace, balance, relaxation into emptiness.

The first night during the evening session, Lama P. announced that the cook's back had gone out again. Could anyone take charge of food service?

Forty pairs of eyes turned to look at me.

"I can do it," I said, waving my hand.

We've all heard about Zen kitchens. The sense of order, focus. Everyone silent, bowing respectfully to each other, to the food, mindful of every minute detail. I've read Zen Master Dogen with delight, applauding the idea that only senior students should be allowed to cook.

But just as Japanese Zen Buddhism is very different from Tibetan Vajrayana, the kitchens of the two differ in the extreme. Forget the bowing, the silence, the respect. Add color, noise, and chaos. Add a kitchen full of people—construction workers looking for a snack, children playing hide-and-seek in the pantry, visitors using the only phone on the first floor, monks making statues out of butter and oatmeal—fit these in the spaces around the cooks and the food, and you've got the sort of kitchen I'm supposed to take in hand.

The idea of a food fair comes to me during the middle of morning meditation the day after I volunteer. Hardly noticing the pain in my knees, I contemplate a variety of booths: salad bar; soup station; potatoes with toppings; rice. . . . Maybe we shouldn't have rice and potatoes on the same day; better on alternate days. When the lunch bell sounds, I am surprised at how short the session has been.

As always, we end a session by dedicating the merit generated by our practice to the welfare of all sentient beings, and I realize that I've done hardly any real practice. But doesn't planning count? Helping to feed real people?

In one of the many ceremonies at Dorje Ling, a specially marked tray is passed around and each person throws a flower onto it. The flower will land to the north or east or wherever, indicating the particular Buddha family with which the individual has the strongest connection. My flower always falls to the north, on the green area of the Karma family, the one involved in activity. In fact, the person representing this family is usually shown in profile, because she doesn't have the time to turn around fully to face you. No matter how hard I try to make my flower hit somewhere else on the tray, it always lands on the Karma Buddha family.

"What doing?" Lama Tashi catches me by surprise as I sit on the floor of the pantry with my laptop and portable printer, surrounded by written-over lists and schedules, books, banners of material that say, "Potatoes," "Salads," and so on.

"Meditating not?" he asks. I shake my head and try to get up, but he motions for me not to. The laptop is indeed on top of my lap. He just stands there, interested, present. I tell him that I am planning the food for the retreat.

"In Tibet. One pot. Big spoon." He picks up a plastic pail from the corner and mimes dishing out a spoonful of food in waiting bowls. Does he really expect me to use a pail and a big spoon?

"Lama Tashi, I'm a professional chef"—it comes out in a rush—"and I thought if I just planned enough that we could have sort of like a food fair with different booths. One for salads, one for soups, another for sandwiches and so on."

I'd actually planned to have the shop make small booths and the sewing group to run up some signs in the colors of the Buddha families and string prayer flags in between, but suddenly I see all this production as the sheerest folly, excessively elaborate in a way that only Southern women can manage.

Lama Tashi doesn't say a word, just stands there in silence as the contents of my mind open to me in a new and not very flattering light.

"You good worker," he says finally, nodding approvingly. "But you so busy being you!"

He flashes a big smile, and is gone.

One morning, I get a postcard from Kentucky with horses grazing by a white picket fence.

"Really envy you all that quiet and peace, but aren't you ever coming home? We miss you. Your friend, Sallie."

Sallie runs the front office at the Horse Center where I used to run the kitchen. All my friends and family seem to think that since I've signed on for the long retreat, I now live in a blissful cocoon, wrapped round with serenity and love.

My mother, with her Presbyterian sniff: "You're being so selfish, going off like that. So self-centered. And those Ricochets of yours . . ."

"*Rinpoche,* Mother."

What did they know? How could I explain that moments of quiet and peace were few and as rare as daytime stars?

I think a lot about anger these days. How the commercial kitchen used to run on rage. Hadn't I worked my way up from kitchen help by being unrelentingly precise and demanding? Hadn't I made a point of never faltering in my zealous control of both the process and the product? The staff, beaten at last into submission, left me alone, didn't talk back. Among themselves, they referred to me simply as "God." "I don't know," they'd say without rancor, "I'll go ask God."

Anger released adrenaline, force. It kept the kitchen going. But it has a big price tag hanging on its toe. People dislike you afterward, so you have to keep feeling angry, feeding it, keep pushing that energy outward in order not to take in the effects of your anger on other people.

A professional chef is almost always furious on some level. Why? Control and perfection. Entitlement. In the kitchen at a Buddhist center all this starts to feel like damage rather than privilege. I begin to track the impact of anger. An inner dialogue rages over the rightness—of my position, my method, my perfect food, my idea of how a dish should look or taste. The center of energy is myself, inside my own being.

Anger comes in waves, say the psychologists. The first wave tends to be fairly mild, but then, after we've pumped it up a bit, it becomes much stronger. I try to remember what the teachings have said. I ask Lama P., head of the local hospice, who has come into the kitchen to melt coconut oil for butter lamps. The oil comes in five-gallon tins from somewhere in Thailand. When visitors melt it, they tend to mess up the stove, slopping it over the burners, creating a fire hazard. Lama P. never spills a drop.

"So, what do you do with anger? Stuff it?"

"Watch it. 'Liberate it in its own ground,' as they say. Don't identify with it. See it as a poison. Different from stuffing it. Oil's melted, got to go."

Lama P. picks up the huge pot of hot oil and heads toward the porch where he's already set out the butter lamps, each with its wick in a brass goblet-like holder.

One thing about this center, the one with lamas rather than horses, they throw you in at the deep end. Sink or swim. Whatever personal assistance I get, I usually receive on the fly, while working by the stove. I sometimes watch the lamas with the newbies, answering questions, being patient, kind, loving. I'm not a newbie anymore. I'm supposed to know what's what.

I begin to think about how much better the newbies are treated than I am. Even though I work long hours in the kitchen while some of them just sit around soaking up the sun, chatting up the lamas. Pretty useless in the kitchen, too, most of those new people.

Oh, grow up, a voice in my head interrupts my rant. I was just given instruction and blew it by concentrating on the newbies and not on my own mind.

During the first month at the retreat center, I'd gone in tears to Lama Tashi, the acting head of the center, saying that I was hopeless, that my mind seethed and wriggled with poisons, that I had the attention of a flea, the motivation of a cat.

He'd smiled very kindly, nodded cheerfully. Oh, yes, he agreed, my mind had always been hopelessly out of control. Now I was beginning to pay attention. This was a good sign.

"Progress having," was the way he put it.

The most recent crisis in the kitchen has to do with Nina, the neurotic teenage sister of our chief mechanic. She enjoys playing the evil elf: switching labels on the spices, turning the oven controls to 500 degrees, putting a cupful of salt in the sugar bin, hiding the masking tape and pen used to mark the leftovers. Then she blames whatever she's done on someone else. After one infuriating day when I made her leave the kitchen, she told her brother Jorg that I wasn't being nice to her and he went to Lama Tashi.

"She crazy, you not," the Lama said to the assembled kitchen staff. The bottom line at Dorje Ling was that everyone had to get along.

"But, Lama Tashi, how can we fix lunch for sixty-five people when she's all over the kitchen getting into everything?"

"Good practice for bardo," he calmly proclaimed.

He said we should thank Nina for showing us the limits of our patience. Most of us hadn't developed what he called large patience, an ease of mind that could see the world like an old man on a park bench watching children at play. At most, what we practiced was restraint, and while that was better than anger, it still wasn't large patience. Some of us hadn't even learned restraint.

"Lama Tashi." I almost said that I was tired of being jacked around by that bad-news piece of Eurotrash, but stopped just in time.

"I have a job to do. In a place this size I have to have things organized, under control. Just yesterday I came into the kitchen to cook lasagna and she's drying her boots in the oven and won't take them out."

Even as I talked, I could see how many times "I" and "my" snuck in, how much of my own suffering came from wanting control. I seethed. And went back to the kitchen.

A few weeks later, after much talk about the Nina situation, I go to see Lama S., a woman originally from Idaho and just out of a three-year retreat. Lama S. has a rare beauty that seems to start deep in her bones. I can sit next to her and never want to be anywhere else.

I show her my list of projects. Most of these entail my transfer out of that damnable kitchen into the relative calm of the Center's office. I'd designed a web site for meditators called QuietSpaces.com and devised a plan to hypertext various *sadhanas* used in morning *puja*.

"When you click on Tara's name," I explain, "you see a slide show of thangkas, hear her mantra, then a menu comes up and you can read up on her historical significance as a female Buddha in Tibet, then go right to teachings on the text."

She looks at me.

"It's not that hard, really. The material is all there in the library. It just needs to be entered into a database."

Lama S. listens intently. When I finish, she flips a few beads on her mala, looks at me, goes back to her mala.

She says: "You know, all these projects, you're just rearranging the clouds. What you really need to do is to concentrate on the nature of sky."

As she speaks, I experience again a sense of unobscured space I'd glimpsed the first day I came to Dorje Ling. I'd been hoping and straining to catch another hint of that openness ever since. And yet sky had been there all along, waiting for me to stop straining, to quit pushing the clouds around.

"How about," Lama S. smiles, "you become Quiet-Spaces.com?"

The Miracle of Camp 60

from *The Hudson Review*

> *(The speaker is a fictive Italian ex-POW revisiting
> the Italian Chapel on the Orkney Island of Lamb
> Holm in 1992.)*

Amici d'arti, amici dei fiori, amici d'amore,
when in our towns they told us *go fight for Il Duce*
we Dolomiti had to go. We were . . . coscritti, we
had no choice. I wept when I departed from Trento,
my poor mother, my so sad new young wife.
Credi in Dio, we embraced each other as the train
stretched us apart. But then in the deeps of misery
I had some luck. My seat-partner, how do you say,
was Chiocchetti. L'artista Domenico Chiocchetti
of Moena, a man very sensitive . . . you understand?
And so he saw my tears. With him he kept always—
like this, around his neck—a spiritual picture,
Madonna delle Olive—Our Lady of the Olives—
of our great Italian painter, Nicolo Barabina.
This medallion Domenico let me hold, for hope,
as the train transported us human meats to Roma,
then to Tunis, to Egitto, to fight the war.
See over the altar, the Madonna of Chioccetti,
Regina Pacis, Ora Pro Nobis. As we prayed many many times
in that desert of death under the stars.
Our prayers were answered when Tommy beat us.

No more did we have to fear the brute Tedeschi.
So we were glad. Not to be prisoners, you understand,
but to be not any longer soldiers, while we were sad
not to go home. We did not know what was happening
in our country, to our families. When we came to Orkeny,
we did not know where we were, so far, so . . . smorta
this terrible island, not one tree, not one flower.
Only polvere, calcina, cemento . . . everywhere
filo barbato—all sunshine strangled in it—and huts
we would use for pigs in Italy, to share.

Only Chiocchetti saw . . . a holy place.
Look, he pointed through the wires, the azure water,
isole, islands, emerald in the sea. He was painting them
already in his head while we worked through rain and wind
to build the barriers. Labour we did not mind.
Better to work than to despair. Even so,
there was too much time to think of home.
Before the war my occupation was giardinere.
I made gardens for the city of Merano.
(After I went back, I was the capo.) One day on Lamb Holm
I spied among the rocks a small flower, an iris rare
in Italy, and I thought, here we could grow plants,
make little beds, walkways, sentieri.

So with some men I went to the Commandante. "Please
may we have some seeds." Seeds? he was surprised.
He found us seeds and bulbs, in some months we had iris,
geranio, calendula, lupini, giglio—you say lily?
We made your desert bloom. Now, why not a piazza with a
    statue?
"OK," says Chiocchetti, "without marble, I carve cemento;

without bronze, I twist barbed wire." Eccola,
the marvel he created! St. George spearing the Dragon.
To show the wish of us Italians to exterminate evil.
Into the base we put our names and coins we saved
from home. Our padre, Gioachino Giacobazzi, swung his
     censer.
We wept for sadness and joy because from memory
we had made in our ugly camp a dream of Italy.

Allora, came winter and the long nights. We found
some space for a teatro; talented men among us played
harmonica, mandolin; always we prisoners had the spirit
to make beauty, but up to that time we had no church,
no place of God to celebrate mass. Yet once again
il padre, Chiocchetti and myself were called to Major
     Buckland,
"Signori, you are Catholics. Do not you need a chapel?"
That English Major was, I think, exceptional. Under his
traditional reserve beat surely the Italian heart.
A short time and two new huts appeared, placed end to end
—like so—to make one bigger one.
And now the talent of Chiocchetti became genius.
He picked skilled helpers and they, too, caught fire.
Palumbo, who studied metal-working in America, contrived
from scrap—gracile, delicato—the screen of iron.
And Bruttapasta whose speciality was concrete.
Regard his altar, made out of just cemento; the same for
la facciata, colonne, campanile, pinnacoli, vetri—
painted in all colori, l'arco, i pedimenti. Also, in sandstone,
la testa di Cristo crocefisso that was moulded by Pinesi.
It was as if, on this far island, by the mercy of God,
we few had been chosen to prepare in a world destroyed

a home for the immortal dove who alone brings peace
to men and women. Regard—on the vault of the sanctuary
in the fresco of Chiocchetti—white dove among angels.

Mi scusate. Excuse me. I am incapable of beholding this place
without tears. War was good to us. We were prisoners
but we were happy, making our chapel beautiful.
Happier than ever again. When the war finished
we had to depart. I sobbed because we had not finished.
I wept again in Merano. La mia madre, morta . . . my poor
   wife,
you know what i bruti soldati did to beautiful women,
we could not have children. To forgive myself for joy
while my loved ones suffered—so many suffered—
it was not easy. Chiocchetti did not come home with us.
He stayed to complete his font, and when I met him in
   Moena—
many many years later—he told me he, too, felt guilty.
But guilt is not right, he said, for art is joy.
Short is our suffering in this life, joy is forever.
Now, an old man, I visit again our joyful chapel
to read, in your language, a prayer of blessed Francis.
"Lord make me an instrument of peace.
Where there is hatred, let me sow love,
where there is injury, pardon,
where there is darkness, light,
where there is sadness . . . gioia, la gioia."

Note: Domenico Chioccetti died at Moena on 7 May 1999.

Religious Consolation

from *The New Republic*

One size fits all. The shape or coloration
of the god or high heaven matters less
than that there is one, somehow, somewhere, hearing
the hasty prayer and chalking up the mite
the widow brings to the temple. A child
alone with horrid verities cries out
for there to be a limit, a warm wall
whose stones give back an answer, however faint.

Strange, the extravagance of it—who needs
those eighteen-armed black Kalis, those musty saints
whose bones and bleeding wounds offend good taste,
those joss sticks, houries, gilded Buddhas, books
dictated by Moroni, each detail?
We do; we need more worlds. This one will fail.

JAMES VAN THOLEN

Surprised by Death

from *Christianity Today*

> James Van Tholen, pastor of the Christian
> Reformed Church in Rochester, New York, was
> stricken in 1998, at the age of 33, with a
> virulent and incurable form of cancer. By
> October 1999, after bouts of chemotherapy,
> he was able to return to the pulpit. This is the
> sermon that he preached upon his return.

*While we were still weak, at the right time Christ died for the
ungodly. . . . But God proves his love for us in that while we
still were sinners God died for us.*

—Romans 5:6, 8, NRSV

This is a strange day—for all of us. Most of you know that
today marks my return to this pulpit after seven months of dealing with an aggressive and deadly form of cancer. Now, with the
cancer vacationing for a little while, I am back. And of course, I'm
glad to be back. But I can't help feeling how strange this day is—
especially because I want to ignore my absence, and I want to pre-
tend everybody has forgotten the reason for it.

But we can't do that. We can't ignore what has happened. We
can rise above it; we can live through it; but we can't ignore it. If
we ignore the threat of death as too terrible to talk about, then the
threat wins. Then we are overwhelmed by it, and our faith doesn't
apply to it. And if that happens, we lose hope.

We want to worship God in this church, and for our worship to be real, it doesn't have to be fun, and it doesn't have to be guilt-ridden. But it does have to be honest, and it does have to hope in God. We have to be honest about a world of violence and pain, a world that scorns faith and smashes hope and rebuts love. We have to be honest about the world, and honest about the difficulties of faith within it. And then we still have to hope in God.

So let me start with the honesty. The truth is that for seven months I have been scared. Not of the cancer, not really. Not even of death. Dying is another matter—how long it will take and how it will go. Dying scares me. But when I say that I have been scared, I don't mean that my thoughts have centered on dying. My real fear has centered somewhere else. Strange as it may sound, I have been scared of meeting God.

How could this be so? How could I have believed in the God of grace and still have dreaded to meet him? Why did I stand in this pulpit and preach grace to you over and over, and then, when I myself needed the grace so much, why did I discover fear where the grace should have been?

I think I know the answer now. As the wonderful preacher John Timmer has taught me over the years, the answer is that grace is a scandal. Grace is hard to believe. Grace goes against the grain. The gospel of grace says that there is nothing I can *do* to get right with God, but that God has made himself right with me through Jesus' bloody death. And that is a scandalous thing to believe.

God comes to us before we go to him. John Timmer used to say that this is God's habit. God came to Abraham when there was nothing to come to, just an old man at a dead end. But that's God for you. That's the way God likes to work. He comes to old men and to infants, to sinners and to losers. That's grace, and a sermon without it is no sermon at all.

So I've tried to preach grace, to fill my sermons up with grace, to persuade you to believe in grace. And it's wonderful work to have—that is, to stand here and preach grace to people. I got into this pulpit and talked about war and homosexuality and divorce. I talked about death before I knew what death really was. And I tried to bring the gospel of grace to these areas when I preached. I said that God goes to people in trouble, that God receives people in trouble, that God is a God who *gets* into trouble because of his grace. I said what our Heidelberg Catechism says: that our only comfort in life and in death is that we are not our own but belong to our faithful Savior, Jesus Christ.

I said all those things, and I meant them. But that was before I faced death myself. So now I have a silly thing to admit: I don't think I ever realized the shocking and radical nature of God's grace—even as I preached it. And the reason I didn't get it where grace is concerned, I think, is that I assumed I still had about forty years left. Forty years to unlearn my bad habits. Forty years to let my sins thin down and blow away. Forty years to be good to animals and pick up my neighbors' mail for them when they went on vacation. *not enough time...*

But that's not how it's going to go. Now I have months, not years. And now I have to meet my creator who is also my judge—I have to meet God not later, but sooner. I haven't enough time to undo my wrongs, not enough time to straighten out what's crooked, not enough time to clean up my life.

And that's what has scared me.

So now, for the first time, I have to preach grace and know what I'm talking about. I have to preach grace and not only believe it, but rest on it, depend on it, stake my life on it. And as I faced the need to do this I remembered one of the simplest, most powerful statements in the entire Bible.

You may have thought that the reason for my choice of Romans 5 lay in the wonderful words about how suffering produces endurance, and endurance produces character, and character produces hope. Those are beautiful words, true words, but I'm not so sure they apply to me. I'm not sure I've suffered so much or so faithfully to claim that my hope has arisen through the medium of good character. No, many of you know far more about good character than I do, and more about suffering, too.

It wasn't that beautiful chain with character as the main link that drew my attention to Romans 5; instead, it was just one little word in verses 6 and 8. It's the Greek word *eti,* and it has brought comfort to my soul. The word means "yet" or "still," and it makes all the difference between sin and grace. Paul writes that "while we were *still* weak Christ died for the ungodly." He wants us to marvel at the Christ of the gospel, who comes to us in our weakness and in our need. Making sure we get the point, Paul uses the word twice in verse 6 in a repetitious and ungrammatical piling up of his meaning: *"Still* while we were *still* weak, at the right time Christ died for the ungodly."

I'm physically weak, but that's not my main weakness, my most debilitating weakness. What the last half year has proved to me is that my weakness is more of the soul than the body. This is what I've come to understand as I have dwelled on one question: How will I explain myself to my God? How can I ever claim to have been what he called me to be?

And, of course, the scary truth is that I can't. That's the kind of weakness Paul is talking about. And that's where *eti* comes in—while we were *still* weak, while we were *still* sinners, while we were *still* enemies of God, we were reconciled with him through the death of his Son. I find it unfathomable that God's love propelled him to reach into our world with such scandalous grace, such a way out, such hope. No doubt God has done it, because there's no hope anywhere else. I know. I've been looking. And I have come to see that the hope of the world lies only inside the cradle of God's grace.

This truth has come home to me as I've been thinking what it will mean to die. The same friends I enjoy now will get together a year, and three years, and twenty years from now, and I will not be there, not even in the conversation. Life will go on. In this church you will call a new minister with new gifts and a new future, and eventually I'll fade from your mind and memory. I understand. The same thing has happened to my own memories of others. When I was saying something like this a few months ago to a friend of mine, he reminded me of those poignant words of Psalm 103:15–16: "As for mortals, their days are like grass; they flourish like a flower of the field; for the wind passes over it, and it is gone, and its place knows it no more." For the first time I felt those words in my gut; I understood that my place would know me no more.

In his poem "Adjusting to the Light," Miller Williams explores the sense of awkwardness among Lazarus's friends and neighbors just after Jesus has resuscitated him. Four days after his death, Lazarus returns to the land of the living and finds that people have moved on from him. Now they have to scramble to fit him back in:

Lazarus, listen, we have things to tell you.
We killed the sheep you meant to take to market.
We couldn't keep the old dog, either.
He minded you. The rest of us he barked at.
Rebecca, who cried two days, has given her hand
to the sandalmaker's son. Please understand
we didn't know that Jesus could do this.

We're glad you're back. But give us time to think.
Imagine our surprise. . . . We want to say
we're sorry for all of that. And one thing more.

We threw away the lyre. But listen, we'll pay
whatever the sheep was worth. The dog, too.
And put your room the way it was before.

Miller Williams has it just right. After only a few days, Lazarus's place knew him no more. Before cancer, I liked Williams's poem, but now I'm living it. Believe me: hope doesn't lie in our legacy; it doesn't lie in our longevity; it doesn't lie in our personality or our career or our politics or our children or, heaven knows, our goodness. Hope lies in _eti_.

So please don't be surprised when in the days ahead I don't talk about my cancer very often. I've told a part of my story today, because it seemed right to do it on the first day back after seven months. But what we must talk about here is not me. I cannot be our focus, because the center of my story—*our* story—is that the grace of Jesus Christ carries us beyond every cancer, every divorce, every sin, every trouble that comes to us. The Christian gospel is the story of Jesus, and that's the story I'm called to tell.

I'm dying. Maybe it will take longer instead of shorter; maybe I'll preach for several months, and maybe for a bit more. But I am dying. I know it, and I hate it, and I'm still frightened by it. But there is hope, unwavering hope. I have hope not in something I've done, some purity I've maintained, or some sermon I've written. I hope in God—the God who reaches out for an enemy, saves a sinner, dies for the weak.

That's the gospel, and I can stake my life on it. I must. And so must you.

Arc of the Lily

from *First Things*

for Susan

The movements of the Madonna—
moment of maternity,
passion of the Pieta
are the same stance.

See first her skyward gaze
open-handed, empty, bloom to full arms.
Follow the arc of her head downward,
beholding the babe.

She wraps the cloth tighter
around hot baby flesh, gathering Him
to her face, her breast.

She wraps another cloth
around his still warm body
broken, gathering Him
to her face, her breast.

His head in her lap has the heft
of her newborn boy. Her hand drapes
over the man. Her white face turns upward,
a lily seeking rain.

Biographical Notes

CHRISTOPHER BAMFORD is editor-in-chief of Anthroposophic Press and Lindisfarne Books. He is the author/translator/editor of a number of books, such as *The Voice of the Eagle: John Scotus Eriugena's Homily on the Prologue to the Gospel of St. John, Celtic Christianity: Ecology and Holiness,* and *The Noble Traveller.* His writings appear frequently in journals such as *Lapis, Parabola, Sphinx,* and *Temenos.* "In the Presence of Death" was first given as a talk at the Fourth Annual Sophia Conference of the School of Spiritual Psychology.

LEONARD BASNEY, poet and musician, was professor of English at Calvin College in Grand Rapids, Michigan, at the time of his accidental death in 1999. His essay in this volume was honored as the best essay published in *The American Scholar* in 1999.

WENDELL BERRY is the author of more than thirty books of poetry, essays, and fiction, including *Entries, Another Turn of the Crank,* and *A World Lost.* He lives in Henry County, Kentucky, with his wife.

SCOTT CAIRNS's poems have appeared in *The Atlantic Monthly, The Paris Review, The New Republic, Image, Mars Hill Review, re:generation quarterly, Spirituality and Health,* and elsewhere. His poetry collections include *Recovered Body* (1998), *Figures for the Ghost* (1994), *The Translation of Babel* (1990), and *The Theology of Doubt* (1985). With W. Scott Olsen, he co-edited *The Sacred Place* (1996), an anthology of poetry and prose. He teaches American literature and creative writing at the University of Missouri.

JIMMY CARTER served as the thirty-ninth president of the United States. He is the author of twelve books, including *Why Not the Best?, Keeping Faith: Memoirs of a President, The Blood of Abraham, Everything to Gain: Making the Most of the Rest of Your Life* (with Rosalynn Carter), *Talking Peace: A Vision for the Next Generation, Always a Reckoning, Little Baby Snoogle Fleejer,* and *Living Faith.* The founder of the nonprofit Carter Center, he also teaches Sunday school and is a deacon in the Maranatha Baptist Church of Plains, Georgia.

DAVID CHADWICK is the author of *Crooked Cucumber: The Life and Zen Teaching of Shunryu Suzuki,* and *Thank You and OK!: An American Zen Failure in Japan.*

ROBERT CORDING teaches English at Holy Cross University. He has published three collections of poems: *Life-list,* which won the Ohio State University Press/Journal award, in 1987; *What Binds Us to This World* (1991), and *Heavy Grace* (1996). His poems have appeared in the *Nation, Poetry, DoubleTake, The Paris Review,* and *The New Yorker.* He has received fellowships from the National Endowment of the Arts, the Connecticut Commission of the Arts, and Bread Loaf. In 1992, he was poet-in-residence at the Frost Place in Franconia, New Hampshire. He lives in Woodstock, Connecticut, with his wife and three children.

ALFRED CORN is the author of eight books of poems, including *Stake: Selected Poems, 1972–1992.* He is the author of a collection of critical essays, *The Meta-morphoses of Metaphor,* and the editor of *Incarnation: Contemporary Writers on the New Testament.* A frequent contributor to *The New York Times Book Review* and the *Nation,* he also writes art criticism for *Art in America* and *ARTnews.* Fellowships and prizes awarded for his poetry include the Guggenheim, the National Endowment for the Arts, an Award in Literature from the Academy and Institute of Arts and Letters, and one from the Academy of American Poets. He teaches in the Graduate Writing Program at Columbia University and lives in New York City.

HARVEY COX is a professor of divinity at Harvard University. His most recent book is *Fire From Heaven* (1994).

ANNIE DILLARD is the author of *For the Time Being,* which includes the selection reprinted here. Dillard considers herself a humorist. Her other books include *The Living,* a novel, and *Teaching a Stone to Talk,* as well as *Pilgrim at Tinker Creek.*

GRETEL EHRLICH is the author of many books, including *Questions of Heaven: The Chinese Journeys of an American Buddhist; A Match to the Heart; Islands, the Universe, Home;* and *The Solace of Open Spaces.*

FRANK X. GASPAR is the author, most recently, of *A Field Guide to the Heavens* (1999), which won the Brittingham Prize. His other poetry collections include *Mass for the Grace of a Happy Death* (1995) and *The Holyoke* (1988). He is also the author of a novel, *Leaving Pico* (1999).

WILLIAM H. GASS, author of *Finding a Form* and *Reading Rilke,* is the director of the International Writers Center at Washington University in St. Louis.

NATALIE GOLDBERG is the author of many books, including *Writing Down the Bones, Long Quiet Highway,* and, most recently, *Thunder and Lightning: Cracking Open the Writer's Craft* (2000). She is a longtime Zen practitioner.

MARY GORDON is the author of many novels, including *Spending, The Company of Women, The Rest of Life,* and *The Other Side,* as well as of *Seeing Through Places: Reflections on Geography and Identity* and *The Shadow Man,* a memoir. Winner of the Lila Acheson Wallace Reader's Digest Award, a Guggenheim Fellowship, and the 1996 O. Henry Prize for best short story, she teaches at Barnard College and lives in New York City.

DEBORAH GORLIN's book of poems, *Bodily Curse,* won the 1996 White Pine Press Poetry Prize. Recent work has appeared in *Bomb, Prairie Schooner,* and the *American Poetry Review.* She is co-director of the Writing Center at Hampshire College.

JEANINE HATHAWAY is the author of *Motherhouse* (1992), an autobiographical novel. Her poetry has appeared in *The Georgia Review, America, River Styx, Image,* and elsewhere. Her personal essays are a regular feature in *The Wichita Times.* She teaches writing and literature at Wichita State University.

LINDA HOGAN, Chicasaw writer and environmentalist, is the author of several novels and a book of nonficiton, *Dwellings: A Spiritual History of the Natural World.* She is also co-editor of *Intimate Nature: The Bond Between Women and Animals.*

ANN HOOD is the author of the nonfiction book *Do Not Go Gently* and seven novels, including *Somewhere Off the Coast of Maine* and *Ruby.* Her essays and fiction have appeared in many publications, including *The New York Times, The Washington Post, Story, GlimmerTrain, Bon Appetit, Travel & Leisure,* and the *Pushchart Prize 2000.* She lives in Providence, Rhode Island.

ANDREW HUDGINS has written five books of poetry, most recently *Babylon in a Jar* (1998), and one collection of essays, *The Glass Anvil* (1997). He has taught at Johns Hopkins University and the University of Alabama, as well as the University of Cincinnati, where he is Distinguished Research Professor.

PICO IYER is a longtime essayist for *Time* and the author, most recently, of *The Global Soul: Jet Lag, Shopping Malls, and the Search for Home,* an investigation of how to lead a settled and directed life in a world ever more mobile and impersonal. Born in Oxford, England, he now lives in suburban Japan.

PHILIP LEVINE lives in Fresno, California, for half the year and Brooklyn, New York, for the other half. He teaches poetry writing each fall at New York University. His books of poems include *The Mercy* and *The Simple Truth,* which won the Pulitzer Prize in 1995.

Jacques Lusseyran is the author of the critically acclaimed memoir *And There Was Light*. Born in Paris in 1924, he lost his eyesight in a school accident at the age of eight. During the Nazi occupation of Paris, he organized the *Volontaires de la Liberte,* a student resistance group. Arrested by the Gestapo, he was deported to Buchenwald, where he remained until liberation by the U.S. Third Army. Two thousand other French inmates were brought to the camp with him; he was one of only thirty survivors. After the war, he became a professor at the Sorbonne, at Western Reserve University in Ohio, and at the University of Hawaii. He died in an automobile accident in 1971. He is survived by four children.

Anita Mathias has written for *The Washington Post, The Virginia Quarterly, The London Magazine, Notre Dame Magazine, America,* and elsewhere. She has received fellowships in nonfiction from the National Endowment for the Arts, the Minnesota State Arts Board, the Jerome Foundation, and the Vermont Studio Center. She lives in Williamsburg, Virginia, with her husband, Roy, and her young daughters, Zoe and Irene.

William Maxwell is the author of many books, including *They Came Like Swallows; So Long, See You Tomorrow; Time Will Darken It; The Folded Leaf;* and *All the Days and Nights: The Collected Stories of William Maxwell.*

Bill McKibben is the author of many books, including *The End of Nature; Hundred Dollar Holiday; Hope, Human and Wild;* and *Maybe One.*

Thomas Moore is the author of the bestselling *Care of the Soul, SoulMates, The Reenchantment of Everyday Life, The Soul of Sex, On the Monk Who Lives in Daily Life,* and many other books. He has also produced several audiotapes, videotapes, and the compact discs *Music for the Soul* and *The Soul of Christmas.* He lives in New England with his wife, Joan Hanley, his daughter, Siobhan, and his stepson, Abraham.

Robert Morgan is the author of ten books of poetry, most recently *Topsoil* (2000). He has also published six books of fiction, most recently *Gap Creek,* a *New York Times* Notable Book of 1999. A native of western North Carolina, where most of his work is set, he has won fellowships from the National Endowment for the Arts, and the Guggenheim and Rockefeller foundations. He has also received the James G. Hanes Poetry Award from the Fellowship of Southern Writers, and the North Carolina Award. Since 1971 he has taught at Cornell University, where he is at present Kappa Alpha Professor of English.

Richard John Neuhaus is president of the Institute on Religion and Public Life and editor-in-chief of *First Things.* He is the author of numerous books, including *Death on a Friday Afternoon: Meditations on the Last Words of Jesus from the Cross* and *The Naked Public Square: Religion and Democracy in America.*

JOHN PRICE's essays have appeared in *Orion, The Christian Science Monitor, Creative Nonfiction,* and elsewhere. He teaches literature and nonfiction writing at the University of Nebraska–Omaha, and lives with his wife, Stephanie, in the Loess Hills of western Iowa.

ROBERT REESE's essays and articles have appeared in *Parabola, Zen Quarterly, Ceramics Quarterly,* and *Sacred Journey.* He is the director of the Carl Cherry Center for the Arts and lives with his wife and daughter in Carmel Valley, California.

DAVID RENSBERGER is professor of New Testament at the Interdenominational Theological Center in Atlanta. He has written a number of books and articles on the gospel and epistles of John. He is also a novice in the Order of Ecumenical Franciscans.

PATTIANN ROGERS has published nine books of poetry, including *Firekeeper, New and Selected Poems* (1994), named by *Publisher's Weekly* as one of the best books of the year. *The Dream of the Marsh Wren: Writing as Reciprocal Creation* appeared in 1999. Her next volume is *Collected and New Poems, 1981–2001. A Convenant of Seasons,* a collaboration with artist Joellyn Duesberry, appeared in 1998. She has received two grants from the National Endowment for the Arts, a Guggenheim Fellowship, a Poetry Fellowship from the Lannan Foundation, five Pushcart Prizes, three prizes from *Poetry,* two from *Prairie Schooner,* and two from *Poetry Northwest.* The mother of two grown sons, she lives in Colorado with her husband, a retired geophysicist.

MARJORIE SANDOR is the author of *The Night Gardener* (1999) and *A Night of Music: Stories* (1989).

JIM SCHLEY is editor-at-large for the book publisher Chelsea Green, former co-editor of *New England Review,* editor of *Writing in a Nuclear Age* (1983), and author of a poetry chapbook, *One Another* (1999). He lives in Vermont.

ROGER SHATTUCK is the author of *Marcel Proust* (1974), which won the National Book Award. His most recent book is *Forbidden Knowledge: From Prometheus to Pornography* (1996).

KIMBERLEY SNOW is the author of *Keys to the Open Gate: A Woman's Spirituality Sourcebook, Writing Yourself Home, My Short but Violent Career As a Chef,* and numerous articles and reviews. Her plays include *Dragon Soup & Other Intense*

Sensations and the award-winning *Multiple.* She and her husband, the poet Barry Spacks, live and teach in Santa Barbara, California.

Anne Stevenson is the author of ten collections of poetry, among them *Collected Poems 1955–1995.* She has been awarded a Cholmondely Prize by the Society of Authors in England. She lives in Durham, England.

John Updike is the author of many books, including *Gertrude and Claudius* (2000) and *More Matter* (1999). He won the Pulitzer Prize in 1991 for *Rabbit at Rest* and in 1982 for *Rabbit Is Rich.*

James Van Tholen is pastor of the Christian Reformed Church in Rochester, New York. A graduate of Calvin Theological Seminary, he has been a minister since 1992.

Loretta Watts is a poet and pastel artist. She has published poems in *Yankee, First Things, Spoon River Review,* and many other journals. She lives in Connecticut with her husband, son, and daughter.

Miller Williams is the author, editor, or translator of thirty books, including *How Does a Poem Mean?* (with John Ciardi), and many volumes of poetry, the most recent of which is *Some Jazz a While: Collected Poems.* He served for many years as director of the University of Arkansas Press.

Philip Zaleski is the editor of the Best Spiritual Writing series. His books include, most recently, *The Book of Heaven* (with Carol Zaleski), as well as *The Recollected Heart, Gifts of the Spirit* (with Paul Kaufman), and others. A senior editor of *Parabola,* he writes frequently for *The New York Times Book Review, First Things, Parabola,* and other magazines. He teaches religion at Smith College and lives in western Massachusetts with his wife, Carol, and his sons, John and Andy.

Notable Spiritual Writing of 1999

JAMES SLOAN ALLEN
"The Mystery of the Smiling Elephant," *The Georgia Review,* Summer

KEVIN J. BARRY
"The Gift of Cancer," *America,* November 20

JAMES STEPHEN BEHRENS, O.C.S.O.
"Kissed and Worded All the Way," *Notre Dame,* Summer

J. BOTTUM
"Awakening at Littleton," *First Things,* August/September

MARK BUCHANAN
"Trapped in the Cult of the Next Thing," *Christianity Today,* September 6

MICHAEL CLARFELD
"Moss," *Tricycle,* Summer

WILLIAM S. COBB
"The Game of Go," *Tricycle,* Spring

A. J. CONYERS
"Beyond Walden Pond," *Touchstone,* December

DAVID COOPER
"Along the Point," *DoubleTake,* Winter

LAWRENCE CUNNINGHAM
"Learning to Pray from the Gospels," *Spiritual Life,* Summer

MICHAEL DOWNEY
"Gifts Constant Coming," *Weavings,* November/December

MARCIA FIELDS
"It Takes a Village to Die," *Whole Earth,* Fall

ROBERT FINCH
"Wilderness Ride," *New Age Journal,* May/June

LARRY MICHAEL FRELIGH
"Sermon in the Barn," *Guideposts,* February

BEDE GRIFFITHS
"Going Out of Oneself," *Parabola,* Summer

ROBERT GURWITT
"Tupelo Money," *DoubleTake,* Winter

L. STEPHANIE HAROLD
"The Cemetary," *Orion,* Summer

ROBERT INCHAUSTI
"That's What a Teacher Does and I Am Going to Be One," *Shambhala Sun,*
January

LIN JENSEN
"Shaking Down Seed," *The Quest,* May/June

B. K. LOREN
"Plate Tectonics," *Orion,* Autumn

HELEN LUKE
"A Blessing of One's Own." *Parabola,* Summer

MELISSA MADENSKI
"Revelations Too Small to Resurrect the Dead," *Northern Lights,* Winter

DAVID MAMET
"Samson," *Tikkun,* September/October

ALANE SALIERNO MASON
"Walking Where Jesus Walked," *Commonweal,* March 26

FREDERICA MATHEWES-GREEN
"The Jesus Prayer," *Sacred Journey,* June

ERIN MCGRAW
"My Father's Religion," *Image,* Twenty-two

ERIC MILLER
"Keeping Up with the Amish," *Christianity Today,* October 4

VIRGINIA STEM OWENS
"What Shall We Do With Mother," *Books & Culture,* July/August

NEIL POSTMAN
"Staying Sane in a Technological Society," *Lapis,* Seven

ROBERT ROYAL
"What Did You Go Out in the Wilderness to See?," *Books & Culture*, July/August

PATRICK RYAN
"Hallowing God at Auschwitz," *America*, November 13

SY SAFRANSKY
"I Don't Have all Night," *Sun*, January

SCOTT RUSSELL SANDERS
"The Force of Spirit," *Orion*, Autumn

DAVID SHI
"The Simple Life," *Lapis*, Eight

ELIEZER SHORE
"The Temple of Amount," *Parabola*, Fall

JANE SMILEY
"A Week's Worth of Sorries," *Civilization*, April/May

RALPH STEELE
"In the Image of Sister Mary," *Tricycle*, Spring

SHUNRYU SUZUKI
"Things As It Is," *Shambhala Sun*, September

DONNA TARTT
"Spirituality & the Novel," *Oxford American*, November/December

BARBARA BROWN TAYLOR
"Boundary Issues," *Christian Century*, December 8

KERRY TEMPLE
"The Thing Is," *Notre Dame*, Summer

SALLIE TISDALE
"Manta Dance," *Sierra*, September/October

CALVIN TOMKINS
"The Man Who Walks on Air," *The New Yorker*, April 5

PTOLEMY TOMPKINS
"My Decade of the Cardboard Box," *Lapis*, Eight

P. L. TRAVERS
"In Search of the World Tree," *Parabola,* Fall

MICHAEL VENTURA
"Homage to a Sorcerer," *Sun,* March

ROBERT WILKENS
"Gregory VII and the Politics of the Spirit," *First Things,* January

LARRY WOIWODE
"The Word Made Flesh," *Books & Culture,* July/August

PHILIP YANCEY
"The Book Jesus Read," *Christianity Today,* January 11

SUSAN ZWINGER
"Tracking Rock Art," *New Age Journal,* September/October

A List of Former Contributors

THE BEST SPIRITUAL WRITING 1998

Introduction by Patricia Hampl
Dick Allen
Marvin Barrett
Rick Bass
Joseph Bruchac
Scott Cairns
Léonie Caldecott
Stephen V. Doughty
Andre Dubus
Gretel Ehrlich
Joseph Epstein
Rick Fields
Frederick Frank
Marc Gellman
Natalie Goldberg
Edward Hirsch
Rodger Kamenetz
Anne Lamott
Madeleine L'Engle
Philip Levine
Barry Lopez
Nancy Maris
Frederica Mathewes-Green
William Meredith
Rick Moody
Thomas Moore
Noelle Oxenhandler
Cynthia Ozick
Kimberley C. Patton
Reynolds Price
Francine Prose
Phyllis Rose

Lawrence Shainberg
Luci Shaw
Huston Smith
David Steindl-Rast
Ptolemy Tompkins
Janwillem van de Wetering
Terry Tempest Williams

THE BEST SPIRITUAL WRITING 1999

Introduction by Kathleen Norris
Virginia Hamilton Adair
Max Apple
Marvin Barrett
Wendell Berry
S. Paul Burholt
Douglas Burton-Christie
Léonie Caldecott
Tracy Cochran
Robert Cording
Annie Dillard
Brian Doyle
Andre Dubus III
Alma Roberts Giordan
Bernie Glassman
Mary Gordon
Ron Hansen
Seamus Heaney
Edward Hirsch
Pico Iyer
Tom Junod
Philip Levine
Barry Lopez
Anita Mathias
Walt McDonald
Thomas Moore
Louise Rafkin
Pattiann Rogers
Jonathan Rosen
David Rothenberg

Luci Shaw
Eliezer Shore
Louis Simpson
Jack Stewart
Barbara Brown Taylor
Ptolemy Tompkins
Janwillem van de Wetering
Michael Ventura
Paul Willis
Larry Woiwode

Reader's Directory

For more information about or subscriptions to the periodicals represented in
The Best Spiritual Writing 2000, please contact:

The American Scholar
Phi Beta Kappa Society
1785 Massachusetts Avenue, N.W., 4th Floor
Washington, DC 20036

The Atlantic Monthly
77 N. Washington Street, Suite 5
Boston, MA 02114–1908

Christianity Today
465 Gundersen Drive
Carol Stream, IL 60188

Commonweal
475 Riverside Drive, Room 405
New York, NY 10115

DoubleTake
55 Davis Square
Somerville, MA 02144

First Things
The Institute on Religion and Public Life
156 Fifth Avenue, Suite 400
New York, NY 10010

Forward
45 East 33rd Street
New York, NY 10016

The Georgia Review
University of Georgia
Athens, GA 30602

Green Mountains Review
Johnston State College
Johnston, VT 05656

Harper's Magazine
666 Broadway
New York, NY 10012

The Hudson Review
684 Park Avenue
New York, NY 10021

Image
P.O. Box 674
Kennett Square, PA 19348

The Kenyon Review
Kenyon College
Gambier, OH 43022–9623

Lapis
83 Spring Street
New York, NY 10012–3208

Mother Jones
731 Market Street, Suite 600
San Francisco, CA 94103

The New Republic
1220 19th Street, Suite 600
Washington, DC 20036

The New York Times Magazine
229 West 43rd Street
New York, NY 10036

Notre Dame Magazine
583 Grace Hall
Notre Dame, IN 46556–5612

Ontario Review
9 Honey Brook Drive
Princeton, NJ 08540

Orion
Orion Society
195 Main Street
Great Barrington, MA 01230

Parabola
656 Broadway
New York, NY 10012

The Paris Review
541 E. 72nd Street
New York, NY 10021

Salon
www.salon.com

Shambhala Sun
1585 Barrington Street, Suite 300
Halifax, Nova Scotia, Canada B3J 1Z8

Spirituality & Health
741 Trinity Place
New York, NY 10006–2088

Tricycle
92 Vandam Street
New York, NY 10013

Weavings
1908 Grand Avenue
P.O. Box 189
Nashville, TN 37202–0189

Credits